In 1980 when *Dylan—What Happened?* was first published, Bob Dylan bought more than 100 copies because he wanted some people he knew to read it. Out of print for more than a decade, it is now available in its entirety within this collection.

Also included are Williams's essay on *Blonde on Blonde*, written when he was barely 18, and later chosen by Dylan's song-publishing company to be the introduction to a collection of his songs . . . and another essay, "Time and Bob Dylan" (1967), written at the request of Dylan's publisher to be the introduction for another songbook. And more recent essays from Williams's column in a popular Dylan magazine, *On the Tracks*, "You've Got to Hear this Tape!", in which he reviews privately circulated concert tapes as though they were as important as new albums.

All of these review essays were written by a contemporary of the artist at the time when the recording (or concert experience) was brand new. They are thus a kind of history of the impact of each new stage of the singer's work, on the audience that was (still is) growing up with him. Dylan is one of those rare artists who never stands still for long, making each new work a fascinating and sometimes confusing episode in an ongoing story. So this book is called *Watching The River Flow*, named after a song in which Dylan sings, "makes you wanna stop and read a book." (Occasionally, in live performance, he has changed it to "write a book!")

Paul Williams's writing about Bob Dylan has been praised by such distinguished Dylan fans as Sam Shepard, Jerry Garcia, and Allen Ginsberg. One member of Dylan's band says he found reading Williams's books on Dylan helpful when he first joined the band and needed to become more familiar with his new boss's huge output of work.

"Anything Paul Williams writes about Bob Dylan—and always in his wonderfully unpretentious, conversational, and heartfelt manner—is worth reading."

—Jonathan Cott, contributing editor, *Rolling Stone*

"The most eminently readable of the Dylan commentators."

—*Record Collector*

"Probably the best general studies of Dylan that have yet appeared. There's no better survey of his output."

—from a description of Williams's books in the Frequently Asked Questions section of *rec.mus.dyl,* the largest Dylan discussion group on the Internet.

Bob Dylan

Watching The River Flow
Observations on his art-in-progress
1966 ★ 1995
by Paul Williams

OMNIBUS PRESS
LONDON · NEW YORK · PARIS · SYDNEY

Exclusive Distributors:
Book Sales Limited,
8/9 Frith Street,
London W1V 5TZ, UK.

Music Sales Corporation,
257 Park Avenue South,
New York, NY 10010, USA.

Music Sales Pty Limited,
120 Rothschild Avenue, Rosebery, NSW 2018, Australia.

To the Music Trade only:
Music Sales Limited,
8/9 Frith Street,
London W1V 5TZ, UK.

Printed in the United Kingdom by Hartnolls Ltd., Bodmin, Cornwall.

A catalogue record for this book is available from the British Library.

Contents

This book is dedicated to
the singer,
the musicians,
the listeners,
and the readers

Introduction

This is a collection of essays about Bob Dylan written in response to his music as I encountered it, as a fan and contemporary, starting with my first published review of one of his records, written in July 1966 when *Blonde on Blonde* was brand new. I was eighteen, had been a great fan of Dylan's since I was fifteen and had my life and my worldview changed by his album *The Freewheelin' Bob Dylan*. People talk a lot about "The Sixties" these days, but in those days we were in the middle of them. So I wasn't writing about *Blonde on Blonde* as an expert on the 1960s but as a participant, the kind of kid who had to buy this new album the day it came out, a member of the audience.

The river was flowing by me, and I was watching. In 1979 there were rumors that Bob Dylan had become a "born-again Christian," a concept very difficult for us his long-time fans to believe or grasp, and then the rumor seemed substantiated by the release of his album *Slow Train Coming* in August. Then in November Dylan came to San Francisco to do a series of concerts in a movie theater, his first performances since whatever it was that had happened to him. I went to the first seven shows and came home and started writing a long essay (published as a short book, "instant" book, only three weeks later) about the shows and the album and my response to them, trying to answer the question all my friends were asking me, which became the title of the book: *Dylan—What Happened?* That book-length essay is included here, along with many other dispatches from the front, from the listener caught up in the drama of a continually unfolding artistic oeuvre, a gripping story about him and me and us, our times, our moment. Big news! There's a new installment of the story. *John Wesley Harding. Blood on the Tracks.* The

Rolling Thunder Revue. The basement tapes. The Supper Club shows. *World Gone Wrong.* Even the first year in six when there was no new Dylan album, 1967, was also news, and you will find herein my report on how it felt at the time. Not how it felt to everybody, but to one member of the audience. These are personal reports. Usually written to others who I imagined felt similar excitement. Sometimes not just reports from the front, but conversations on the front. Did you hear what I heard?

Of course I didn't know at the time I was writing this book. I was always writing something to be read quickly. A magazine or newspaper review or, in the case of *Dylan—What Happened?,* a book to be read immediately, while the news was still fresh. Some of the more recent pieces here are columns from a magazine aimed at Dylan fans, in which I talked about live tapes that I'd heard recently and become excited about. The name of the column was "You've Got to Hear This Tape!" Which is how fans talk to each other. I've never really thought of myself as a journalist, except in the sense that new art is news. Maybe the best kind of news. Planet drum. Planet waves. Something is happening and we don't know what it is. But we think we know. And we want to know. And we want to share our feelings. So these essays are me trying to share my feelings about how it felt when the artist tried to share his feelings with me, or us. Or just tried to express his feelings, get them out, spread the news. In public. And since he did it in public (the concert hall, the record store), you and I have the right to talk about it too. It happened to us. Indeed, the whole point of appreciating a living artist, a contemporary, and following the story he or she tells from installment to installment, record after record, show after show, is that what's happened to him always seems connected to or simultaneous with what's happened or is happening to us. We are alive at the same moment. And when we hear the singer, we feel this truth, so reassuring, so inspiring, so consciousness-expanding. And mind and heart expanding. I'm not talking only about Bob Dylan. I'm talking about the power of music, and expressive art. Bob Dylan just happens to be the living artist who has most caught and held my attention during my lifetime, so far. And this collection is my document of that experience. A fan's notes.

So since it's a document, I haven't rewritten any of these pieces or tried to second guess myself, even if I'm occasionally embarrassed by what burst from my mouth back then. Oh well. They're arranged chronologically, and I've tried to be fairly complete. I do apologize for the great moments (hanging out with the artist backstage in 1980, or hearing him and The Band at the Woody Guthrie Memorial Concert in 1968) that didn't get written about at the time. But when I did write something, and I still have a copy of it, I've included it here, even if in hindsight I may not have been at my most articulate that day. Oh well. Missing from this book is the first Dylan essay I remember writing, a "review" of *Bringing It All Back Home* written in early 1965 and handed in to my high school English teacher (he hated it). I lost the manuscript years ago. And maybe just as well, because I still remember the foolishness of some of my comments, particularly when I complained about his previous album, *Another Side of Bob Dylan,* which I came to appreciate much more some years later. Which reminds me that you shouldn't take the generally positive tone of most of these pieces as an indication that I always loved everything Bob Dylan did as soon as I heard it. There were certainly moments when I was disappointed, rightly or wrongly. *Shot of Love* infuriated me at first, but after a while my expectations and initial prejudices got out of the way and I came to appreciate this new music. God, I remember that back in 1965 I thought "Subterranean Homesick Blues" was amateurish rock and roll. And I thought some of Dylan's best songs were too long and sloppily-written. Fortunately for me, perhaps, that 1965 manuscript is lost, and most of the time when I didn't like a new album (*Budokan, Down in the Groove*) I was less inclined to share that news by writing a review-essay . . . because I knew I might change my mind later and meanwhile really embarrass myself, but mostly because disappointment was not the kind of news I felt compelled to spread. I never needed to write a column called "You Don't Have to Hear this Tape." So this collection is mostly a collection of good news. Gospel. And no, gospel songs are seldom about the things He can't do for you.

Then there were other times when I didn't write about a new album because I didn't have a place that would publish what I wrote, or that I thought might possibly publish it the way I wanted to write it. Most editors consider my style too personal or unprofessional or self-indulgent. Oh well. But I could defend myself by pointing out that most A&R people and record producers would not have been inclined to let Bob Dylan get away with doing things in the unprofessional and unpredictable manner he's always favored, but for his great success and reputation they wouldn't have allowed it, not in the 1960s or any other decade. That doesn't mean my self-indulgence is as inspired as his, but anyway I got around the problem early by starting my own rock music magazine and being my own editor and publisher. Dylan, I think, got around the problem by being essentially his own producer while working with someone from the record company (Tom Wilson, Bob Johnston) who stayed out of Dylan's way while filling the "producer" position nominally and thus keeping the businessmen from interfering.

So anyway, this is a collection of fan's notes, contemporary observations, that did get written. "People disagreeing everywhere you look, makes you wanna stop and write a book." (When he first recorded the song, Dylan sang "read a book," but he has rewritten the line in many subsequent live performances. Thereby writing his own book. Still painting his masterpiece.) And I reserve the right, even though this collection is out, to rush to my typewriter or computer every time I hear more great new musical news from Bob Dylan. "This ol' river keeps on rollin', though . . ."

1. Understanding Dylan

This essay/review was written in July 1966 for the fourth issue of my magazine Crawdaddy! *and was a personal breakthrough, the first time I found a way to write about music that really satisfied me. Because Dylan was on the cover, my friends and I were able to sell 400 copies of #4 walking around at the 1966 Newport Folk Festival; and this piece was soon reprinted in* Hit Parader *and in a M. Witmark & Sons songbook called* Bob Dylan . . . a collection. *So I started to feel like a "real" writer.*

Perhaps the favorite indoor sport in America today is discussing, worshiping, disparaging, and above all interpreting Bob Dylan. According to legend, young Zimmerman came out of the West, grabbed a guitar, changed his name and decided to be Woody Guthrie. Five years later he had somehow become Elvis Presley (or maybe William Shakespeare); he had sold out, plugged in his feet, and was rumored to live in a state of perpetual high (achieved by smoking rolled-up pages of *Newsweek* magazine). Today, we stand on the eve of his first published book *(Tarantula)* and the morning after his most recent and fully realized lp *(Blonde on Blonde)*, and there is but one question remaining to fog our freshly minted minds: what in hell is really going on here?

Who is Bob Dylan, and—this is the question that is most incessantly asked—what is he really trying to say? These are not, as such, answerable questions; but maybe by exploring them we can come to a greater understanding of the man and his songs. It is as an approach to understanding that I offer you this essay.

* * *

Everyone knows that Dylan came east from the North Country in 1960, hung around the Village, and finally got a start as a folksinger. If you're interested in biographical information, I recommend a book with the ridiculous title of *Folk-Rock: The Bob Dylan Story.* The authors' attempts at interpretations of songs are clumsy, but the factual portion of the book is surprisingly reasonable (there is no such word as "accurate"). The book perpetuates a few myths, of course (for instance, the name "Dylan" actually comes from an uncle of Bob's and *not* from Dylan Thomas); and it has its stylistic stumblings. But for just plain (irrelevant) biographical info, the book is worth your 50¢.

There are a few things about Dylan's past that *are* relevant to understanding his work (or to not misunderstanding it), however, and these appear to be little known. His roots are deep in country music and blues: he lists Curtis Mayfield and Charlie Rich among the musicians he admires most. But he did not start out as a "folksinger," not in the currently accepted sense. From the very beginning his desire was to make it in the field of rock 'n' roll.

In 1960, however, rock 'n' roll was not an open field. The songs were written in one part of town, then sent down to the recording companies in another part of town where house artists recorded them, backed by the usual house bands. A country kid like Dylan didn't stand a chance of getting into rock 'n' roll, and it did not take him long to find that out. The only way he could get anyone to listen to him—and the only way he could keep himself alive—was to start playing the coffeehouses. This got him a recording contract and an interested audience, as well as a reputation as a folksinger, and it was one of the luckiest things that ever happened to him. First of all, it put him under pressure to produce; and nothing better can happen to any young writer. Secondly, it made him discipline his songwriting, and though he may have resented it at the time, it was this forced focusing of his talents that made them emerge. You have to learn the rules before you can break them.

But it was inevitable that "folk music" would only be a temporary harbor. "Everybody knows that I'm not a folk singer," he says; and, call him what you will, there is no question that by the time *Another Side of Bob Dylan* appeared he was no longer thinking his songs in terms of simple guitar accompaniments (to a certain extent he never had been). He was straining at the bit of folk music's accepted patterns, and fearing, perhaps rightly so, that no one was interested in what he wanted to say any more. But then "Tambourine Man" caught on, and people began responding to him as a man and not as a politician. The light was green: he'd been working very hard on a very important song, and he decided he was going to sing it the way he heard it. That was "Like a Rolling Stone," and its success meant that from now on he could do a song any way he wanted. "I knew how it had to be done," he says; "I went out of my way to get the people to record it with me."

It was a breakthrough. He was into the "rock 'n' roll field" for real now, but of course he is no more a "rock 'n' roll singer" than a "folksinger." He is simply an artist able to create in the medium that for him is most free.

I have gone into this background only because there continues to be so much useless misunderstanding, so much talk about "folk-rock," so much discussion of the "old Dylan" and the "new Dylan." Until you, as a listener, can hear *music* instead of categories, you cannot appreciate what you are hearing. As long as people persist in believing that Dylan would be playing his new songs on a folk guitar instead of with a band, except that recording with a band brings him more money, they will fail to realize that he is a creator, not a puppet, and a creator who has now reached musical maturity. Dylan is doing his songs now the way he always wanted to do them. He is a bard who has found his lyre, no more, no less; and if you're interested in what he's saying, you must listen to him on his own terms.

It is my personal belief that it is not the artist but his work that is important; therefore, I hesitate to go too deeply into the question of *who* Bob Dylan is. Owl and Churchy once had a fantastic fight over whether a certain phrase actually fell from the lips of Mr. Twain, or Mr. Clemens. And someone has pointed out that nobody knows if the *Odyssey* was written by Homer or by another early Greek poet of the same name. Perhaps I don't make myself clear. I only want to point out that if we found out tomorrow that Bob Dylan was a 64-year-old woman who'd changed her sex, and a proven Communist agent, we might be surprised, but the words to "Mr. Tambourine Man" would not change in the slightest. It would still be the same song.

I will say, to dispel any doubts, that Mr. Dylan is not a 64-year-old woman or an agent of anything. I met him in Philadelphia last winter; he is a friendly and straightforward young man, interested in what others are saying and doing, and quite willing to talk openly about himself. He is pleased with his success; he wanted it, he worked for it honestly, and he's achieved it. We talked about the critics, and he says he resents people who don't know what's going on and pretend they do. He named some names; it is my fervid hope that when this article is finished, and read, my name will not be added to the list.

It is difficult to be a critic; people expect you to *explain* things. That's all right if you don't know what's going on . . . you can make up almost any clever-sounding explanation, and people will believe you. But if you do understand a poem, or a song, then chances are you also understand that you're destroying it if you try to translate it into one or two prose sentences in order to tell the guy next door "what it means." If you could say everything that Dylan says in any one of his songs in a sentence or two, then there would have been no point in writing the songs. So the sensitive critic must act as a guide, not paraphrasing the songs but trying to show people how to appreciate them.

One problem is that a lot of people don't give a damn about the songs. What interests them is whether Joan Baez is "Queen Jane," or whether or not Dylan dedicated "Tambourine Man" to the local dope peddler. These people, viewed objectively, are a fairly despicable lot; but the truth is that all of us act like peeping toms now and then. Dylan himself pointed this out in a poem on the back of *Another Side*. He wanders into a mob, watching a man about to jump off the Brooklyn Bridge: "I couldn't stay an look at him/because i suddenly realized that/deep in my heart/i really wanted/t see him jump." It is a hard thing to admit that we are potential members of the mob; but if you admit it, you can fight it—you can ignore your curiosity about Dylan's personal life and thoughts, and appreciate his generosity in offering you as much as he has by giving you his poems, his songs. In the end you can know Bob Dylan much better than you know your next door neighbor, because of what he shows you in his songs; but first you have to listen to his songs, and stop treating him as though he lived next door.

Another problem, and in a way a much more serious one, is the widespread desire to "find out" what Dylan's trying to say instead of listening to what he is saying. According to Bob, "I've stopped composing and singing anything that has either a reason to be written or a motive to be sung . . . The word 'message' strikes me as having a hernia-like sound." But people go right on looking for the "message" in everything Dylan writes, as though he were Aesop telling fables. Not being able to *hear* something, because you're too busy listening for the message, is a particularly American malady. There's a tragic lack of freedom in being unable to respond to things because you've been trained to await the commercial and conditioned to listen for the bell.

Take a look at a great painting, or a Polaroid snapshot. Does it have a message? A song is a picture. You see it; more accurately, you see it, taste it, feel it . . . Telling a guy to listen to a song is like giving him a dime for the roller coaster. It's an experience. A song is an experience. The guy who writes the song and the guy who sings it each feel something; the idea is to get you to feel the same thing, or something like it. And you can feel it *without knowing what it is*.

For example: you're a sixth grader, and your teacher reads you Robert Frost's "Stopping by the Woods on a Snowy Evening." The poem sounds nice; the words are perhaps mysterious, but still powerful and appealing. You don't know what the poem "means," but you get this feeling; the idea of having "miles to go before I sleep" is a pretty simple one, and it means a lot to you. The poet has reached you; he has successfully passed on the feeling he has, and now you have it too.

Years later you read the poem again, and suddenly it seems crystal clear that the poem is about death, and the desire for it. That never occurred to you as a sixth grader, of course; does that mean you originally misunderstood the poem? Not necessarily. Your teacher could say "We want the peace death offers, but we have responsibilities, we are not free to die"; but it wouldn't give you anything. It's a sentence, a platitude. You don't even believe it unless you already know it's true. What the poet does is something different: walking through the woods, he gets a feeling that is similar to the idea your teacher offered you in a sentence. But he does not want to tell you what he believes; that has nothing to do with you. Instead, he tries to make you feel what he feels, and if he succeeds, it makes no difference whether you understand the feeling or not. It is now a part of your experience. And whether you react to the poem as a twelve-year-old kid, or an English professor, it is the feeling you get that is important. Understanding is feeling . . . the ability to explain means nothing at all.

The way to "understand" Dylan is to listen to him. Listen carefully; listen to one song at a time, perhaps playing it over and over to let it sink in. Try to see what he's seeing; a song like "Visions of Johanna" or "Sad-Eyed Lady of the Lowlands" (or almost any of his more recent songs) is full of pictures, moods, images: persons, places and things. "Inside the museums," he sings, "infinity goes up on trial." It doesn't *mean* anything; but you know what a museum feels like to you, and you can see the insides of one, the particular way people look at things in a museum, the atmosphere, the sort of things that are found there. And you have your image of a trial, of a courtroom: perhaps you don't try to picture a lazy-eight infinity stepping up to the witness chair, but there's a solemnity about a trial, easily associable with the image of a museum. And see how easily the feeling of infinity slips into your museum picture, endless corridors and hallways and rooms, a certain duskiness, and perhaps the trial to you becomes the displaying of infinity on the very walls of the museum, like the bones of an old fish, or maybe the fact that museums do have things that are old in them ties in somehow . . . there's no *explanation,* because the line (from "Visions of Johanna," by the way) *is* what it is, but certainly the line, the image, can turn into something living inside your mind. You simply have to be receptive . . . and of course it is a prerequisite that you live in a world not too unlike Dylan's, that you be aware of museums and courtrooms in a way not too far different from the way he is, that you be able to appreciate the images by having a similar cultural background. It is not necessary that you understand mid-century America and the world of its youth in order to understand Dylan; but you do have to be a part of those worlds, or the songs will lose all relevance. This is true of most literature, in a way; and of course Dylan has his elements of universality as well as his pictures of the specific.

I could "explain," I suppose. I could say that "Memphis Blues Again" is about displacement, and tell you why Dylan would think of a senator as "showing everyone his gun." But the truth is, that wouldn't give you anything. If you can't feel it, you can't get anything out of it; you can sneer and say "it's commercialism" or "it's about drugs, and I'm above it," but not only are you dead wrong, you're irrelevant.

In many ways, understanding Dylan has a lot to do with understanding yourself. For example, I can listen to "Sad-Eyed Lady of the Lowlands" and really feel what the song is about, appreciate it; but I have no idea why "a warehouse eyes my Arabian drums" or what precise relevance that has. Yet it does make me feel something; the attempt to communicate is successful, and somehow the refrain "Now a warehouse eyes my Arabian drums" has a very real relevance to me and my understanding of the song. So it isn't fair to ask Dylan what the phrase means, or rather, why it works; the person I really have to ask is the person it works on—me. And *I* don't know why it works—i.e., I can't explain it. This only means I don't understand me; I do understand Dylan—that is, I appreciate the song as fully as I believe is possible. It's the example of the sixth grader and Robert Frost all over again.

If you really want to understand Dylan, there are perhaps a few things you can do. Read the poems on the backs of his records; read his book when it comes out; read the brilliant interview that appeared in last April's *Playboy*. But above all listen to his albums; listen carefully, and openly, and you will see a world unfold before you. And if you can't see his songs by listening to them, then I'm afraid that all the explaining in the world will only sink you that much deeper in your sand trap.

We have established, I hope, that art is not interpreted but experienced (whether or not Dylan's work is art is not a question I'm interested in debating at the moment. I believe it is; if you don't, you probably shouldn't have read this far). With that in mind, let's take a cursory look at *Blonde on Blonde,* an excellent album which everyone with any admiration for the work of Bob Dylan should rush out and buy at once.

Two things stand out: the uniform high quality of the songs (in the past Dylan's lps have usually, in my opinion, been quite uneven) chosen for this extra-long lp; and the wonderful, wonderful accompaniments. Not only is Dylan's present band, including himself on harmonica, easily the best backup band in the country, but they appear able to read his mind. On this album, they almost inevitably do the right thing at the right time; they do perfect justice to each of his songs, and that is by no means a minor accomplishment. *Blonde on Blonde* is in many ways—the quality of the sound, the decisions as to what goes where in what order, the mixing of the tracks, the timing, etc.—one of the best-produced records I've ever heard, and producer Bob Johnston deserves immortality at least. Certainly, Dylan's songs have never been better presented.

And they really are fine songs. It's hard to pick a favorite; I think mine is "Memphis Blues Again," a chain of anecdotes bound together by an evocative chorus ("Oh, Mama, can this really be the end, To be stuck inside of Mobile with the Memphis blues again?"). Dylan relates specific episodes and emotions in his offhand, impressionistic manner, somehow making the universal specific and then making it universal again in that oh-so-accurate refrain. The arrangement is truly beautiful; never have I heard the organ played so effectively (Al Kooper, take a bow).

"I Want You" is a delightful song. The melody is attractive and very catchy; Dylan's voice is more versatile than ever; and the more I listen to the musicians backing him up the more impressed I become. They can't be praised enough. The song is lighthearted, but fantastically honest; perhaps what is most striking about it is its inherent innocence. Dylan has a remarkably healthy attitude toward sex, and he makes our society look sick in comparison (it is). Not that he's trying to put down anybody else's values—he simply says what he feels, and he manages to make desire charming in doing so. That is so noble an achievement that I can forgive him the pun about the "queen of spades" (besides, the way he says, "I did it . . . because time is on his side" is worth the price of the album).

"Obviously Five Believers" is the only authentic rock 'n' roll song on the record, and it reflects Dylan's admiration of the early rock and rollers. Chuck Berry and Larry Williams are clear influences. "I'd tell you what it means if I just didn't have to try so hard," sings Bob. It's a joyous song; harp, guitar, vocal and lyrics are all groovy enough to practically unseat Presley retroactively.

"Rainy Day Women #'s 12 & 35" (the uncut original) is brilliant in its simplicity: in a way, it's Dylan's answer to the uptight cats who are looking for messages. This one has a message, and it couldn't be clearer, or more outrageously true. But somehow *Time* Magazine still managed to miss the point: they think "everybody must get stoned" means everyone should go out and get high on drugs. Evidently they didn't hear where Bob says (about 200 times) that "*They* stone ya . . . ." Oh well. Everybody must get stoned.

20

I could go on and on, but I'm trying hard not to. The album is notable for its sense of humor ("Leopard Skin Pillbox Hat" and "Pledging My Time" and much else), its pervading, gentle irony (in "4th Time Around," for example), its general lack of bitterness, and above all its fantastic sensitivity ("Sad-Eyed Lady of the Lowlands" should become a classic; and incidentally, whoever decided it would sound best all alone on a side instead of with some other songs before and after it deserves a medal for good taste).

"(Sooner or Later) One of Us Must Know" is another favorite of mine: in its simplicity it packs a punch that a more complex song would often pull. "Visions of Johanna" is rich but carefully subdued ("the country music station plays soft but there's nothing really nothing to turn off" . . . I love that). Dylan's world, which in *Highway 61* seemed to be bubbling over the edges of its cauldron, now seems very much in his control. Helplessness is still the prevalent emotion ("honey, why are you so hard?"), but chaos has been relegated to the periphery. Love (and sex, love's half-sister) are all-important, and love, as everyone knows, has a certain sense of order about it, rhyme if not reason. No one has to ask (I hope) what "I Want You" is about, or "Absolutely Sweet Marie." Or "Just Like a Woman," which I want to cut out of the album and mail to everybody. The songs are still a swirl of imagery, but it is a gentler, less cyclonic swirl; more like autumn leaves. The nightmares are receding.

Blonde on Blonde is a cache of emotion, a well-handled package of excellent music and better poetry, blended and meshed and ready to become a part of your reality. Here is a man who will speak to you, a 1960s bard with electric lyre and color slides, a truthful man with X-ray eyes you can look through if you want. All you have to do is listen.

2. Time and Bob Dylan

In the summer of 1967, Dylan's song publisher (Witmark, soon to become Warner Bros Music) asked me to write an introduction to another Bob Dylan songbook they were planning. I wrote this essay, which first appeared a year later (as "Time and Bob Dylan," not an introduction but a kind of afterword) in a songbook called Bob Dylan, the Original, *with an "Editor's Note" that explained: "Although the following article is a year old, its commentary is so pertinent that we decided to include it in this volume." The same essay appeared in my first book,* Outlaw Blues, *under the title "The Period of Silence."*

As I write this—August 1967—Bob Dylan has been silent for more than a year. It's been a curious calm. Between *Highway 61 Revisited* and *Blonde on Blonde* was a gap of some ten months—but a gap broken up with the release of several 45's of exciting new material, a winter concert tour, a fascinating interview in *Playboy,* and finally the cheerful, triumphant "Rainy Day Women"—"everybody must get stoned."

1967 has offered no such relief. Dylan suffered severe damage—three broken vertebrae—in a motorcycle accident in August '66 and retired from public view. All concerts were cancelled—first till January, then March, then—perhaps—forever. *Tarantula,* Dylan's much-promoted first book, never appeared. TV specials scheduled for ABC-TV and the BBC in Britain were cancelled amid bad will and lawsuits. MGM Records announced it had signed Dylan, discovered it hadn't, and prudently shut up; and meanwhile Columbia issued a Greatest Hits lp, just to be on the safe side. And still no sign of a new recording.

And why should we be so concerned? It has been Dylan's unwilling, unfortunate fate to be somehow held responsible to the world for every move he makes. A year is not a long time in an artist's life—some writers have been silent for twenty—and surely a man deserves as much time to do his work in private, and as much time to simply relax, as he can possibly obtain. This is the least any of us might ask; and yet if Dylan retreats he is considered not hard-working but somehow cowardly, unwilling to show the world his rough drafts, unwilling to work and create in a fishbowl mounted on a pedestal in Times Square. Dylan is our most-loved living poet, and the public that has embraced him now believe they possess him—he must behave according to their will.

They hold him responsible for the passage of time; sometimes he must think that. At Newport, Forest Hills, 1965, his fans dictated what he could and could not play, and with what instrument! The "folk music boom"—actually an early stage of modern pop music and not deserving of the name "folk" at all—progressed properly into a freer, more complex form of creative music; and *Sing Out!* and the mad dogs of the "folk boom" led a witch hunt against the man most prominently identified with the changes music was undergoing. Bob Dylan and his electric guitar were held respon-sible for the plight of every ambitious "folk" singer who found himself out of fashion. "Dylan did it!" they screamed. "You got a lot of nerve . . ." answered Bob, but he was deeply hurt. He'd been concerned with his music, his poems—he'd never tried to carry the world on his shoulders.

But the world wants to be on his shoulders. We expect our artists to take care of us. Or so it has been; but maybe, just perhaps, this last year of silence has been a time of learning, not just for Dylan but for his fans. Deprived of a new lp, we return to what he's done before . . . at some point *Highway 61* or *Another Side of* or *The Times They Are A-Changin'* has crept back on the phonograph, and the songs have been heard a new way. "It ain't me babe . . . no, no, no it ain't me babe; it ain't me you're looking for." Does the girl who first heard that at nineteen, a champion of Peace, defender of the Negro and veteran of her first traumatic freshman affair, now discover the song at twenty-two? It doesn't seem as sad, perhaps; she's come and gone and discovered that sometimes it just ain't him, or it just ain't you, and there's nothing anyone can do about it. She suspects that maybe the words mean a little less than she thought they did, but maybe they evoke a little more . . . And the young glue-sniffer who so proudly uncovered "Mr. Tambourine Man" as a song about a pusher now hears it again, and the thought strikes him that if the word "pusher" was supposed to have risqué connotations, or if he thought the song incomprehensible without its "secret meaning," then he was a silly child and as wrong as the night is dark. For now he listens to Dylan's song and hears the singing joy, feels it all on the surface and true with no need of a secret decoder, realizes that whether Mr. Tambourine Man is a connection or a Cub Scout den mother, or just a close, close friend, what counts is the feeling, the surrender and the joy, the sense of wonder and discovery and the bright jingle-jangle morning all around you.

Dylan has been silent. But songs are never silent—they speak long after they've been spoken. Dylan's songs do not decay in time; rather, time flows over them, enriches them, filling in the little cracks we did not understand. "My Back Pages," "Baby Blue," "One Too Many Mornings"—these songs have meaning now, and always will. Dylan owes us nothing; we owe him already more than we can give.

3. God Bless America

The first new Dylan album since Blonde on Blonde *was released at the end of December, 1967. I started listening to it immediately, of course, and a few weeks later wrote this offbeat "review" for the 14th issue of* Crawdaddy! *Professor Betsy Bowden in her 1982 book* Performed Literature *studies every review of* John Wesley Harding *she can find—18 altogether—and kindly calls mine "the most articulate and thorough." Not bad for a college dropout! But what really thrills me is she goes on to point out that Dylan in an interview published ten months later specifically confirmed my analysis of the structure and intended impact of "All Along the Watchtower." Dylan: "The song opens up in a slightly different way, in a stranger way, for here we have the cycle of events working in a rather reverse order." Bowden: "So Dylan put it in there, indeed, and Williams figured it out." I did so (now it can be told) on an acid trip in a Manhattan apartment with Van Dyke Parks, Parks's wife Durrie, and legendary comix artist Trina Robbins (our conversation is documented in the "Paranoid X" section of the review).*

So stop what you're doing, and hello to *John Wesley Harding*. The medium is the messenger, and wicked is as wicked does, anyway. Don't ask me nothin' about nothin'. Bob Dylan welcomes us all back to the center ring, with many pithy wisdoms which we can take at surface value, surface value at a depth of ten feet, surface value at a depth of twenty feet, and on. "Nothing is revealed." Which is not to imply that the whole album may be unfathomable; at least the soundings are good. But why all these nautical jokes?

I don't know what it means not to understand. It's really an intransitive verb. Transitive stuff like "interpret" might hang you up with all sorts of doubts about will and the ability to choose and all, but there's no freedom involved in understanding. You've gone and done it even if you chose not to. And since you and I never quite see through the same eyeballs anyway, what do you care who understands which? We'll all grow old together.

But I know what you mean. When you're out on the balcony saying run come see the lovely sunset and I look out commenting that's a three-winged caterpillar and anyway the woods are full of them, there *is* a sense of communications loss which undermines togetherness. A drag. And people who *know* they don't perceive the same whatever as the rest of us generally have trouble with the feds. Crazy is not putting on a good enough act. Too many caterpillars, and they take you away.

So let's run *John Wesley Harding* through the analysis mill and see if we can grind it down to oatmeal wretched enough to be universally palatable. All gazing at the same Waterloo Sunset. And how come nobody ever talks about Madison Avenue any more? Like, John Wesley Hardin at fifteen killed a nigger for being uppity, and kept up that kind of bullshit until 1878, when, foolish move or no, he got stuck in jail for sixteen years, missing his twenty-sixth through forty-first birthdays and the inaugurations of Grover Cleveland. Bob Dylan is nobody's fool. He knows about John Wesley Hardin (and added the "g" to his name presumably to compensate for all the g's he's dropped from other words over the years). Don't underestimate him, and he'll scratch your back too. But dear landlord, this is a mighty intentional record. Intentional and accessible, and that's a tricky combination. Because if Dylan really knows how accessible it is, then maybe he's playing around with the ways that we're going to access it. Wheels within wheels, generating spheres if you're clever enough to tilt them, and at this point there's a lot of control being exercised over the unpredictable. Said Frankie Lee with a smile.

So the way you react might be part of the *STOP PRESS! STOP PRESS! 3&77##seven minutes* Stand By. PARANOID X, with a message from your sponsor:*

"Let us not talk falsely now, the hour is getting late." Mr. Parks thought it "very nice" of Mr. Dylan to say this, and we all concurred. Trina noticed "two riders were approaching, the wind began to howl," and in our several ways we tried to remember how the song had begun.

THERE MUST BE SOME WAY OUT OF HERE . . .

THERE MUST BE SOME WAY OUT OF HERE . . .

"All along the watchtower . . .", and it somehow bothered me that the line only appeared once in the song. It had seemed like twice, but . . . And, kindly! The Thief he kindly spoke! Certainly was seeming Meaningful . . .

"There are many here among us who feel that life is but a joke." Well, we laughed and laughed.

But if Bob Dylan is nice enough to empathize with Mick Jagger (". . . no relief"), then thieves might be all right too, and you can feel sorry for a joker with claustrophobia. Naturally if you start in the middle it seems like you need to look for a way out, and all; no reason to get excited, that's okay, only, now that we've done that, well, the hour is getting late . . .

And it's a real feeling of friendship when he can say, let us not talk falsely now; Mr. Parks appreciates that sort of thing, and maybe we all wouldn't mind being polite. If the hour really was getting late, and the thief was sympathetic to our occasional panic.

But this isn't "the hour that the ship comes in." And even though it sounds like Bob Dylan's 115th dream, it's not the same. There's some business to take care of, folks, and Dylan can make the song more pleasant for you by starting in the middle, but in the end you've got to start at the beginning, if you know what I mean. Just a joke. But let us not talk falsely now . . .

There must be some way out of here. There must be some way out of here.

End of flash. But where does this leave *The Notorious Byrd Brothers?* Well, for one thing, it's obviously the same Bob Dylan, even though he's hard to find on the cover, and curiously enough it's the exact same Byrds even if there's two in the bush. And mainly you have this incredible self-awareness, the artist knowing what he wants to do, and why, and just churning it out, just like any old accepted creative type. In addition to which you have the good old America of science fiction and Tom Paine; and the Byrds have completely let go to bossa nova and square dance and eight miles high the same way Dylan has delightfully done a total Percy Mayfield, Sonny Boy Williamson Live in London (at the Crawdaddy Club!) with the Yardbirds, Eric von Schmidt, Geoff Muldaur, everything you could possibly want if we'd finally gotten around to just digging music. Sort of like Love doing their movie music album, and Van Dyke Parks just being accepted on all fronts. We really are set free.

And on a straight sociological level, that's important. When Dylan started playing Those Instruments, back in the Forest Hills/ Newport days, he really did make it possible for a lot of serious and also okay music listeners to begin making that tough transition into rock. And now the general importance of listening to a Dylan album, even if it does sound like some half-country half-blues guy with clever old Nashville cats helping him along, some guy who might in fact just be on the verge of inventing rock and roll in say 1954, even if it sounds like all that nice ethnic music that everyone can dig but no one can really get into, well, you've got to get into it because it's a Dylan album. And now I can start giving all my rock friends Percy Mayfield records. Because you can only listen to music openly and comfortably if you *want to* listen to it; and you only used to want to listen to it if it was Folk Ethnic, but it turned out then that you wanted to also if it was Bob Dylan, so you got stuck finding out about rock. And now you wouldn't want to listen to Sonny Boy Williamson, though you might say "that's nice" if I played you a little, but since nothing could be more exciting than a new Dylan album, why, here you are getting into it. Good old rock, expanding our minds, opening us up to the world, making us comfortable with and therefore able to appreciate more and more subtle, good stuff. Rock, the friendly music. Bob Dylan, frontier scout. Sociologists, take note.

And it all has to do with contexts. Like everyone else, I'm sure you have flashed one way or another on the realization that all things are related to all other things. That thing A, transcendental meditation, can always be related to thing B, spider crabs, if you do it step by step: APE ARE ARM AIM DIM DIN DEN MEN MAN. So it stands to reason that folksong A and rock-song B are always related, can always be made to share *some* sort of fairly specific category. There are more categories, therefore, than there are songs; so why categorically dislike things? To say (even to yourself) I only really enjoy classical music, is like saying, I only enjoy songs whose second verses begin with the letter "m." To have an open mind is to be unrestricted by the arbitrary, at least some of the time. Without such occasional indiscriminate behavior, how could sunsets and caterpillars be made to coexist? How would we talk to each other?

And you wanted to read about Bob Dylan. A friend of mine confided that he felt considerable tension in listening to this album, and I think I can understand why. I get the same feeling. It has to do with everything on this album's being at least relatively accessible, and at the same time so damn intentional; so any time you happen to say to yourself, "I wonder why he did that," you really feel obliged to work at figuring it out. 'Cause you know he did it on purpose. Earlier Dylan records seemed hard to listen to, at first, because so much was baffling; but we quickly overcame that by not getting uptight about what we didn't understand—instead, just listening and enjoying what we felt. This new album, which could be called merely a new arrangement of all those earlier names and prepositions, is so easy to just listen to that you can't help absorbing all the words and getting involved in their implications; and pretty soon you're all tense wondering what in hell he meant by that? When few things are baffling they become all-important.

Which is, I think, what Paranoid X was trying to tell us. "All Along the Watchtower"—a nice song. But certain minor questions arise. Why does it end "two riders were approaching . . ."? Why does the phrase "all along the watchtower" seem somehow out of place? Why is "There must be some way out of here" so incredibly successfully claustrophobic? Why are we drawn to "so let us not talk falsely now, the hour is getting late"? On an lp that is so very comprehensible on an objective level, you can't help getting involved in these subjective questions. And that's why I say Dylan-as-artist is even playing around with our personal reactions to the stuff.

Because, without these subjective questions, I would never have discovered the most delightful aspect of the song. Its ends have been twisted, and taped together. In another universe, Dylan would begin: "All along the watchtower, princes kept the view . . . Two riders were approaching, the wind began to howl." The second and third verses would then be conversation between the two riders, the Joker and the Thief; and "Let us not talk falsely now . . ." would close the song with comfort.

But only in this universe, with the song dissatisfying because the end seems to be in the middle of things, and the beginning stuck in there on the third verse, only in this world can the real claustrophobia of the Joker come through to us all. Because indeed, "There must be some way out of here"—what more natural reaction, caught on a Mobius strip?

When people ask me why I get scared on trips, I can point to this song.

And of course it has to do with Time. As more and more people get off the trolley ride, fewer and fewer are aware of 9 to 5, and SMTWTFS. And people's ages. And which album came first. The existence of the jet doesn't mean you can be everywhere at once, but it certainly allows you to think of your life in space as more than a point on a line. And the more we read Borges and Pynchon and listen to rock, the more we ignore the supposed directionality of Time. After months and years, lovers continue to say "hello." Time only takes place in our minds . . . and as we realize this, our minds become more than one-dimensional. We don't have to always hear "Like a Rolling Stone" as after "Subterranean Homesick Blues" and prior to *Blonde on Blonde*. We retain that feeling of progress, but discard the "future" and "the past."

And the music makes it seem so easy. It's all incredible, probably the best electric bass playing on record and truly brilliant, virtuoso work by the drums and steel guitar. Dylan's voice on this album is so good, is put to such excellent use, that the stubbornest of doubters will be knocked out more than once. His piano makes "Dear Landlord" the work of one of the world's finest blues combos. And the guitar and harmonica provide that persistent link with the other albums, droning along and shaping everything in Dylan's own image. Jes' fine. The whole album offers this sense of shelter, of quietness and ease and protection with everything else that exists in the world ever-so-gently implied in the knotty wood of the cabin walls. "Down Along the Cove" is just about as nice as music can be.

I think I copped out. Looking back on this discussion, I don't think I ran *John Wesley Harding* through the analysis mill at all; I seem to have circled it warily, poking at a theme here or there but never really pouncing on the beast. I haven't told you why this strikes me as the most American record I've ever heard; I haven't described these songs as being Dylan's usual stuff but in different focus; I haven't even gotten onto such grand topics as The Folk Process in Woodstock and Hibbing, or Will the Real John Wesley Hardin Please Stand Up?

But what the hell. I just might be doing it on purpose. Without the deceptions of Time, who really knows the shortest possible distance between two points, and anyway how would it be possible for me to bring up a subject that *didn't* relate to Bob Dylan? If you gaze long enough to see *both* caterpillars and sunsets, whole universes might open up; which is, I think . . .

Enough of that. In *Lot 49* is a lawyer, a child actor turned lawyer whose friend the lawyer-turned-actor is playing the part of him in a movie; and, as Metzger, the lawyer, points out, to portray the role properly the actor must act like a lawyer, who, after all, becomes an actor in the courtroom in front of the judge, and in this case was in fact an actor previously . . . "The film is in an air-conditioned vault at one of the Hollywood studios, light can't fatigue it, it can be repeated endlessly."

Pynchon calls this the "extended capacity for convolution" (or anyway Metzger does) (or I just did); Dylan says, "There must be some way out of here," and . . .

No, come to think of it, the Joker said it.

"You can be in my dream if I can be in yours; *I* said that . . ."

So the way you react might be part of the

this is the way

out of here →

4. *Nashville Skyline*

In the fall of 1968 I left Crawdaddy!, *moved from New York City to Mendocino California, and when* Nashville Skyline *came out in April 1969 the only writing I did about it was a few lines within a larger piece (published in a fly-by-night underground paper called* Planet) *titled "I'm Beginning to See the Light." I'm proud of the essay for the following prophetic sentences, on the occasion of the release of the third Velvet Underground album and Philip K. Dick's novel* Do Androids Dream of Electric Sheep?: *"The Velvets now world's finest. Better than the Stones. Dylan alone remains. But is Phil Dick really the Herman Melville of this century?"*

By way of documenting my written responses to Bob Dylan's albums as they arrived, the piece began with the phrase "Nobody had ever talked to us like that before:"— followed by a long quote from "Just Like a Woman," starting with "It was raining from the first" through "I was hungry and it was your world" to the end of the chorus. And then: "It isn't often that people, strangers or friends, reach in to where we really feel stuff and speak gently and openly . . . How deeply is Bob Dylan into your life?"

Then lots of talk about the Velvet Underground, sex, the population explosion, and finally only these four lines, near the end of the piece, about Nashville Skyline:

If you like Bob Dylan's new album, move to the country. If you're already in the country, I suppose the proper response to the record is to make love more, and better. Shine on brightly. Relax.

5. *Before the Flood*

The next time I wrote about a newly-released Bob Dylan record was at the beginning of July, 1974, when the live album from his January '74 tour was released. The main reasons I didn't write about Self Portrait *or* New Morning *or* Pat Garrett & Billy the Kid *or* Planet Waves *were that I wasn't writing record reviews at all from 1969 to 1974, and maybe also that I wasn't so sure what I thought or felt about each of those records as they came along. In '74 I was back in New York, and this review was written for* The Soho Weekly News.

In 1969 or 1970 I visited my neighbor Bob Novick, and he was deep into *Another Side of Bob Dylan*—just listening to the same album over and over again for three weeks steady. When I saw him a few weeks later, he had progressed (retrogressed?) to *The Times They Are A-Changin'*. The point is, at that moment I began to realize that there's always a Dylan retrospective going on somewhere.

The 1974 concert tour and this new double-album re-creation of that tour are part of the greatest Dylan retrospective ever, the first conducted publicly by The Man himself.

Retrospectives are a Good Thing, as is well-known and widely accepted in the art world. It's not a matter of nostalgia, not when you're dealing with living art. Rather, at the only significant level (who cares how many Dylan dolls were sold?), it's a matter of re-evaluation, *self*-evaluation, by the listeners, the viewers, the audience. We are given a chance to see the span and scope of the artist's work taken as a whole; at the same time we are given a chance to open ourselves anew, find new and deeper responses inside ourselves, as a product of our own maturing.

Dylan encouraged this attitude of rediscovery and reappraisal of the work as a whole ("the 60s period") when he put together and arranged for the publication of *Writings and Drawings by Bob Dylan* (Knopf, 1973). The state of mind that brought him to devote a lot of attention to the publishing of his collected works probably also contributed to his decision to tour again, and affected the choice of songs and the general structure (and character) of his performance.

The man is proud of what he's done. Quietly proud, in fact, despite all the inevitable hoopla that surrounded "tour '74." If Dylan is still in any way a hero/symbol of our "generation" (persons born again in the 1960s), then his sane and loving acceptance of himself is good news for one and all.

And so is this album good news, a welcome and unexpected slap in the face for those of us who believed that all the best Dylan lps were behind us. (His last first-rate lp in terms of impact on me and my friends—the only way I can really judge—was *John Wesley Harding*, six and a half years ago.)

Before the Flood is a record, the record of a moment when a great artist "saw daylight" (quote from a *Rolling Stone* interview) and swam for it. It's also a phonograph record (literally an album, because there's more than one disc) and a great one. I recommend it unreservedly—no light statement in these days when a double album costs $10, and $10 is not easily come by, and Dylan lps are no longer automatic purchases. Buy it, give your money to the rich as long as you have it, you're better off with the music.

The grace notes are terrific. After all, these guys have been playing these songs for a long time. Dylan and The Band began performing together nine years ago. And when I first heard of Robbie Robertson (from Michael Bloomfield), he was talked of as this "really great guitarist." That he is, but that's not the image he projects of himself with The Band. So even if Bob Dylan couldn't squawk a note, it'd be worth it to drag him out of retirement now and then just so we could see the easygoing, oh-so-clever Band transform itself back into the Hawks, world's finest electric back-up band, breathtaking, fucking geniuses.

Impact? After a dozen times through, I feel I'm just *starting* to hear this album. *Planet Waves* was sweet, but *Before the Flood* is swallowing me alive. In a move typical of the tour, the record jacket does not reveal where these songs were recorded. But at least one of them I feel certain is from the afternoon concert I saw at Madison Square Garden. I was in a bum mood, and about a mile in back of the singer's head, and I didn't exactly have a transcendent experience (vaguely wishing I was still back in the second row of the Back Bay Theatre in Boston in 1964) but I remember noticing through my fog that it was a really superb performance and hoping there would be a record. Well there is, and for me (not to mention millions of people who weren't at any of the concerts) the impact of *Before the Flood* is and will be much greater than the thrill of just being there. Because damn it when all is said and done it is the music and not the person or the "historicity" we respond to, isn't it? And the music is here, and sure enough those guys down there in the middle of that monster crowd were just playing their asses off. And somehow Dylan became the Muhammad Ali of the stage and took all that energy all those people were directing at him and threw it back at them, quick and strong, singing like fire and ice.

The album is structured just like most of the concerts: six songs by Dylan with The Band, then The Band alone for another five, Dylan does three acoustic magnum opuses, The Band does three more of theirs with the Kid helping out on some harmonies sometimes, and finally Dylan & Band together do three big ones, plus an encore. There are no introductions, lots of applause, and absolutely no flaws in the recording that I've noticed. Simply as re-creation, it must be judged a remarkable piece of work.

But what really makes it is the quality of the concerts being recorded. The choice of songs is inspired, satisfying both the needs of the audience and the needs of the moment, always a tough trick. The programming is unique and completely effective. The egoless style of The Band without Dylan is sometimes stirring, sometimes soporific, but it's a perfect foil for the overwhelming power of the Dylan/Band performances and the impossible expectations of the audience. The whole situation was a clumsy collection of impossibilities that Graham, Dylan et al miraculously turned into a triumph and made it look easy. Bill Graham, for one, really deserves a credit line on the record jacket.

And it ain't no poetry reading. So fuck the lyrics, and forget the memories, and listen to this music! That singer, that guitar, those drums . . . oh God. If "Highway 61" is cut to three minutes and rush-released as a single, I got $20 says it's a number one record. When have we *ever* heard drums like that on a live recording? (Congratulations to Rob Fraboni and Village Recorders, who did the recording. They should be up to their armpits in work for the next three years when the musicians hear this one.)

"Like a Rolling Stone" is extraordinary. I think I like it better than the original—this year, anyway. Listen to the sweetness of that opening, the fullness of Dylan's voice—fine, fine punctuation— the power of the chorus, drums, voices and organ, a lilting, roaring, beautiful arrangement and performance.

"Knockin' on Heaven's Door" is another favorite. Great singing —ominous, energetic, soulful, heartbreakingly evocative—great song, written in '73 but transcendent and universal like that early stuff. Hey, does this mean he can still do it? Fine bass.

"It's Alright, Ma" stands out for its enormous power and un-diminished relevance, although it's terribly rushed. Dylan's vocal style this time around is always aggressive, as though he's psyched himself up to sing these songs and perform before this audience —and he's done a fine job, he sings convincingly and well, but always with that edge of tension, because he can't relax his guard. He relaxes *within* the structure, plays with it, performs brilliantly within it (as he once did within his ridiculously affected but effec-tive rural drawl). But that edge is always there, reminding us what time it is.

And though one could wish he would have been able to open up and actually *feel* "Don't Think Twice" and "Just Like a Woman" while singing them, there are silver linings aplenty—who cares how speedy "It's Alright, Ma" is once you're caught up in the wonder that he can still spit it out, which means it's still true? And listen to his guitar-playing! And the harmonica solo on "Just Like a Woman." And The Band's fine performance of "The Shape I'm In" is the perfect and only possible follow-up to "It's Alright, Ma." Everything works.

"All Along the Watchtower" is too fast, too, but did you *ever* hear Bob Dylan rock like that? Sheer joy. And "Lay Lady Lay" isn't the song it used ta be, but it's another one. "Rainy Day Women" also perfect.

And more. But I leave it to you. With this warning: we ain't heard nothing yet. The purpose of a good retrospective is to bring the artist and the audience into the present. Here we are. Bravo.

6. *Blood on the Tracks*

Another Soho News *piece, Thursday, January 30, 1975. Written a couple of days earlier—what fun to be sitting at a typewriter in New York City and know that people will be reading your comments around town before the week's over.*

I have already played this record more times in the past week than I play most records in a year. I love it. It is one of Dylan's best albums. It is probably the best album of the last five years. No matter how broke and busy you are—aren't we all?—you can't go wrong by going out and purchasing this record right now. End of review.

Still here? Okay, I'll mumble on. The record review is clearly an exhausted form, but so is the network news program (for example) and that doesn't stop those dummies from earning their livings—it doesn't even stop this dummy from watching them do it, often. Bob Dylan mumbled for years, collecting residuals, making children, and probably cleaning off his desk now and then. Now here he is again speaking like Zeus on the Mountaintop, or maybe some Italian poet from the fifteenth century.

It just goes to show.

"Life is sad/Life is a bust/All you can do is do what you must/You do what you must do, and you do it well/I do it for you, honey baby can't you tell?" (BD, "Buckets of Rain")

I watched Helmut Schmidt talking to Bill Moyers the other night, and I must say I was awfully goddamn impressed. Considering the competition (I mean Gerry, and Giscard, and Harold and Chou and all those guys), I'd give him my vote in a minute.

Every song on *Blood on the Tracks* is about or addressed to a woman, usually a woman who is now or soon will be separated from the singer or the protagonist, who continues to love her. This could be a rather limiting matrix, but it's not, or it's one of those cases of limitation resulting in abundance. Lyrically, melodically, emotionally this is a rich, varied album; it offers a lot, makes a great many unabashed statements, covers a lot of ground. It is as rich and rewarding as Dylan's brilliant recordings from 1965 and 1966, not as cosmic but more universal (you know what I'm saying; rephrase it any way that makes sense to you).

Bringing It All Back Home inspired my first record review/essay, just about ten years ago. My English teacher hated it—or maybe he just said he couldn't comment because he hadn't heard the record. As I recall it, the record had an intense impact on me, although I had trouble getting into the electrical stuff. I thought "Subterranean Homesick Blues" a rather poor attempt at rock 'n' roll. Changed my mind later, of course . . .

Blood on the Tracks is so fucking beautiful. Just to focus in on one aspect, where is there anyone around today who can sing half this well? I wanted to slug someone at a party recently who was repeating that old canard about Dylan being good in spite of his singing. People don't know what singing is. It's delivery. So-and-so may have a pair of vocal chords that should be put under glass and kept in the Smithsonian; what I want to know is, how much do I hear when that voice speaks to me? Is there an audible, complex consciousness present in the enunciation of every noun, verb, and pronoun? When there is, it's not because of the words. Any fool can think, and most can write; *delivering* those thoughts intact to another mind, another consciousness, is the extraordinary talent. Every singer currently working the rock circuit would be well-advised to shut up for a year and just listen to and consider Dylan's diction on this album, like for example when he says "waking up" and "cup" on "Simple Twist of Fate." Analyse the words all you want, folks, but remember how those words reached you. Every word on this record is a hundred times bigger because of the awareness and skill with which it is spoken. Music is singing (all those instruments are just imaginative forms of the human voice), and singing can be described when it's good as an advanced form of speaking. Encodes more information, is all, and information of precisely the sort that computers (useful, crude tools) can't even index.

Off the top of my head, the only singing/speaking that I even want to compare with *Blood on the Tracks* is Lou Reed's performance on the third Velvet Underground album (which should sell a million copies if reissued by MGM under the title *Pale Blue Eyes*).

(I should be in bed. I don't know what I'm doing here, sharing my precious opinions with people all editors assure me are idiots.)

Speaking of idiots (you'd be in a foul mood too, if you had to earn a living by trying to communicate through mass media) (especially in this decade of deep soup), I was talking to some guys the other day who said the musicianship on this album was not very good. I think they mentioned Mike Bloomfield (lead guitar on *H. 61 Revisited*) as an example of somebody with better, uh, musicianship. What a crock. I know these guys; they think "musicianship" is measured by how difficult it might be for somebody else to repeat the same riff. They probably say things to each other like, "Eric Clapton still has musicianship even when he plays slow."

The musicianship on this album is superb, it couldn't be better, and that's measurable by the *music* and nothing else. When a song comes out right, it means everybody was playing great. When a song comes out right, it's a miracle and we should be filled with love and fear of God.

I love this record. Word has it that it was partly recorded by unknown musicians in Minnesota, and I say thank the Lord that there are still unknown (and famous) musicians in this country who can do the right thing at the right time (M. Bloomfield, Al Kooper, R. Robertson and others were unknown musicians when they did their great studio work with Mr. D).

The only other thing that must be said is something about the magnificence of the humor in these new songs. I don't know if I should cite examples, because I laugh in different places every time, but the point is I crack up constantly every time I hear the record, which means even or especially when I'm playing one side over and over for five hours straight. That humor, I guess I don't have to say, is the sign of great art, it's like what you get from *Moby Dick* or Zen koans. It's the richest pleasure going.

Okay, some examples: "a creature void of form" in "Shelter," every perfect piece of the story in "Lily, Rosemary & the Jack of Hearts" (like for instance, "the boys finally made it through the wall"), "mine have been like Verlaine's and Rimbaud" from "You're Gonna Make Me Lonesome When You Go," plus thousands of other magical moments.

And did I mention the melodies? I guess I mentioned Dylan's arrangements by implication when I praised the "musicianship," but just to avoid ambiguity . . .

I happened to hear an earlier recording of this album, the one done in New York, and the two together sure taught me (retaught me) a lesson about doing things right and following hunches and taking chances, etc.

I know you'll be titillated to know that the first "Idiot Wind" was 65 seconds longer, and that "Lily, Rosemary etc" was a minute longer and actually *boring* if you can imagine such a thing. Phrases from "Idiot Wind" that didn't make it into the second recording include "I threw the *I Ching* yesterday" and "Imitators steal me blind," neither of which I miss; and "Idiot wind, blowing every time you move your jaw/From the Grand Coulee Dam to the Mardi Gras . . . We pushed each other a little too far," which I thought was terrific. I also have a note here that I got chills the first time I heard "Idiot Wind"—still do. A *tour de force*. I have some things to say about what the words mean to me, but fuck it. Buy me a drink sometime.

Hello to all you songs I didn't mention by name, I want you to know I care for you just as much as the others, I really do (special kisses to "Buckets of Rain," with that jumpy Mississippi John Hurt feel plus great steel guitar sound, and the opening moments of "Meet Me In The Morning," because they were my first loves). Mmm, "Tangled Up In Blue," "You're a Big Girl Now," "If You See Her, Say Hello" . . . ten beauties. Oh, that voice of "If You See Her" . . .

Beats the hell out of discotheques.

A few days later, Rolling Stone *asked 13 critics (including Greil Marcus, Dave Marsh, Robert Hilburn, Janet Maslin, Robert Christgau) to contribute a paragraph each about* Blood on the Tracks. *Here's mine:*

Make no mistake. It's the best album of the last five years by anybody and, beyond all the intelligence of the words and the beauty of the melodies and arrangements, it's the *performance* here that lifts this music so high. Dylan at his best is our finest singer; he delivers his heart. At last the Seventies have something musical to be proud of, to measure up to; this one record will pull better work from all of us. Bravo.

7. On Learning to Listen

The new publishers of Crawdaddy *asked me to write a column for the magazine, and I decided to write about a record I'd already written about, but that I felt they and some listeners had overlooked.*

Bob Dylan recorded two great albums in 1974. One of them was reviewed here last month, so I'll hold my tongue and just say that I consider *Blood on the Tracks* a masterpiece—I've been listening to it day and night for two weeks now and I still can't get enough. I love it.

The other album, though it didn't feature new material, was also a superb piece of work, and the first major album by Dylan since *John Wesley Harding.* I was surprised, therefore, that this magazine chose to ignore the record completely, printing a scatological lampoon of a Dylan review (funny, but inappropriate) instead of any sort of commentary on *Before the Flood.*

Before the Flood is Dylan's first official live album (there have been numerous bootlegs, and I once saw the promotional cover of a Columbia album called *Bob Dylan in Concert* which was scheduled and then canceled in 1964 or '65). It followed hot on the heels of *Planet Waves* (which bored me) and the massive, empty media coverage that accompanied the Dylan/Band Tour '74. I didn't expect much from it, a live album is an "iffy" proposition even from highly professional live performers, which Dylan is not—he's too private a person, and for a very long time he's been far too important to his audience for them to allow him to relax on stage.

But *Before the Flood* is extraordinary! Dylan sings like a man possessed. It's scary, and disorienting at first, to hear the aggressiveness in his voice; when you've had eight or ten years to get used to how a particular song sounds, you don't easily warm to reinterpretation. A number of people have told me they played this record once or twice and just couldn't listen to it.

41

Once or twice is not enough. The quality of popular rock music hit an all-time low in 1974, and more and more I've been thinking that it's not simply the fault of the times, or the business, or even the artists—the primary blame belongs with the audience. We've forgotten how to listen.

Listening to music is as important a part of the musical act as writing or performing. You have to do it right, or good music doesn't come into existence. That doesn't mean that you have to put on a coat and tie and sit in a straight-backed chair—or put on faded blue jeans and sit cross-legged smoking hash from a chillum—*doing it right* is not a matter of following the custom or the rules. What it is, is a matter of the heart. You've got to listen—sometimes, whenever you can, often enough to make it mean something—with an open heart. An open mind and wax-free ears aren't half enough.

For example: my experience with the first Buffalo Springfield album. I had never heard of Neil Young, Stephen Stills, or Richie Furay. And the first three or four times I listened to the record it didn't do anything for me, it sounded clichéd, and the production was really lame. Later, some of my friends reported similar reactions, and I suggested they keep on listening, give it a chance to grow on them. I myself had kept on listening to this unknown album by an unknown group because once, just once, I had heard the single "Nowadays Clancy Can't Even Sing" on a Buffalo radio station (audible in Boston sometimes late at night) and it killed me, I fell in love with it. My heart was open in those days, wide open, you could drive a train through it, and several people did.

So I kept listening to the Springfield album ("For What It's Worth" was added to the lp later) because I wanted to like it, and after five or six or seven spins the songs started hitting me, one after another, my barriers broke down or my senses woke up but anyway I found myself into it, way in, in enough to never want to get out. (". . . If crying and holding on/And flying on the ground is wrong/Then I'm sorry/To let you down/But you're from/My side of town/And I miss you . . .")

Similar experiences with many other albums and songs formed the basis of my love for rock music.

Today rock music is mass media on a scale few dreamed of nine years ago. I'm sure there are still people who buy only one record a month, and listen to it over and over on their primitive phonographs, as I did when I was 16, but I don't know those people and it's hard for the musicians to remember they're there—they sure don't write record reviews or work for radio stations. The din of the mass media commenting on the mass media (politics, music, business, everything becomes the same thing) is everywhere these days; people are deafened to the sound of heartbeats underneath the pandemonium.

If you, dear reader, happen to be one of the last of the great listeners, if you haven't lost your capacity for discovery and passion, if you can respond openly even to something as mythified as the songs of Bob Dylan, then you must listen to *Before the Flood.* Here is an album that speaks rock and roll heart language fluently. I can no longer even remember the earlier versions of many of these songs. Bob Dylan, Robbie Robertson, Garth Hudson, Rick Danko and Levon Helm, working together, form the core of one of the greatest live rock and roll bands ever. They seem to enjoy the pressure of absurd situations—the Royal Albert Hall concert in 1966, the Madison Square Garden concerts in 1974—and they respond by generating a tension in their music that is strong enough and sharp enough to cut human hairs and blocks of steel in mid-air.

Sit down and listen. Never mind the crap about how you don't like the sound of Dylan's voice on this record—I've heard that one before and so have you. Dylan's voice on this record is perfect, utterly accurate and devastatingly contemporary. Learn to love it. Learn to hear it. Have some respect. Listen to "Ballad Of a Thin Man," "All Along the Watchtower," "It's Alright, Ma," "Like a Rolling Stone" . . . There is such great music, guitar playing, drumming, singing, everything, saying so incredibly much all the time, on the Dylan/Band parts of *Flood* that you could listen to nothing else for the next eighteen months and still come back for more.

Now and then a record we think we don't like turns around and kicks us in the pants, humbles us, gives us some lessons on learning to listen again. I wish it would happen to me more often. I miss a lot of records. Somehow, I didn't miss this one.

8. Dylan's in the Basement

In June 1975 Bob Dylan released a set of recordings he and his friends in The Band had made at home eight years earlier, recordings that had partly circulated as song demos sent out by Dylan's publisher, and then as underground tapes passed on from listener to listener, and later as bootleg lps. I can't find the source, but I remember reading an article some months later in which Dylan expressed shock that the album sold well enough to get into the top ten: "I thought everybody had it already!" This review/essay was written for the Soho Weekly News *soon after the "official" album became available (I had not previously owned any of these recordings).*

Words. Humor. Nonsense a cover for deeper levels of communication. Cover necessary because Dylan had already taken language to its limits in the direction of recognizable "meaning" and "significance" & was now stuck with audience wanting mere more of the same. No point writing more verses to "Memphis Blues Again," right? But how far or rather where can mere words go? Well, after recognizable stories or anecdotes of ambiguous implication, strung together either randomly as in "MBA" or "Just Like Tom Thumb's" (random but with definite sense of motion towards climax) ("going through all these things twice") ("do believe I've had enough") or else in the form of an apparently sequential ("Johanna") or semi-sequential ("Des. Row") narrative, after this comes verses/anecdotes and choruses that are in recognizable English structure but made up of word-combinations that are *de facto* not valid (for example "yea heavy & a bottle of bread" or "looking for my lo and behold!"), i.e., nonsense. A la Edward Lear or many American folk songs of the sort that turn up on Burl Ives records.

And of course it worked; I mean even though the resulting stuff seemed too weird or inappropriate to release at the time (and note that it's the most cognitive songs from this set, not necessarily the best ones, that were picked up by other artists at the time . . . The

Byrds could certainly sing "You Ain't Going Nowhere" & "Nothing Was Delivered," PPM "Too Much Nothing," Hamilton Camp—best—and Julie Driscoll et al. "This Wheel's on Fire," etc., but who among them or anywhere else would have had the guts to sing, "Don't you tell Henry, apple's got my fly"?), there can be little question now, at least in my mind, that this stuff we have here, taken as finished product, performance, penetrates at times even deeper than anything that came before, "Visions of Johanna" or "Gates of Eden" or whatever your fave rave happens to be. "Memphis Blues Again" is one of mine, and yet I wouldn't hesitate to mention "Lo and Behold!" in the same breath; I mean, it's just that good.

In his most intense work, Dylan has effectively created new language. People who've listened to a lot of Dylan can and do incorporate this experience into their regular verbal communication with each other, both by direct quotation ("she breaks just like . . .") and indirectly by enhancing or altering the meanings of words ("Meantime life outside goes on all around you" might cause a person to use the words "life outside" to express an awareness/feeling subtly different from anything those words would have meant without the song's existence). Images and bits of phrasings from Dylan songs are liberally sprinkled throughout the daily conversation of many persons these days, and certainly show up often with and without credit (why credit what's become part of the language?) in all forms of contemporary writing. This is not unique to Dylan of course, the Beatles and the Rolling Stones have the same effect on us, and Shakespeare's been doing it to us, and to the language, for a very long time.

Anyway obviously the phonograph record TV transistor radio jet airplane etc. makes it all happen a hell of a lot faster (geometrically faster) now than in Shakespeare's time. Dante fixed a language by writing a poem in it, modern minstrels are breaking through the walls of language like firemen with axes and definitely the cumulative effect of all this is considerably more important than the mere messages any of these speakers may think they're trying to convey. In a sense, Dylan, always plagued by the word "message" (you remember he suggested a Carnegie Hall concert starring 1000 Western Union kids, if that was what people wanted), has consciously gone beyond the act of conscious statement in many of his

Basement Tapes songs, a massive major courageous last move into the unknown before his inevitable arrival at the post-paradoxical stage of simple statement as in *Nashville Skyline*. (*John Wesley Harding*, recorded immediately after or almost simultaneously with *The Basement Tapes*, is a transmogrification of the energy expressed in the Basement Tapes music into the intellectual realm, brilliant riddles, some solvable, some not, musically crude in comparison to expectations and the trends of the times (certainly not musically crude in any true sense) but intellectually complex enough to offer protection against those who would have insisted that Dylan broke his brain on the pavement if they'd had to analyse "Million Dollar Bash.")

Performance is essential to all this; this is the point I want to come back to again and again. The performance of the music and the performance of the words, that is, the singing. There is a magnificent book, which too few people seem to own or be aware of, called *Writings and Drawings by Bob Dylan* ; it was published several years ago, and most of the Basement Tapes songs are included, as printed words, in the section "from *Blonde on Blonde* to *John Wesley Harding*." I read most of these songs at one time or another, glancing through the book, and I heard many of them either on the bootlegs (which I guess because of sound quality or else context never attracted my intense attention, with the exception of the superb Royal Albert Hall concert) or on other people's recordings of them (learned from the bootlegs, or copies of the tapes); and so I learned that the profundity which I insist permeates "Yea Heavy & A Bottle of Bread" cannot be felt simply by reading the song *qua* poem. At least, not until *you've already heard it.* (The fascinating corollary of this is the realization that "It's Alright, Ma," for example, is also pretty inconsequential as words on a page until one has heard it sung and therefore *knows what it means.*)

In other words, the meaning we feel in the words is imparted to us by the performance: melody, rhythm, inflection, and simply performance-as-a-whole, that unnamed effect of music on the nervous system. The words enter as part of the music, the performance, and are never really heard alone again.

So: when I heard the perfect rolling tension of the first few bars of "Lo and Behold!" my hair stood on end, and by the time the chorus came around I was singing along like a madman. The way he says "Moby Dick" made me want to fall off the planet. Right away before I knew what the words were I heard much more than was there, and (this is familiar to any Rolling Stones fan) then began the rather effortless task of dragging the words up to the level of the performance, forcing them (they submit soon enough) to accommodate the intense sensation of meaningfulness that the song invokes. Specifically, within a day of first hearing the record, I was walking around telling myself that I was "looking for my lo-and-behold" and I understood myself perfectly, I mean that's just what I'm doing, and I sure wouldn't have known how to say it until I heard the song. The language I use to talk with myself has been altered, therefore; and I'd use the same words to talk to other people if I felt the need to say anything that intimate.

Get me out of here, my dear man.

The further one goes beyond cognition, still holding onto that primal power that comes from having something to say (so it comes out in your voice even if you're reading the phone directory, though it helps a lot if you wrote the phone directory in the first place, out of your subconscious, you know), the less encumbered one is with what people think words mean, which is another way of saying, with what people think is going on. If you can speak to them and get them to listen on that trans-cognitive level, you can tell them stuff or talk about stuff that is outside of the arbitrary limits they put on their own perception of their experience. You'll open them up, hit them at readily recognizable deeper levels of their soul, and they'll love it. I love it. This album really does me in.

How does he do it? He reaches us with the music, and his way of talking (which is the same thing), but the source of the music is his sense of humour, that is the sustained note he plays off of throughout most of these songs. And as Greil Marcus suggests in his excellent and informative liner notes, there is a conversation, a competition, a friendship going on between Dylan and The Band on these tracks that is the forge of the musical brilliance and of the extraordinary level of awareness in the singing, no audience can be imagined sharp enough to deserve this, but they have each other, high on the moment down in the basement, riffing and showing off their total awareness of the cosmos for fun and excitement till the cows come home.

Williams' Law states that the best performances are never

recorded, and the best recordings are never released. So it's a fucking miracle we have this record; & of course you know it's still just a hint of that highest level of communication between human beings, which whatever it is I assure you never gets on wax (or vinyl).

Dylan and The Band make nonsense meaningful; by doing so they show us how meaning is created—if we can dig it, we're given front row seats to a demonstration of the workings of the central mystery of our existence.

But I digress. This is just a mad rap, of course, and as is probably clear the sort of songs I'm mainly thinking about are "Lo," "Yea, Heavy," "Million Dollar Bash," "Open the Door, Homer," "Please Mrs. Henry," "Tiny Montgomery," "Don't Ya Tell Henry," and "Long Distance Operator." There's other stuff going on here too. I'm not going to hardly talk about most of it (I don't even know anything about most of it—for one thing I've only just started listening, and for another thing I probably never will), but there is another song that flipped me out right away that is right on a consciousness level with "Lo and Behold!" but doesn't fool with nonsense words at all. I'm not sure what it fools with. It's called "Clothes Line."

"Clothes Lines" has the same narrative-with-dialogue structure and the same sort of vocal intonation as "The Balled of Frankie Lee and Judas Priest," but it's—to borrow a phrase from Ken Kesey— much closer to the bone of my contention. It's a short story set to music written in ABCB rhymed quatrains, performed as a one-act play. Everything is right on the surface, perfectly straightforward, but what a devastating little skit, what an extraordinary performance! The stuff that isn't said, all those awarenesses between the lines of the story and in the holding-backness of the music, is enough to kill me. How does he do it? How do they do it? How can I even listen to it? Recorded six years before Agnew's fall, incidentally . . . I love the first and last lines. And, "Sometime, not all the time" is one of those phrases that just can't help changing our language and lives. It says it.

I've made my point. I'm in love with this record. I'll even issue a warning: if you're too busy worrying about money to take the time to really listen to this album, then you're done for. Tonight's the night. I've got to go listen to "Tears of Rage" and "Going to Acapulco." And "Apple Suckling Tree"! "Apple Suckling Tree" is simple proof that rock and roll and American folk music are one and the same. Dance, little sister! And "Lo and Behold!" again.

I can't split without at least mentioning that The Band deserves equal credit with B.D. for the genius & success of these recordings. Their performances on their own songs are excellent & very pleasurable; but their performances on Dylan's songs are unbelievable. Like Al Kooper on *Blonde On Blonde,* Garth Hudson has attained musical immortality on the basis of these sessions alone, whatever else he may achieve. And the relationship between vocalist and "accompanists" on this album, simply judged by what I can hear, is unique in my experience of music. He's working off them and they're working off him in such a way . . .

See you later.

9. *Hard Rain*

My "freewheeling" review-writing style has never been in demand at most peri-odicals. I can remember listening to Desire *the first few times and wishing I had a place where I could write about it and share my responses. Later that year (Sept. '76) I got so excited about* Hard Rain *(the TV special and then the rather different album) I decided to write whether I had a for-sure outlet or not. I sent this review to* New Age *magazine, but I guess it was too new age even for them. I think I sent it to some other places, but no luck. This is its first publication.*

Two factual notes, since I'm not rewriting these pieces for this book (in order to preserve their value as documents of a fan's reaction at that time): it turned out the Hard Rain *album includes a few tracks from a show a week before the one that was filmed for television (Fort Worth, Texas in addition to Fort Collins, Colorado). And that bootleg of "Maggie's Farm" from '65 must have been the Newport Folk Festival performance (with the Butterfield Blues Band, not The Band).*

> "I try my best to be like I am
> But everybody wants you to be like them."
> —Bob Dylan 1976, quoting Bob Dylan 1965

What it is about Bob Dylan, he *still* ain't working on Maggie's Farm no more. Very soon, I think, he's going to be just as con-troversial a character as he was the first time around. Right on, baby, right on! And what we got here is, in my opinion, as import-ant and successful an album as any Bob Dylan has ever made.

Play it loud. If you can't play it *loud*, keep the record in its jacket and just look at the cover picture until you think you're ready.

This is a record about sex.

It's about, uh, well, biting through ... "The storm with its thunder and lightning overcomes the disturbing tension in nature; energetic biting through overcomes the obstacle that prevents joining of the lips." (Wilhelm/Baynes *I Ching*, Hex. 21.) It's about—no, it *is* the energy that we find whenever we go forward with the work at hand.

Hard Rain is a live album, recorded on the eve of Dylan's 35th birthday in intermittent rain in front of 25,000 people and a handful of TV cameramen, Hughes Stadium, Fort Collins, Colorado, May 23rd, 1976. The TV special—the first real rock 'n' roll concert I have ever seen on television—was broadcast Tuesday September 14th, and this album was in the stores three days later. There's only about a 50% overlap between the songs chosen for the lp and those shown on television; still, it may be the first time most of us have had a chance to *see* a great rock concert and then go out a few days later and buy the record. One more global village experience . . .

Dylan, who is famous for his words, has become in the last few years a master of speaking without words, of communicating messages that are greater than words can hold, and that's what this album is about. Where before—in the first age of Dylan—the words were the final focus of attention, now the performance is everything. The sweat on the man's brow—and you can *hear* that sweat in the singing—speaks more than a thousand songs.

What is sex? It is I and thou, it is energy exaltation. Let's say it's a way of focusing one's attention. Dylan, in the extraordinary performances captured on this album, focuses his own attention with incredible intensity on a single, imaginary person: "I'm . . . singing just for you," he says, "I hope that you can hear . . ." You'd better believe he means it.

What are you going to say, now that you've looked and seen that burning intensity, that passionate youthful energy we supposedly lost with the 1960s, on the face of a 35-year-old millionaire?

You've either got to deny the existence of passion altogether (a popular stance), or else admit that your own life might not be over yet.

Side one. "I ain't gonna work on Maggie's Farm no more." Magnificent. A recent bootleg turned up a 1965 live performance of this song—very important song, major gut-level statement, not overly famous & a perfect opener for this lp—the '65 live version, presumably with The Band, is hot, all the extraordinary "this is the moment!" excitement and creativity of early electric Dylan from the golden age, but the 1976 performance is even hotter, the song has been opened up musically in a new way (so has the singer), and more energy gets through. Dylan's moaning at the end of each verse is uplifting; Mick Ronson (electric guitar) busts all his chops

51

trying (bravely but unsuccessfully) to match him.

"One Too Many Mornings." Always loved this song—so did Dylan, he started playing it as a rock number back in '65 or '66. This arrangement is fabulously orchestrated—the rhythm of the whole thing blows me away—"noble" vocal, somehow sounds like Jackson Browne's "Late for The Sky," which of course was influenced by Dylan's original. (Throw in "The Last Thing on My Mind," Tom Paxton, for perfect trilogy on the subject.) What punch! New meanings always in human relationships, the music says it all, no possible exhaustion of subject matter here.

"Stuck Inside of Mobile with the Memphis Blues Again." You wanted to hear this one again, admit it . . . well, *I* did, and got more than I bargained for. Bringing a song back to life—born again, new squalling baby with no chains on—requires a hell of a lot more than a great singer and a fine hot band. It requires total reabsorbtion, like the Borges character who reproduced *Don Quixote* word for word and made it better. How is it done? Well it's like lovemaking, see, tonight is the night of all nights and everything that's come before just leads up to it, I am all my energy ever and I'm going to give it to you. Something like that. Watch out.

"Oh Sister." Oh sister! Stop, you're tearing me apart, I can't stand it any more. No, on second thought, turn up the volume.

Unquestionably a fine record for singing-along.

"Lay Lady Lay." No way I can mention one tenth of what I feel listening to these performances. What guts it takes to push flat out like that—of course, it's the only way to go with stuff like this in front of 25,000 people, but what other performer has realized that and tried even half as hard? If singing is something one does from the heart (like breathing from the stomach), this album contains some of the best singing I've ever heard. "Forget this dance, let's go upstairs!" Indeed.

Side two. "Shelter From The Storm." New intensity level reached, and sustained throughout side two. This is the third re-take of *Blood on the Tracks*. I love it. The man uses his own words as so many boxes to stand on, fills them and transcends them, see him up on tiptoes peering through heaven's keyhole. Now he's brought the whole band up with him, everybody wants to get a better view.

"You're a Big Girl Now." Every time I hear this I want to get stoned, it has that incredible fine detail beauty, messing with the fabric of time itself, one wants to savor every millisecond. (Jesus, I think this album might be better than *Royal Albert Hall 1966.*) When I first heard this song it was impressive because it began to approach "Just Like a Woman." Now it far outdistances the latter, at least for 1976, cuts deeper, seems even more impossibly true and beautiful. This is my kind of music: every note in place, and could never be duplicated in a thousand years. And always the vocal looms over everything else like the smile of a small child on a big man's face.

"I Threw It All Away." Fabulous arrangement, fabulous vocal. Even *Nashville Skyline* (*especially Nashville Skyline*, there's method in this madness) can be resurrected and made Godlike. The profane becomes profound. Makes you think, doesn't it? (Do you scream out wordless squeals while listening at high volume? I do.)

"Idiot Wind." If this album needed a reason, here it is. Something to say? Yeah, I got something to say. You don't have enough orifices in your body to take in all the stuff I have to say. But never mind; here's just the smallest taste, served up on a platter. If you can swallow this, there's more where it came from.

. . . I suppose we don't have to say it's his best rock 'n' roll album, one of the all-time greats in that broad category. And "Idiot Wind" the definition of what a band and a singer can do even while leaving the vocal predominant. It would be good to note the recording quality of all this, close to sublime, I seldom wish I had better speakers but this is one time. Also especially note the quality of the *pressing*, so hard to get hot sound on a 25-minute side, *Desire* was a disaster in that respect (so many returned copies too), this time on my copy at least the pressing plant seems to have made some kind of breakthrough. Is it in the mastering? The PVC? Christ, I wouldn't know. But it does *sound* like an lp with 13 minutes on a side, and that's really saying something.

And finally (since I dare not begin really *talking* about "Idiot Wind" and some of the things it conjures up), perhaps a word about Dylan's, uh, aggressive stance. Looks and sounds like he's just about to beat up you and your mother too, right? "Idiot Wind" especially full of that wonderful old-fashioned (*Highway 61*) vicious bitterness, tempered with self-knowledge perhaps but still so gratifying, his special skill . . . all that grimacing on the TV show.

Somebody told me recently when I go to sign books and meet people I shouldn't smile, the public wants you to look serious. Well, I dunno. But could it mean that underneath all that seething earnest hostility Dylan is just trying so hard *not to laugh?* Hey, it's a glorious posture, as effective for opening up the performance as the weird accent he used to affect, and just as inexplicable . . . it works, never mind why, we'll never know, it's like the Ay-rab headgear, it looks good, never mind what it "means," it just works for the moment to help get the energy through . . .

"Everybody wants you to be just like them." Don't be like that. Enjoy the man for who he is, for how hard he tries to be he. We're just so lucky to have this music. It's a privilege. And an inspiration. Fight about Dylan if you want to, it's good for the soul. Me, I'm just so happy I could cry.

10. Who Pagan Became

As it says, this piece was written the week I saw the shortened version of Bob Dylan's film Renaldo & Clara, *which I had seen and loved nine months earlier when it had its first showing in three cities at once. I saw it (opening day) in San Francisco, since I was now living in northern California. I wrote this I think because I was more and more feeling that Bob Dylan in the late 1970s was a misunderstood and underappreciated artist. The feeling began, I recall, when I found that many of my friends and contemporaries were not open to or excited about Dylan's 1976* Hard Rain *TV show and album.* Blood on the Tracks *and* Desire *and the radical, free-form Rolling Thunder tour were all very well-received by the public and the press, and then suddenly it seemed to me (and it must have seemed to Dylan) the public and the press really turned against him, starting in 1976, confused by and critical of his every move.*

In any case, I wrote this with no idea how I'd get it published—or maybe I knew I'd do what I eventually did, publish it myself. I sent it out in early April 1979 in a small newsletter I was writing for 50 or 100 friends. A few weeks before that I decided to change the piece so as not to refer to the person I was writing about as "Dylan"—maybe I intuited that people were tired of hearing his name. I came up with the name "Pagan" because it had two syllables and ended -an and seemed a clever choice. I had no idea, of course, that for the past three months Dylan had been attending Bible school in southern California, and was about to start recording an album called Slow Train Coming. *My intent was to write about who "Pagan" had already become, as indicated by his recent film and album and interviews . . . In hindsight, I now think I was unconsciously and intuitively starting work on the book I would write later in 1979,* Dylan—What Happened?

(Renaldo & Clara)

Late 1978. I liked Sam Pagan's *Renaldo & Clara* the first time I saw it (the four-hour version), saw it again two days later and liked it just as much. This week, after nine months, I saw the movie for the third time. My wife Sachiko and I felt some apprehension about how we'd like the new two-hour version—there were a lot of things in the original film we badly wanted to see again, and obviously it wasn't all gonna be there. 50% is a big cut.

I (both of us, actually) came out of the theater feeling that the short version was even better than the long one, and that *Renaldo & Clara* in whatever guise is one of the best movies ever made. Certainly it's the movie I most want to see again—if it were playing anywhere remotely near here right now I'd be watching it instead of writing this essay. It is superb. I'd say it's as good as *Gravity's Rainbow*, as good as "Visions of Johanna" followed by "Sooner or Later One of Us Must Know" with "I Want You" and "Memphis Blues Again" on the other side.

I saw it two days ago, and I don't know of anywhere that it's playing tonight (or in the next month). I think I'm having withdrawal symptoms.

I want to see that movie.

I'd forgotten what a great stimulus it is to be misunderstood. Very few of the people I meet understand my enthusiasm for Pagan's recent work. The result is, I'm writing. I feel like there's something that needs to be said that no one else is saying, and it's a rare feeling, and it sure does push me around (forces me to work) but I sure do like it. I like to work, even though I resist it fiercely. I think I'm normal.

I also think Pagan's normal. That tells you what kind of nut I am.

I also think someone who's reading this knows what I'm talking about, or I wouldn't be able to go on.

(who Pagan became)

None of us ever change, of course. But the rest of the world doesn't realize that. In regard to Sam Pagan, I'm just part of the rest of the world, playing his albums on my phonograph, reading the magazines, lining up to see the show. Smart enough to see (partway) through the myth, but hungry enough to embrace it anyway (all the more so) because it gives off sparks for me, because I've seen the best myths of my generation turn to stone and Pagan's to the contrary breathes stronger than ever. Recalled to life. It's a hell of a story (Pagan in the 70s), and for those who haven't ears to hear I just hope you'll wake up right now.

Pagan's reputation at present rests in most people's hearts squarely on the songs he wrote and the records he made circa

1963–1966, an awesome era; and many of the brightest and most sensitive people I know are ready (sometimes eager) to write him off as a has-been. A hundred years from now it'll be obvious to anyone who gives a damn that Pagan in the 70s (let's say 1974 onward, starting with his difficult comeback tour January '74, with a nod to that '73 advance warning tour de force two-minute movie single "Knockin' on Heaven's Door") effectively broke through as an artist, did much of his best work and (in his live performances particularly) added a depth and breadth to his total work that, much more than his original floodtide of genius, assures his immortality as a musician and an artist of the human soul.

(mystery)

Mystery? Yes, but this time it's less focused in the words—more in the presence, which includes the music, the arrangements, the singing, the situation, contexts within contexts. Mystery true as his finest 60's meanderings but not in the same place and never a rerun. Everybody ten years older wants to relive high points but Pagan can't sell that thrill. Saying he ain't what he was is like trying to crawl back to the womb. Most people ('specially over the age of 22) prefer memory of mystery to the real thing, but the artist by definition goes on offering reality regardless. New mysteries are the only evidence of actual creation.

(The person who goes on living encounters ever-deepening mysteries. If your work is a reflection of your life, mystery will shine from the pages of your songs like lovers' eyes sparkling in dreams. No answer will occur too often, or ever really make sense. No one will agree exactly, but everyone will want to be there.)

(timing)

Timing, his timing is impeccable. Even when it's off it's on. I think this is achieved by swallowing the world. If you have a total vision you can really live the moment on stage. Like standing in the right place in a room, everything fits because everything lurches forward from an accurate and conscious center of this particular universe.

(arrangement)

Arrangement is order out of chaos, it's taking the internal pulse and giving it an external form, making it rememberable. Arrangement turns experience into information. What distinguishes the second decade of Pagan—as words from nowhere characterized the first—is new arrangements of existing material. This has been the realm of greatest creativity, this is the setting for the statements he most wants to make, this is where he's most freely exercising his genius. (*Renaldo & Clara* is sheer arrangement.) One walks away from a concert (or live recording) of Pagan '78 humming the arrangements.

(Street-Legal)

Pagan's new album. What's he talking about? For the sake of simplicity (and to avoid oversimplification), let's start with the three-song suite at the end of side two: "True Love Tends to Forget," "We Better Talk This Over," "Where Are You Tonight?" Favorite themes—marriage & lovers, too close & too far away, familiarity breeds absence which makes the heart grow and so forth. I can dig it. The man speaks for me & mine.

Wait a minute. What am I doing here? (Don't get upset.) This isn't a review; don't write it like one. This is a collection of insights, with a purpose. Purpose is to make statement. Statement is:

Mystery. Marriage. Sex & timelessness. Timing. Arrangement.

> "I try my best to be like I am
> But everybody wants you to be like them"
> — Sam Pagan, *Hard Rain* album, 1976

What it is about Sam Pagan (I wrote in 1976), he *still* ain't working on Maggie's Farm no more.

(sex)

"We Better Talk This Over" is about two people and sex is what brings them together. Or (and) forces us apart. "I think/we better talk this over/maybe/when we both get sober" is a tremendously charming line. One could go for a guy like that.

It's important to be funny in bed.

58

Renaldo & Clara (the short version) is fabulously passionate. Never seen anything like it. So's the album *Hard Rain*. This is the sort of work that makes the century look good, work that'll last a long, long time. From the poet's horniness whispers the voice of God.

(marriage)

Marriage provides the subject matter for much of Pagan's best work in the 70's. "Isis" ("Here's a song about marriage. This is called 'Isis.'"—spoken intro from a Rolling Thunder concert). "Sara." "True Love Tends to Forget." "Tangled Up in Blue." "Idiot Wind." "You're a Big Girl Now." *Planet Waves. Renaldo & Clara.*

"Marriage is the hottest furnace of the spirit today"—Leonard Cohen, 1975. This is a subject for mature audiences only. Eternal adolescents, get lost.

(timelessness)

Pagan's greatest accomplishment is his ability to evoke a state of timelessness. It's a place, another world. *Blonde on Blonde*, mostly because of the instrumentation, is filled with timelessness. "Mr. Tambourine Man." "Senor." "Where Are You Tonight?" "Changing of the Guards." "One More Cup of Coffee." "Lily, Rosemary and the Jack of Hearts." "Don't Think Twice, It's All Right." "Tangled Up in Blue." "Knockin' on Heaven's Door."

It's a place, a place. You've been there. Now come on, don't misunderstand me. "Timelessness" doesn't mean "so good it'll never go out of date." It's a *place*. We can go there right now.

You're reading the paper, see, and you hear this news from Berlin. You don't know anybody in Berlin, but somehow it catches your eye. Your baby sneaks up behind you and puts her wings around your heart. You dive for cover, but it's too late: the afternoon is gone.

You're out in the woods when you hear the fire alarm. You turn it off and go back to sleep, but later you wish you hadn't done that. A telephone is ringing. If only she'd tell you her name one time, maybe you could go back and see her again.

You're in the movie theater and they bust you for wearing sandals. You figure you could make your escape but someone's standing on your toes. Up on the screen you're tied and gagged but that's not really real. Her eyes are burning a hole in your trousers and the phone's not ringing any more.

I'm trying to write an essay that will be more or less than obvious. I don't want to just fall in the usual holes. New realities are the only information worth repeating. And the newer they seem the older they turn out to be. Maybe it's time for some history here.

Pagan returned to the stage at the beginning of 1974. This is immediately after the recording and release of *Planet Waves*, which particularly in the context of *Renaldo & Clara* can be seen as trying to tell your lady how much you love her before you go out on the road. There's plenty of guilt involved. And fear, to face those audiences that expect so much that has nothing to do with nothing. Which implies courage on both accounts, and a sense of inevitability, or maybe a grim determination to escape from nowhere in spite of the pain it'll bring. Not that your wife and kids are nowhere. What you really want to do is bring them along, and be on your own as well.

What you really want to do is stay home, but it's not time for that no more.

So you deal with it. "Pagan's vocal style this time around is always aggressive," I wrote in 1974, "as though he's psyched himself up to sing these songs and perform before this audience—and he's done a fine job, he sings convincingly and well, but always with that edge of tension, because he can't relax his guard. He relaxes *within* the belligerence, plays with it, performs brilliantly within it (as he once did within his outrageously affected and effective rural drawl). But that edge is still there, reminding us what time it is."

(Pagan's gift of timelessness is perhaps what makes it seem to me he's *always* singing about the moment.)

My idea is that the belligerent stance of the singer on the '74 tour was more or less consciously assumed, as a way to deal with his paranoia/stagefright/wholly appropriate fear of the combination of his inner uncertainty (hey I ain't done this for a while) & the audience's ferocious need. That's why he sings so fast, he's tense but he's got it formalized, this spit-it-out conscious approach gives him room, riding the tiger, the only other choice was stay home and you know in the face of erosion standing your ground can be no choice at all.

Presumably (I'm really fantasizing here) working on the movie the year before, with Peckinpah, and the fun and stimulus out there, planted the seed and gave him the goad to get back to his work again. And not coincidentally after all those years (six, I'd say) to find himself having written a song every bit as powerful as the stuff he used to do back before he left the world behind.

"Knockin' on Heaven's Door" is a vision of impending death or life. I can listen to it twenty times in a row. Here I am out in the void, feeling the desire to break through. Knock knock knockin'. "It's getting dark, too dark to see . . ." This is the whole thing, boys. Oh yeah!!!

Timelessness has to do with camaraderie, it's that extra ingredient slipped into the ordinary that makes our lives worth living. This song is the eternal brink of revelation.

The comeback tour, with The Band backing Pagan and doing a set of their own, ran for about seven weeks, Jan-Feb '74, in big arenas across the country. A live album from the tour, *Before The Flood*, was released that summer. In September a new studio album, *Blood on the Tracks*, was recorded in New York; half the tracks were then recut with different musicians in Minneapolis at Christmastime, and the album was released in January '75.

Autumn '75 brought a second tour, very different from the first. The Rolling Thunder Revue, featuring Pagan, Joan Baez, Roger McGuinn, Jack Elliott, a house band & others, was thrown together with the speed and spontaneity Pagan strives for in his recording sessions; they played small clubs and occasional arenas in the Northeast for six weeks, starting at Plymouth Rock and ending up in New York City. Most of *Renaldo & Clara* was filmed during this time. Part two of this tour, with most of the same crew, played colleges and arenas in the South from Florida to Texas, then drifted north to Oklahoma, Kansas, Colorado and Utah. This was another six-week stint, April-May '76. The May 23rd concert in Fort Collins, Colorado was filmed for a network TV show under Pagan's supervision; and an album, *Hard Rain*, was released featuring live recordings from Fort Collins and from a show a week earlier in Fort Worth.

A studio album, *Desire*, had been recorded in New York in July '75, and was released in January 1976.

1977 was devoted to the editing of *Renaldo & Clara,* easily the most ambitious and extended creative effort Pagan's ever got himself involved in. In 1978 the movie was released, and a new tour & new band took shape. The tour kicked off in Tokyo in February '78, proceeded to Australia & New Zealand, a week in L.A., on to Europe for shows in England, France, Germany, Holland, Scandinavia, back to the States for a two-month break and then three months of arena shows in 62 cities in the U.S. and Canada. The band, eleven musicians including three backup singers, also worked with Pagan on his 1978 studio album *Street-Legal,* recorded in May in Santa Monica and released at the end of June. (Only two members of the '78 band—David Mansfield and Steve Soles—were part of the Rolling Thunder Revue.)

That's enough history I hope. Basically the discography of this period includes the three studio albums (four if you include *Planet Waves,* which to me is transitional), two live albums with a third presumably on the way (in which case all three tours will be represented), and an indeterminate number of bootlegs featuring live recordings from the three tours plus a miscellany of studio outtakes, TV performances, one great single not included on an album ("Rita Mae") and so forth. Four songs from *Renaldo & Clara* were released by Columbia on a disc for radio stations only; four more Pagan performances can be seen or heard in the movie and album of *The Last Waltz.*

Then there's *Renaldo & Clara* short and long, and three lengthy interviews (in *Rolling Stone* and *Playboy*). Output. Product. The man is elusive even when you're in the room with him they say, but he does leave a lot of footprints. And this product is on what I base my claims that Pagan's second period of intensity easily rivals the first, his myth reborn in a subtler and richer guise, musical achievement reaching new heights and his total opus during the two decades possibly more substantial than that of any other artist in any medium during the same period of time.

The more I listen the better it sounds. Any minute now I hope to break through and start speaking in tongues of my own. I want to tell you what I hear. What I hear is what I want from you is intimacy. That's my purpose. That's what sex & marriage & timelessness are for.

11. Dylan—What Happened?

In early November, 1979, I attended seven Bob Dylan concerts in a row, and decided to write an "instant book" that would be a review of the concerts, and of the new album, and a look at the available information about his sudden and bewildering enthusiasm for Jesus (because everybody I knew was asking me). I also saw it as a chance to write at length, and maybe for a larger audience, about this subject I'd been wanting to talk about: Bob Dylan in the 70s. I'd been wanting to talk about him as an artist in this poorly understood period, but suddenly because of his conversion people had urgent questions about him as a person, again, as they had had in the 60s. I felt qualified to try to address those questions only because it seemed to me he had been and still was telling us a lot about his personal life in his songs.

The book was literally written in two weeks, Nov. 9th to 23rd, and thanks to the extraordinary efforts of my publishing partners at And Books (and The Distributors) in South Bend, Indiana, the book was printed less than a month after I started writing it, and the first copies were actually on sale in some bookstores in the midwest by Dec. 11, 1979, and in stores throughout the U.S. before Christmas. Without the immediate enthusiasm and support for this crazy idea from my friends in South Bend, I probably wouldn't have had the chutzpah to write it. Thanks, Steve, Patty, Mark, Janos, Mike . . . I took the title from a book that was published shortly after Elvis Presley's death. As you'll see, the essay was broken up into sections, or chapters, unnamed or -numbered, but with a quote at the top of each section. The essay that follows is the entire text of the long-out-of-print book (which also included 16 pages of photos from the San Francisco shows).

> "And if you don't underestimate me,
> I won't underestimate you."
> —Bob Dylan, 1968

Something has definitely happened to Bob Dylan. This isn't the first time he's transformed himself, certainly not the first time his fans have had a "new Dylan" to puzzle over. But could anyone have imagined in 1965, when Dylan fans were howling and booing that their hero had sold out by walking onstage with an electric guitar, that fourteen years later Bob Dylan would walk out on stage and sing seventeen songs every one of which makes reference to and centers around the singer's special relationship with Jesus Christ?

November 1st, 1979: Bob Dylan did his first show of fourteen sold-out nights at San Francisco's Warfield Theatre. He played all the songs from his recent *Slow Train Coming* album, plus eight new ones never heard before. He didn't play a single song written before late 1978.

("All old things are passed away," he told the audience halfway through the fourth concert, in response to scattered shouts for "Lay, Lady, Lay" and "Like a Rolling Stone.")

Dylan's face looked tired and puffy through binoculars opening night; for the first time he looked old, much older than his 38 years. He was tense, and the performances of the songs from the new album were forced, unconvincing. The magic only started when he got to the newer songs—the first of them, "Covenant Woman," was instantly stunning, and it was followed by a handful of other great moments.

The second night the weariness was gone from his face, and the music was a lot better. Same songs.

The fifth night (still same songs, same order) was the equal of any concert Dylan has ever done. It was fabulous. The seventh was as good or better. Dylan sang, and his band played, with gut-wrenching conviction; and his new songs were unmistakably revealed as among the best he's ever written.

It's a lot to swallow, I know. But Dylan has done it to us before. I'm not a born-again Christian, or any kind of Christian, particularly. But I'm a stone Bob Dylan fan, now more than ever after hearing these latest concerts. The sum total of the work he's done, the ground he's broken and the stages of creativity he's gone through, is staggering. There is no performer, no artist alive to match his achievement.

It was hard for me to accept Mick Jagger saying, "stick my knife right down your throat, baby," even though he said it on my favorite Rolling Stones album ever. It is equally hard for me to come to terms with and identify with Bob Dylan singing, "I've been saved by the blood of the lamb."

What happened to Dylan, anyway? I'll tell you what I know, what I think, what I feel. I'll tell you the story as best I can piece it together. After that, you're on your own.

* * *

"I believe in you
Even on the morning after"
—Dylan, 1979

Today is November 9th, 1979. Last night my wife Sachiko and I returned from our seventh Bob Dylan concert in eight days. We drove an hour and a half each way every night to get to the theater, arranged a week's worth of babysitting, paid the full $15 plus service charge for each ticket every night. Dylan and his entourage did the same songs in the same order every time.

So last night at 11:00 pm, after listening to the same show seven times, we walked to the parking garage, got in our car and put a Dylan tape into the cassette player. And listened to the show an eighth time, twice in one night! And loved it.

We're out of our minds, of course. ("Are we drunk?", Sachiko wondered. If we were, it wasn't on any of the usual intoxicants. We were drunk on music, which according to a long tradition is something very close to being drunk on God.) But really, if the person you believe to be the greatest living performer and artist schedules a week of live performances in a small theater 55 miles from where you live, and all it takes to go see him is an act of will (spending money you don't have and time you can't afford), what sense could it possibly make *not* to go?

I want to go again tonight. But I'm going to stay here and try to write it all down for you instead. (As he says in one of the new songs, "I've got a covenant too.")

There's no ambiguity, although some have desperately tried to create one, about Dylan's being a born-again Christian. Does he say he is? No; as is normal for him, he says almost nothing between songs. He has given no recent interviews that I know about. But, as is also normal for him, the songs say it all. And the songs say that Jesus Christ is the Lord, and that He died so that Bob Dylan, among others, might live and be saved. The language of the songs is all straight from the Bible, definitely fundamentalist, evangelical, apocalyptic. The album is certainly unambiguous, but the live show goes even further: Dylan, at least the public Dylan, expresses a set of awarenesses that seem totally consistent with the mainstream of contemporary born-again Christian attitudes and beliefs.

There's also no ambiguity, at least to this member of the audience, about Dylan's sincerity in all this. He clearly believes and feels what he's singing; more than that, he clearly loves Jesus. His gratitude to his Lord and to the woman who showed him the way are beautifully and humbly expressed, and even though I'm an outsider I can't help but be moved.

And there are also lines and implications in some of his new songs that make me very uncomfortable. I'll try to explore all this in detail as we go on, but first I'd like to give you a quick rundown of the structure of each night's show.

The Warfield is an old-fashioned, attractive, comfortable down-town theater, presumably designed for drama and vaudeville. It's small (2200 seats) compared with the 20,000-seat auditoriums Dylan and other "superstars" usually perform in. I don't think there's a bad seat in the house. Producer Bill Graham's staff were courteous and efficient; a bar in the balcony lobby busily served drinks throughout the show. Most of the audience seemed to be in their late twenties and early thirties.

The curtain goes up about 8:20, and Regina Havis, a short vibrant black woman (most nights she wore a curly wig, but I liked it better when she didn't), walks up to the microphone and starts telling a story. An old woman wants to go see her dying son, but she has no money and the conductor won't let her on the train. She prays to the Lord for help; the conductor tries to start the train but it won't go; finally he asks the woman to get on the train. "But conductor, you said if I didn't have no ticket I couldn't ride on your train." "Old woman, Jesus got your ticket, now come on this train." Two other black women, Monalisa Young and Helena Springs (all three are beautiful; over the course of the week my heart was totally won by Helena, who's been touring with Dylan since the beginning of 1978), step up to the microphone. Terry Young, a young black man, is at the piano and he accompanies the three women as they run through an energetic opening set of superbly arranged traditional gospel songs.

So, *part one* of the concert consists of:

intro: Regina
1) If I've Got My Ticket, Lord, Can I Ride? (1st song)
2) It's Gonna Rain
3) Lord Please Hold My Hand
4) Look Up And Live by Faith
5) Oh Freedom
6) This Train

This set goes over extremely well with the audience every night, as well it should, and is followed immediately by Dylan and the rest of the band walking on stage (in darkness). The lights go up and without introduction (much applause, of course) they roar into "Gotta Serve Somebody."

Dylan's band for these shows is made up of four highly-professional, seasoned recording/touring musicians: Tim Drummond on bass (played on *Slow Train Coming*, played with Neil Young on *Harvest* and numerous other albums and tours), Jim Keltner on drums, Fred Tackett on guitar, and Spooner Oldham on keyboards (famous for his Muscle Shoals session work); plus, as mentioned, Terry Young on keyboards and back vocals, and Monalisa Young, Regina Havis and Helena Springs (high, middle, and low voices respectively) on backup vocals (Regina and Helena are on *Slow Train Coming*). Dylan does vocals and (mostly) rhythm guitar, for a total of nine people on stage most of the time.

Part two of the show consists of songs from *Slow Train Coming*, plus one new song, followed by an interlude in which one of the three female vocalists does a solo song with the band:

1) Gotta Serve Somebody
2) I Believe In You
3) When You Gonna Wake Up?
4) When He Returns (Oldham on piano, Dylan on electic guitar)
5) Man Gave Names to All the Animals (Helena strums an acoustic guitar on this one)
6) Precious Angel
7) Slow Train

8) Covenant Woman

(interlude) Regina singing "Man from Galilee" or Monalisa
 singing "(God Uses) Ordinary People" or Helena singing her
 own composition, "What Are You Doing with Your Heart?"

Dylan comes right back on stage (he can usually be seen in the
wings watching the solo and smoking a cigarette) with no pause in
the show, and they move right into *part three,* two *Slow Train Coming*
songs and then five new numbers:

1) Gonna Change My Way of Thinking
2) Do Right to Me Baby (Do unto Others)
3) Hanging on to a Solid Rock Made Before the Foundation of
 the World
4) The Saving Grace That's Over Me (Dylan lead guitar solos)
5) What Can I Do for You? (Dylan harmonica solos—a show
 stopper)
6) I've Been Saved (by the Blood of the Lamb)
7) When They Came for Him in the Garden

Dylan puts down his guitar and walks off near the end of this last
song, then is called back for two encores:

encore 1) Blessed Be the Name of the Lord Forever
encore 2) Pressing On (Dylan plays solo piano, then walks
 forward halfway through and sings without his guitar,
 a rare moment)

Dylan says goodnight with a very interesting semi-bow, walks off
while the chorus and band complete the song, and the show is over.
Twenty-four songs in all, seventeen written and sung by Dylan;
duration is slightly over two hours. Some people missed the old
songs, but on the whole the audience seemed well satisfied with
Dylan's 1979 born-again musical offering, at least at the shows we
saw (the engagement continues for another seven nights, a total of
fourteen shows in sixteen days).

Still one can't help wondering, why twenty-four songs out of
twenty-four about the glory of the Lord God Jesus? Why has Bob
Dylan, of all people, turned in this particular direction?

* * *

"I been broken
Shattered like an empty cup
And I'm just waiting on the Lord
To rebuild and fill me up."
      —"Covenant Woman"

Dylan tells us, a slightly different way in each new song, that he was in pretty sad shape before Christ came into his life. He tends to see all the rest of us as being terminal cases too ("Can't help but wonder/what's happening to my companions"; "my so-called friends have fallen under a spell"), which is an arrogance wholly consistent with the postures he's taken throughout his career, and which makes things especially hard for those of us whose method of appreciating Dylan over the years has been to identify 100% with most everything he says and feels. But that's a problem we'll dive into a little later. Right now I want to engage in some entirely called-for privacy invading (using the public record; I don't have no inside line) in order to speculate on just exactly what kind of terrible Dylan's life had become.

Sex, marriage, restlessness, interpersonal relationships and the demands thereof are definitely at the heart of this matter. *Planet Waves, Blood on the Tracks, Desire, Street-Legal, Renaldo & Clara—* Dylan's entire body of work this past decade—all speak directly and in interconnected fashion to the subject at hand. Finally I think Dylan couldn't stand it that he was telling us so much about Bob and Sara—in the movie he changes their names and tries in half a dozen ways to draw a film of ambiguity over the stark beautiful nakedness the movie (to its everlasting credit) reveals.

Incidentally (and very few critics or fans have come to grips with this yet), it is Dylan's work in the seventies—the above-mentioned material plus his live performances—that, even more than his extraordinary and better-known creations of the 1960s, gives him his claim to immortality. Once this is appreciated (and it will be, by and by) it becomes much easier to see Dylan's latest direction in the context of his whole career.

What happened? Well, in the very simplest terms, the divorce happened. Simple terms are misleading, however. Bob and Sara Dylan were divorced in 1977, following a separation in 1974 (*Blood on the Tracks*) and a reconciliation in 1975 (*Desire*). There were irreconcilable differences. And ultimately, I think, the failure of the marriage (augmented by the frustrations of single life), led Dylan the Gemini to a painful and inescapable confrontation with the irreconcilable differences within himself.

Dylan has always believed, not unreasonably, in the power of Woman. When he finally lost faith in the ability of women to save him (and he seems to have explored the matter very thoroughly, in and out of marriage, in the years 1974 through '78), his need for an alternative grew very great indeed, and he found what people in our culture most often find in the same circumstances: the uncritical hospitality of Jesus Christ.

What the man needed to save himself from, I surmise, was guilt, unendurable restlessness, alcohol, self-hatred.

This story is told to me by a fascinating sequence of songs and images beginning with "Wedding Song" and "Going, Going Gone" on *Planet Waves*, climaxing in the movie *Renaldo & Clara* and anticlimaxing gracefully in the scary but hopeful triplet on *Street-Legal*, "True Love Tends to Forget"/"We Better Talk This Over"/"Where Are You Tonight?" And it's all set in relief and given retroactive clarity by the conversion and the new songs and images that have followed.

Let us work backwards at first, by examining the images of Dylan's pre-conversion life that show up in his post-conversion songs. Who does he think he was, what was he saved from?

Dylan is still secretive; mostly what we get are little hints and suggestions. The most revealing new song, "Trouble in Mind," was left off the album and is not performed in his live show. (It shows up as the flip side of the single "Gotta Serve Somebody.") "I been broken/Shattered like an empty cup" from "Covenant Woman" is perhaps the most direct acknowledgement of something having gone wrong in Dylan's life before he found Jesus. In "Precious Angel" he says, "I was blinded . . . (You showed me) how weak was the foundation I was standing upon." And, "I just couldn't make it by myself." "By myself" means without the Lord, but of course it also implies that part of the problem was being "by myself," i.e. without a wife, a woman, without Sara.

"There's so much depression, can't keep track of it no more" in "Gonna Change My Way of Thinking" is meant to be a social observation, but it sounds personal to me. "Gonna stop being influenced by fools" suggests he sees himself as having been under

such influence until he made his change. "Sons becoming hus-
bands to their mothers" tells us the plight of children in a broken
marriage is on his mind. "I've got a God-fearing woman, one I can
easily afford" again implies that, spiritually as well as financially, he
couldn't afford the woman he used to have.

More clues can be found in "Do Right to Me Baby," the Golden
Rule song. Dylan tosses off a lot of lines here, but a few of them seem
to cut to the bone of who he is. "I don't want to be judged . . . don't
want to be betrayed . . . don't want to be winked at . . . don't want to
be hurt." Clearly he feels he has been betrayed—it's in his voice.
"Don't want to be winked at" is the false intimacy his fans press on
him, which is a constant pressure anywhere he goes. "Don't want to
treat nobody like they was dirt" suggests some awareness on his part
that he's done a lot of that in his time. "Don't want to marry nobody,
if they already married" says to me that not coveting thy neighbor's
wife is a commandment he's only recently subscribed to.

In "I've Been Saved" we hear the powerful line, "For so long I've
been hindered/For so long I've been stalled," which states in no
uncertain terms the frustration he felt inside by the time of *Street-
Legal* and the 1978 world tour.

The clue in "I'm Hanging on to a Solid Rock" is in the title
(chorus) line; as he told us in a muttered introduction to the song,
two or three of the nights I saw him, "We're living in perilous times,
the end of the end times . . . you're going to need something
strong to hang onto. This song is called 'I'm Hanging on to a Solid
Rock Made Before the Foundation of the World.' You're going to
need something just about that strong." Well okay. At any rate we
know Dylan felt and feels such a need. He may feel it now because
of his gut-level awareness of the truth of the Book of Revelation, but surely he first grabbed onto the rock out of some more
immediate and personal need. Again, reading backwards to find
the situation that the song's truth is an answer for, we know that the
man must have felt a rather desperate lack of security and support
in his life. (The song that results, incidentally, is sure to become
one of his all-time classics.)

In "What Can I Do for You?" Dylan says to the Lord, "You
have/given me life to live." This is repeated in "Saving Grace" when
he says, "I've escaped death so many times, I know I'm only living/By
the saving grace that's over me." And in the next verse, "By this time

I'd've thought that I'd be sleeping/In a pine box for all eternity." So: coming to Jesus not only saved his soul, it saved his life. And I can believe it, actually. Increasing use of alcohol, increasing loss of self-worth, life on the road and no other home in this world any more ... the strongest among us get tired, and what he's saying is he'd lost all sense of what he was doing it for. This can indeed be fatal, and Dylan has been there before. I'm willing to believe that he knew, with a sense of helplessness and defeat, that he was going down for the third time. And then some precious angel threw him a line.

One more quote from "What Can I Do," and this one's a shocker: "The search for love is no more than vanity." He's right. Love is not to be searched for, and when we do think of it like that we're really just looking for gratification: that this good-looking person is attracted to me, he or she is someone new to be dazzled by my virtues and who doesn't yet know me well enough to start reflecting my flaws as well. And when things do start getting a little too close to home: pack my bags and go on with the search. This wasn't the one. Vanity, indeed.

Lucky Bob: love has found him. He don't have to search no more. (Couldn't he have just broken himself of the habit? No, he couldn't. He wasn't able to. Not without the Lord's help. That's what he's trying to tell us, you see. And naturally he assumes— vanity again—that everyone else is in the same boat.)

But was it really so terrible, to be rich, attractive, acclaimed for his work, free to do whatever he wanted? How desperate could he have been? Pretty freaking desperate, in my opinion. Because Dylan in 1978 had finally reached—again—what Mel Lyman has called "the mirror at the end of the road."

* * *

"I got to know Lord
When to pull back on the reins
Death can be the result of
The most underrated pain.
Satan whispers to ya
'Well I don't want to bore ya.
But when you get tired of that Miss So-and-so
I got another woman for ya.'"

—"Trouble in Mind"

"Trouble in Mind is easily the most naked of Dylan's recent songs, at least in the personal sense (the singing on "When He Returns" represents a more exalted kind of nakedness—naked spirit—but it's the messy everyday nakedness of human affairs and human emotions we're peering into right now). This song, unlike any of the others, seems to be a catalog of the singer's own troubles, his fears, guilts and doubts. Maybe I'm cynical, but it seems to me these are usually the strongest factors influencing a person who's turned to religion. My assumption is that Dylan turned to Jesus for sanctuary—and that falling in love with God was an unexpected bonus.

I can understand not wanting to include this song in the show. "Trouble in Mind" is, superficially, the most preachy of the new Dylan songs, and it might well offend people. It's a fine recording, an ominous, traditional urban blues riff and vocal that sent me running for my Howling Wolf records (thank you Bob; it's been a long time since I pulled them out), and it shows off that great band and Muscle Shoals sound of the *Slow Train Coming* sessions just delightfully. But it might come across a little heavy ("you're all the time defending/what you can never justify"). And one of the surprising virtues of Dylan's born-again evening of song is that it never turns into a harangue (unless you're unusually sensitive—I do know some people for whom the very mention of the word Jesus is like fingernails on a blackboard. But they're gonna have to learn to get over their cultural prejudices like everybody else).

What is ironic is that the song, which might come across as arrogant, is one of Dylan's humblest: not one of those songs where he calls attention to his humility, but one where he actually reveals his own vulnerability and distress, transparently covering himself by saying "you" instead of "I." The man has courage; this has always been true, and he's showing as much courage now as he ever has. A lot of people exploit Christianity; but in Dylan's case it's clear that he's out there testifying not because it's an easy road—it's not—but because it's the only road for him right now, the way of the challenge. Dylan's energy has been reborn too, and that's the good news as far as I'm concerned.

(It was fun to go to the whole week of concerts, and see Dylan's face get younger and stronger, more self-confident and relaxed every night. He was obviously pleased and given strength by the warm response of the audience to his new music. On the sixth night the band just couldn't get themselves together, but Dylan kept his cool, sang extremely well in spite of real obstacles, and stayed good-natured about the whole thing. I was amazed. He clapped Tim Drummond on the arm at the end, smiling as if to say, "Don't take it too hard," and I couldn't help feeling that here was evidence of a real personality change. The next night the band was terrific.)

"Trouble in Mind" tells us the agony this new liberation was born from. The chorus says it all: "Trouble in mind, Lord, trouble in mind. Lord take away this trouble in mind."

> "When the deeds that you do
> Don't add up to zero
> It's what's inside that counts
> Ask any war hero."

I had to think about the above verse for a moment. I think—in fact I'm quite sure—that he's saying the war hero is praised and admired for his deeds, but inside may feel shatteringly empty. He's telling us that he reached a point, and we could too, where all the things he's done, the songs and records and so forth, didn't mean anything to him, disappeared without a trace when dropped into the pit of empti-ness inside. And he's saying the sense of loss and lostness that results is devastating beyond what we may be able to imagine.

Trouble in mind is something real and specific—it's described in many a country blues song, and I know it well, I've been through it. It's an almost physical thing, a pain you wake up with in the morning and go to sleep with at night, thoughts that tear you in two or more directions at once with no resolution possible, usually because all choices are equally unacceptable and equally hard to avoid. The *I Ching* nails it well: "It is very difficult to bring quiet to the heart." (In Chinese and Japanese and old blues songs, "heart" and "mind" are not separate concepts.) "The heart thinks constantly. This cannot be changed, but the movements of the heart—that is, a man's thoughts—should restrict themselves to the immediate situation. All thinking that goes beyond this only makes the heart sore."

This song "Trouble in Mind" acknowledges the fact that sex is a central issue—central to Dylan's trouble in mind, and there-fore central to his conversion. "Well your true love has caught you/Where you don't belong./You say everybody's doing it/So I guess it can't be wrong." I don't want to say more about this right now—it's too big a subject, and needs to be approached starting back at the *Planet Waves* songs which first revealed the stresses pulling at Dylan's marriage.

Dylan also offers in this song an unnerving portrait of his own rockstar vanity and corruption-by-power:

> "Here comes Satan
> Prince of the power of the air
> He's going to make you a law unto yourself
> Build a birds-nest in your hair
> He's gonna deaden your conscience
> Till you worship the work of your own hands
> You'll be serving strangers
> In a strange and forsaken land."

An exaggerated portrait, perhaps, but who has more right? And he does succeed in giving us, in this song, a detailed and very tangible picture of the sort of pain he was going through.

> "Trouble in mind, Lord
> Trouble in mind.
> Lord take away
> This trouble in mind."

*   *   *

"90 straight minutes of poorly played, poorly presented and often poorly written sounds . . . is a pretty grueling experience."
—Philip Elwood, *San Francisco Examiner,* Nov. 2, 1979

"Dylan has written some of the most banal, uninspired and inventionless songs of his career for his Jesus phase. Years from now, when social historians look back over these years, Dylan's conversion will serve as a   concise metaphor for the vast emptiness of the era."
—Joel Selvin, *San Francisco Chronicle,* Nov. 3, 1979

The newspaper reviews of Dylan's opening night in San Francisco were savage (one headline called the show "God-awful"). These reviews are so far from my own feelings, and from the general audience response to the shows, and they had such a measurable impact on so many of the people I've met who weren't at the concerts (partly because the reviews were picked up and parroted by radio disc jockeys), that I must confess to an unworthy and unChristian desire to feed both these men through a meat grinder. "Vast emptiness of the era," indeed! Well poor baby, I'm sorry we don't have a War in Vietnam right now to make your life seem meaningful.

Critical response in the influential media to most of Dylan's major work in the last six years has been overwhelmingly negative (with some exceptions, notably the general acclaim for *Blood on the Tracks*). This year the critics, and some of the people in the audience (fewer each night), were upset because he didn't do any old songs. Last year, when he did a show that was almost entirely old favorites (carefully chosen from the whole range of his career), he was widely attacked for having changed the arrangements! It seems there are a whole lot of people out there who are so hopelessly mired in their own long-gone adolescence that they have no interest in living art at all: they want their performers to be time machines for them. Return with me now to those thrilling days of yesteryear . . . Predictably, a lot of the critical venom directed at Dylan is simple resentment of the man's popularity and stature. Envy is a common emotion, particularly among writers, and when a contemporary figure piles up achievements the way Dylan has, and refuses to rest on his laurels to boot, you can be sure any perceived vulnerability on his part will be jumped on with a vengeance. Some of the more vocal critics never related to Dylan's work in the first place (though they now proclaim he's lost his power). I met one of *Rolling Stone*'s most respected reviewers—who wrote a vicious put-down last year of *Street-Legal* and Dylan's '78 tour—back in 1974 at a preview of *Blood on the Tracks*. He admitted at the time that he'd never been able to listen to all of side two of *Bringing It All Back Home*!

It is true that opening night, which is the show the critics saw, was the least successful of the performances. Dylan, for reasons that aren't hard to understand, is afraid of his audience—their relationship with him is so intense, they expect so much and more than once over the years they've turned really nasty when he chose to deliver something other than their notion of who "Bob Dylan" should be. And this was certainly one of those historic evenings when a "new Dylan" would be unveiled to an unready world.

People were pre-warned, of course. First the rumors about Dylan becoming a Christian, never confirmed, and then the *Slow Train Coming* album, released at the end of August, with images of the cross on the front and back covers (a pick-axe on the front, sailboat mast on the back) and songs that made Dylan's new position unavoidably clear to anyone who listened carefully to the lyrics. It was strange, the first few days of listening to that new album, so powerful and attractive musically and so challenging in its lyrics, letting it sink in . . . yes, he really says, "You either got faith or you got unbelief, and there ain't no neutral ground," but how narrow is his new definition of faith? "Gotta Serve Somebody"—yes I can relate to that. "Slow Train"—a great song, magnificent recording, but why that dumb line about the Arabs? We played the record over and over again, just fell in love with it despite mixed feelings— every time I got in my car, for two months, I'd look through the tapes and that would be the one I wanted to hear.

I don't usually read the newspaper, but I was lucky enough to catch the announcement that Dylan would do seven concerts at the Warfield Theatre as rehearsal for a tour. I immediately decided to get tickets for the whole week of concerts, if possible. It seemed too rare an opportunity to let it go by. (Later an additional seven concerts were added—we decided to let those pass, though we still hope to go to one of the last shows—and the national tour was postponed or cancelled.)

The final preview of the new show was Dylan's surprise TV appearance on Saturday Night Live, October 14th. He and his band did three separate segments of one song each. "Gotta Serve Some-body" was first, and it was disappointing—Dylan was nervous and sang without conviction, the band was unsure of itself and the guitar player was particularly timid. But Dylan's singing in the second segment, "I Believe in You," turned things around: it was a moving performance, deeply felt. And finally "When You Gonna Wake Up?" showed that the band was capable of doing something—Terry Young was outstanding, passionate, on organ, and the backup singers were really hot. I liked the way they looked at Dylan with open admiration. Dylan's singing had turned mechanical again on this number, but after all, this was TV—the show left me feeling apprehensive but still hopeful about the concerts we were going to see.

Nervousness. I remember seeing Dylan on the Johnny Cash Show around the time of *Nashville Skyline*... he looked absolutely terrified. All those people looking at him, wanting something from him (at that time he'd been out of the public eye for three years). The next time he was on TV was in 1975, the tribute to John Hammond. Again he started out real stiff, but he was determined to get "Hurricane" and its message out to the world—he performed with tremendous conviction, and I remember thinking how strong he was, that his real greatness as an artist came from that strength, belief in himself. I wrote at the time that seeing him made me feel that "God-given talent is nothing without the stamina and the will to activate that talent again and again in the face of all odds, in the face of doubts and terrors that ordinary people (those who don't make superhuman efforts of will over and over) can never imagine ... To me a great artist is someone who says 'I am' more honestly, more powerfully, more beautifully, more straightforwardly, more inclusively than anyone else except other great artists."

Fade to 1979. Opening night. Regina bravely walked on stage, with no one in the audience knowing what to expect, and just started talking into the mike, telling her story about the old woman and the train. She and her "sisters" were in top form, holding the stage and our attention and enthusiasm even as we wondered when *he* would come on stage and what he would do when he got there. I knew these were Dylan's backup singers, having seen them on TV, and it made sense for a born-again Dylan to open his new show with gospel music.

Hearing them sing "Oh Freedom," their fifth song, was a flash: suddenly I remembered the days when I first encountered Bob Dylan's music, via Pete Seeger at the Boston Arts Festival and my friend David Hartwell who played "Hard Rain" on his guitar, days when we would go to civil rights demonstrations in Boston and sing "Oh Freedom" and "We Shall Not Be Moved" and "We Shall Overcome," black and white, a thousand voices together. I was very young—so was Dylan—but I could see that for these women at least the connection was very clear between what he was doing then and what he's doing now.

Another connection was made with their final song, Woody Guthrie's "This Train Is Bound For Glory" done up as a gospel number: "This train is a clean train, this train" and "I was lost in sin/I had no peace within/Until I met my Jesus on this train." Would Guthrie have approved? But of course he'd borrowed the inspiration for the song from gospel music in the first place—he could hardly complain.

Train imagery everywhere. In *Renaldo & Clara* Dylan sings "People Get Ready (there's a train a-coming)"; it's always been one of his favorite songs. The liner notes to *Highway 61 Revisited* begin, "On the slow train time does not interfere"; and continue, "the songs on this specific record are not so much songs but rather exercises in tonal breath control . . . the subject matter—though meaningless as it is—has something to do with the beautiful strangers . . . the beautiful strangers, Vivaldi's green jacket and the holy slow train."

So the lights went down and Dylan and the rest of the band came on stage and started "Gotta Serve Somebody." There he was. It's a little like all the other people that you would be just as excited to see standing in the flesh in front of you are long dead—Shakespeare, Beethoven—and so seeing Dylan there feels like a dream. It's a rush—you don't really get used to the idea as the night wears on, you just forget about it and remember again, ha, there he is.

He was wearing a black leather jacket, open in front, over a white T-shirt, black levis, trace of a Fu-manchu moustache. His face was puffy, tired, tense—he looked like he'd just got up. He played rhythm guitar (electric) and sang in a clipped voice, as though he knew all the words and when to sing them, but didn't necessarily remember what they meant. He was tight, nervous. He had that characteristic dour look on his face, and wouldn't look at the audience or the other members of the band. The band played the song better than they had on TV, but with none of the power of the recorded version. Mostly you could hear a lot of bass.

The next two songs were not as good as they'd been on TV. The fourth song, "When He Returns," was a sort of breakthrough, with only Dylan and Oldham (playing grand piano) on stage; Dylan's voice didn't soar like it does on the record, but it had some power, he was starting to open up. "Man Gave Names to All the Animals" helped loosen up the band, and it was a pleasure to hear him sing

"Precious Angel." Even so that nervousness dominated, so that it almost seemed to change from line to line whether he was mouthing the words or really singing them. Still afraid of what he might feel if he opened himself up to feeling—concentrating real hard on just getting through the songs. "Slow Train" was a disappointment, hurried and underarranged and I really missed the superb guitar lines Mark Knopfler plays on the album.

And then he sang "Covenant Woman" and the show finally came alive. It was as if he were tired of all the other songs already, they were too old to get excited about and too new to change the arrangements around. And so this was the first song that was really a challenge, an uncertainty, something he could throw himself into. It's a beautiful song—bright, attractive melody that pulls you right in. I couldn't hear many of the words first time—thought it was called "God-made Woman"—but the lines that jumped out were powerful ones, especially the chorus, with its complex rhythmic build: "And I just want to tell you I intend/To stay closer than a friend/I just want to thank you once again/For making your prayers known unto Heaven for me/And to you always so grateful I will forever be." Dylan's voice as he sang it was just as humble and warm and penetrating as the lyrics are, and Oldham's organ swells between verses filled the heart with joy (the organ makes it sound a little like something from *Blonde on Blonde*, although there are also moments when it reminds me of the Stones' "Moonlight Mile").

The concert got a lot better after that, with the high points being "Hanging on to a Solid Rock" and Dylan's harmonica solos in "What Can I Do for You?" (as though he were answering the question even as he asked it: let me play the harmonica for you, Lord, it's the best way I know of just pouring out to you everything that's in my heart). Yes, and the second encore, seemingly unrehearsed (the applause went on and on, maybe because people thought if they could bring him out once again he'd do an old favorite, but mostly because people really liked the show and were glad to see him in spite of everything). He sat at the piano, almost out of sight, accompanying himself singing "Pressing On": "I'm just pressing on to the higher calling of my Lord." It was clearly meant as a sort of explanation: hey, I can't stop, can't go back, just got to keep going and this is where it's taking me to. A moving tune, real simple, real effective—the audience was clapping rhythm, Dylan sang a verse—his best singing of the night, super—sang the chorus again and got up. We assumed he was walking off for the night, but he came around the piano and then made his way to the mike at the front of the stage. He beckoned, and other band-members started to come back on. Dylan seemed really pleased, it was like he was discovering to his surprise that a good part of the audience had liked the concert, were with him, weren't just calling out for old songs. He clapped his hands together a few times, and went on with the song (it was the first time all night he'd stood before us without his guitar). The chorus joined in, then the guitar player and organist. Dylan sang a second verse: "Shake the dust off your feet/Don't look back" (his voice seemed to smile at this last line) "Ain't no one can hold you down, ain't nothing that you lack . . ." He finished the song and said goodnight. I left feeling really satisfied, with the tune to "Pressing On" running through my head.

The opening songs were much better the second night—again "When He Returns" was the early standout—the band was tighter, the arrangements were starting to evolve, and mostly Dylan was starting to open up. The third night was a fabulous show, very high energy; fourth night was off a little, better than the first two but everyone was getting tired and it showed. They'd gotten better at what they were doing, everyone, but some of the energy was missing. Then there was a night off, no concert, and when they came back for the fifth night they were terrific. Things had reached the kind of pull-out-the-stops energy level I associate with Dylan's 1966 tour with The Band, or the Rolling Thunder shows. And Dylan had relaxed and opened up to the point where he was really getting into it, holding the long notes, allowing his voice to soar and bite and growl and caress. The shows had been good, almost from the beginning. Now they were becoming ecstatic. No more calls for old songs. Instead the show-stopper had become "Hanging on to a Solid Rock," which on several nights prompted a spontaneous standing ovation.

Dylan opened up during the course of the week like a flower, curled tight in a bud at the beginning, blooming like the brightest rose of spring by the end. On the third night, with the band really cooking and the audience getting more and more enthusiastic (and showing it) with every song, Dylan grinned for a split-second into the wild applause after "Saving Grace" and told us, "Don't read any more newspapers." The audience understood, and howled its approval.

In seven nights, there was never a moment when I was bored. At first, I was excited to see him—after that the music and the performance carried me, and it just got better all the time. I got so I couldn't wait to hear the new songs again. It was quite a week. Whatever happened to Dylan, it hasn't hurt his music any.

*   *   *

"It's the ways of the flesh
The war against the spirit
24 hours a day
You can feel it, you can hear it"
—"Hanging on to a Solid Rock"

Bob Dylan married Sara Lowndes in November of 1965. It was a secret. He was at the height of his popularity—he had released *Highway 61 Revisited* and *Bringing It All Back Home* in the same year, and "Like a Rolling Stone" had been a number one single. Things were getting real crazy. He married Sara and then he went on the road for six months.

Two months after he got back, he had an accident on his motorcycle and disappeared. He badly needed to disappear, and I guess you could say God gave him the cue, the opportunity.

That was the summer of '66, just after the release of *Blonde on Blonde.* For seven and a half years, as far as we know, Bob was a family man. He stayed home, mostly—didn't do any touring—didn't write many songs and, as time went by, fewer and fewer good ones.

Then in November of 1973, Dylan went into the studio and recorded an album called *Planet Waves.* Shortly thereafter he said goodbye to his wife and five kids and went out on tour again.

To the public it was Dylan's big comeback. And sure enough, the songs he wrote while he was on the road turned out to be his best in eight years (they appear on the album *Blood on the Tracks*). Looking at it selfishly, you'd have to say it was nice for all the rest of us that he gave his old lady the slip.

But I wonder what it was like for her and for him.

It's a nasty paradox, that suffering makes for good art. I don't like to admit it, don't want it to be true, but the evidence is against me. In the case at hand, Dylan's fallow period coincides with his peaceful days at home with his family. I don't say it was bad for his art—he needed the rest, she saved his life, he fathered four children (the fifth she had already)—but certainly it was good for his art that he left when he did. Everything in the songs that followed tells us that the suffering of separation from loved ones and the stimulation of being loose in the world were factors that combined to bring about overnight a reawakening of Dylan's greatness as a word-writer, music-creator, performer, singer.

And in the long run, I suspect, they were also the factors that brought him to a point where his choices were madness or death; at which point it seems he was fortunate enough to be able to choose Christ instead.

This is not some theory I've constructed. This is simply what I hear when I listen to the man's music; and I listen to his music a lot.

On *Planet Waves*, three songs stand out: "Dirge," "Wedding Song," and "Going, Going, Gone." "Wedding Song" is the most explicit of the various love songs to Sara on this album; both the title and various internal references leave no doubt at all who he's speaking to. What's interesting is that he seems to be saying I love you so many times because he's trying to convince her of it, convince her of something: "Oh can't you see that you were born to stand by my side?" Something has happened, it seems, to cause her to doubt. "What's lost is lost, we can't regain what went down in the flood." And finally: "I could never let you go, no matter what goes on" (a very revealing line—he could never let her go is not the same as saying he wouldn't leave himself) "Cause I love you more than ever, now that the past is gone."

"Wedding Song" is clearly for Sara; the other two songs are far more ambiguous. Still, it's interesting to contrast all those "I love you more than ever" lines with the repeated line in "Dirge" (not repeated so often; it doesn't need to be), "I hate myself for loving you." Could it be possible that this is the same man speaking to the same woman? It does happen in human relationships that we sometimes feel two sharply conflicting emotions at the same or almost the same time. It's also interesting that a dirge is a funeral song. So we have a funeral song and a wedding song. What died?

It almost sounds to me like a marriage died, and the man is saying, let's take our vows again. Some other lines from "Dirge": "We stared into each other's eyes/Neither one of us would break." And "I can't recall a useful thing you ever did for me" (phew—sounds like a preview of "Idiot Wind"). And "I've paid the price of solitude/But at least I'm out of debt." (I'm free of guilt now, you can't touch me.) (Wanna bet?)

And then there's a fine song I didn't appreciate when this album first came out. "I've just reached a place/Where the willow don't bend/There's not much more to be said/It's the time of the end./I'm going/I'm going/I'm gone." So here's this man who's saying, I love you, I hate you, I'll stay with you forever, I'm going away now. And this is good, because we really do feel all these things at the same time. I guess what I hear in *Planet Waves* is something like: "I can't stand it any more, I've got to get out of here. But I love you very much, I want to be married to you, give me enough room and I know it'll be all right. Gosh you're beautiful. 'Bye . . ."

And then he went on tour. We don't have to wait long to find out what happened next, because ten months after recording *Planet Waves* he recorded another album of new songs, *Blood on the Tracks*. Ten months after "Wedding Song" it's "If You See Her, Say Hello" (which sounds casual, but it's sung by a man with a broken heart). And this time we *know* he's talking about the same girl.

We know partly just because the feeling is too strong for him to be talking about anyone else. "Wedding Song" is nice, but it's unconvincing. There's something he wants—I would say he wants to avoid a divorce but still keep his freedom, but in any event it's clear that there's a *reason* why he's trying so hard to convince her of his love. Which in turn makes it hard for her or us to know if he really means it. "If You See Her, Say Hello", on the other hand, is sweet, sad, friendly, relaxed, and full of anguish. He's not pleading now—he's not trying to convince anyone of anything, instead he's saying he accepts the situation, it's all right, it had to be, it just hurts a lot. And the result is we can't help but believe him—the song is a masterpiece, it fills the listener with that sweet anguish of separation and (demonic) one can't help feeling a tenderness toward the person singing. Yes, he admits he was a bastard, but look at the suffering he's going through . . .

And indeed, sometime in the year following the release of *Blood on the Tracks*, Sara and Bob got together again.

Blood on the Tracks is amazing; it sounds good and feels good right from the top, but the closer you look at it the better it gets. "Idiot Wind" is one of the greatest essays on marriage ever written. I know, it's awfully negative, but so is "Like a Rolling Stone." "Like a Rolling Stone," which everyone loves, is a song of hatred, bitterness, revenge. But it is so real, so deeply felt, that in a sense it conjures up that whole passionate state of being in which one lives this hard and cares this deeply—the bitter outburst at the end of the affair somehow implies and contains all the other intense feelings we shared together.

"Like a Rolling Stone" is the "I am" that the wounded lover (of a person, of life) shouts to the other and to the world, the ultimate declaration of existence, passionate rediscovery and proclamation of selfness, you can't take this away from me (translation: you did take it away from me, but the hell with you, I've got it back again, I've repossessed my heart, broken though it may be, I am free, so you got what you wanted how does it feel?, I don't care, I am me again now, I AM). Catharsis. And "Idiot Wind" dives into the hatred side of what two people who've been living together long do feel towards each other when the buttons are pushed and the screaming starts (some people scream loud, some scream quiet) and the gloves are off. "I can't feel you any more, I can't even touch the books you've read./Every time I crawl past your door, I've been wishing I'd been somebody else instead./ . . . You're an idiot, babe . . ." And conversely, "You'll never know the hurt I suffered, nor the pain I rise above./And I'll never know the same about you, your holiness or your kind of love./And it makes me feel so sorry . . ." The intensity, the bitterness, confirms that they really did live together, really did share and impinge on each other's space, if you don't somewhere cop to and acknowledge this aspect of the experience of living with another person then in a sense you're denying the whole thing ("she just acts like we never have met"). "Idiot Wind," along with the pain-filled love songs and timeless histories on the album, is an affirmation—I wasn't sleeping those seven years, I was involved in the most intense and intimate and difficult scene any person can be a part of, a world that can't be spoken of or communicated while you're there ("marriage is the hottest furnace of the spirit today"—Leonard Cohen, 1975) and at best can only be hinted at through the recriminations and regrets that erupt when it's over and broken and there's nothing to keep private any more. "Idiot Wind" touches on other relationships as well—business partners, audience/artist—but its greatest triumph is its revelation of the fierce struggle implicit in the heart of even the happiest marriage. That the two should be one was never meant to be easy, and oh what can't be said does eventually build into an incredible head of pressure, which when and if it blows is far beyond any question of what you or I did wrong: we're idiots, that's all, insensitive louts, at best we can admit it and be friends, at worst we can resent it in each other forever.

Why did the marriage break up? Well, whoever we're talking about, it wasn't because he did this or she did that. There's a deeper level.

"You're a Big Girl Now" is another kind of revelation: "Oh I know that I can find you/In somebody's room/It's a price I've got to pay/You're a big girl all the way." He'd probably been demanding for years to know when she was gonna grow up . . .

Blood on the Tracks, in a thousand different ways, is explicitly about the breaking up of a long-term relationship (often treated as though it were her move that made it happen, he pushed her too far and she finally walked out, it's always true both ways of course but it's interesting how he chose to present it); it is a musical and creative work of extraordinary maturity. The singing, voice as an instrument of subtle communication, is enough by itself to qualify this album as a masterpiece. It's not hard to see the ways that "Tangled Up in Blue" is (and, cleverly, isn't) about Dylan's marriage to Sara and about how only by standing outside of time can we see things (& feel them) as they really are. "Simple Twist of Fate"—another love song, so much more subtle, deeper, more effective than anything on *Planet Waves*. Because he wasn't yet free to speak ("the naked truth is still taboo whenever it may be seen") when he recorded the earlier album. And also because he hadn't dived that deep into himself yet; whatever happened when he finally embraced that pain it sure had an impact on his work.

But the story goes on, other women, then the same one again, then a nastier and more final break, other women and finally so much desperation that he couldn't go on any more. In retrospect, the long movie of a song called "Lily, Rosemary and the Jack of Hearts" (on *Blood on the Tracks*) is a useful clue to this, because it shows us part of what seduced Dylan away from marriage (partly he was driven away, partly seduced away, it must always be thus): an image of himself too dreamlike and perfect a fantasy-realization and too obviously attainable to be resisted. Dylan as the Jack of Hearts, in the midst of things and outside it all, irresistible to women, impeccable in his timing, living by his wits and charm and awareness of the cosmic joke. And yes he could pull it off. What a marvelous temptation—far beyond any ordinary offer of wealth or women or fame. How could he refuse to try out for the part?

And I'm not here to say he was tempted, though of course he was, but I'm not here to say he was wrong. It's all just a fabulous story as far as I'm concerned, what a saga, that was just the next door that opened in front of him. Pressing on. Suddenly he could sing, write, perform, talk, think, move around, make things happen, at least as well as he could back at the peak of his madness and creative powers, only he could do it consciously this time. He could control it. When you've got a gift, you've got to go out there and use it, see what happens.

New innocence, new power. Wild times in the world again. And after all, it did ultimately bring him to God.

"Jack of Hearts" is a portrait of the life Dylan imagined for himself as an alternative to marriage (of course the way he set it up in his head, he only needed an alternative because Sara had walked out, he hadn't chosen to end it, oh no—he shared the blame certainly, but it was all her choice, said he) with Sara. He could write "Jack of Hearts" because he could be "Jack of Hearts" (as he could be the clever seducer who sings "Buckets of Rain": "everything about you is bringing me misery"—wow, what a great and attractive description of desire). And all the girls would say, "I'm glad to see you're still alive, you're looking like a saint." Mmm. And meanwhile of course he'd have his eye out for the one who, like Sara in the timeless past or possibly even future, could offer "Shelter from the Storm." ("Now there's a wall between us," he explains, "Something there's been lost. I took too much for granted, got my signals crossed. . . . Try imagining a place where it's always safe and warm. 'Come in,' she said, 'I'll give you shelter from the storm.' ")

It was the storm he lusted after now—time to go to sea again—shelter would surely come along again when the time was right.

* * *

"I know all about poison; I know all about fiery darts
I don't care how rough the road is, show me where to start
Whatever pleases you, tell it to my heart
I don't deserve what I have come through
What can I do for you?"

—Bob Dylan, 1979

The songs on *Desire* (released 1976; written summer '75) indicate a reconciliation with Sara; they also show us a Dylan trying consciously to be concerned with the world, to put some balance into his choice of subject matter (the last two albums had dealt exclusively with the joy and pain and struggle of marriage and love). So this time we have "Hurricane," one of Dylan's most passionate performances on record, about the unjust imprisonment of a man; "Joey," another story-song, this time painting a romantic portrait of the life of a Brooklyn gangster (all the songs on this album except "Sara" and "One More Cup of Coffee" were co-written with Jacques Levy); and four travelogues or mini-movies, "Mozambique," "Romance in Durango," "Black Diamond Bay," and "One More Cup of Coffee" (the latter is a combination mood piece/evocation of place and love song; anyway definitely the penultimate scene of a movie, kind of a cross between "Don't Think Twice" and "The Drifter's Escape." This time neither the pain of leaving nor the need to get away is as strong as it used to be; it's just that with the passage of years it's getting a little harder to go back out on that lonely road and face the darkness again).

But although "Hurricane" is sincere and tremendously powerful, and though Dylan stuck with this cause longer and more tenaciously than he's been known to in the past, in the end this didn't turn out to be an answer to Dylan's need for a place to direct his energy, a way to use his power (power as a songwriter, not just power as a rich & famous person) towards satisfying and worthwhile ends. Neither "Hurricane" nor The Rolling Thunder

Revue, the touring community Dylan formed in autumn 1975 to go on the road and invent a movie (if not a cultural revolution) with, turned out to be a rock solid enough to hang onto for more than eight months at the outside.

Dylan's marriage, on the other hand, seemed to be outliving and transcending all the obstacles and separations described in *Blood on the Tracks.* Sara traveled with Bob during much of the Rolling Thunder tour, and as a result plays a major role in the movie *Renaldo & Clara.* And two songs (both of exceptional quality) on *Desire* address themselves specifically to the subject of the ever-changing relationship between these now-legendary lovers.

"Isis," interestingly, is about a man who marries the same woman twice. It's a story song, a western with middle-eastern influences, somewhat along the lines of the traditional folk song "Buffalo Skinners." The man who's telling the story has married a woman who is too much for him—the Goddess Isis—presumably her very presence makes him go "aw shucks" and look at his feet, and she in turn gets bored, so it's not working out: "I married Isis on the fifth day of May, but I could not hold on to her very long. So I cut off my hair, and I rode straight away to the wild unknown places where I could not go wrong."

Basically the narrator meets a stranger and they ride out on a dangerous and fruitless adventure, ostensibly fueled by greed but in fact what's motivating our hero is his headlong flight away from and towards this awesome woman: "She told me that one day we would meet up again, and things would be different the next time we wed . . . if I only could hang on and just be her friend. I still can't remember all the best things she said."

They find what they're looking for, but the sarcophagus is empty and his partner has died of exposure. The narrator rides back to find Isis "just to tell her I love her." He finds her, and although he doesn't say so somehow the words he does say ("she was there in the meadow where the creek used to rise, blinded by sleep and in need of a bed") tell us she looks more ravishing than ever. This song is an example of extraordinary use of and control over language. Dylan performed it during the Rolling Thunder tour with phenomenal energy, like a Shakespearean actor ripping into his favorite soliloquy; the recording from the Montreal concert which CBS put out as a disc jockey sampler from the soundtrack of

Renaldo & Clara has got to be one of the hottest live tracks ever recorded.

When he sees Isis, he curses her and rides on past. In a way it's his only choice—falling at her feet ain't gonna do him any good—and anyway he's a different man since his adventure, the sarcophagus was empty but he turned out not to be, maybe he finally regained some sense of himself and his own power and worth, which we presume is what attracted Isis to him in the first place. Only he was too overawed by her presence to do her any good.

They have this wonderfully spare conversation: "She said, where you been? I said, no place special; she said, you look different—I said, well, I guess. She said, you been gone . . . I said, that's only natural. She said, you gonna stay? I said, if you want me to, yes."

So now he's found himself, and they can really get married—she's no less a goddess, but now he's worthy of her. "Isis, oh Isis, you're a mystical child," he sings, then offering a line which cuts through to why the album is called *Desire* and why I say women are central to this man's trouble in mind: "What drives me to you is what drives me insane." And then this beautiful denouement, bringing us back to the original wedding day, the moment that would bring him bliss or madness, all depending not on her grace but on his will power: "I still can remember the way that you smiled on the fifth day of May in the drizzling rain."

You have to hear the power of the music, and his voice, and see the furious strength he poured into this performance (another rare case of his standing before an audience with no guitar between them); it's nice that on the Montreal recording he starts by saying, "Here's a song about marriage; this is called 'Isis'." And then, "This is for Leonard [Cohen, he who called marriage 'the hottest furnace of the spirit'], if he's still here." Larry Sloman reports in his book about the Rolling Thunder tour that Sara was wearing an Isis amulet around her neck that night, a medallion of her own design.

And the other marriage song on *Desire* is a starkly beautiful ballad called "Sara." (Dylan, 1978: "When people say 'Sara' was written for 'his wife Sara'—it doesn't necessarily have to be about her just because my wife's name happened to be Sara. Anyway, was it the real Sara or the Sara in the dream? I still don't know.") Again Dylan has performed his favorite trick of slipping out of time: this song is simultaneously about a relationship that's ended and a relationship that's still going strong, with no way to separate the two, and I guess we should draw the obvious conclusion that that's the way things were at the time he wrote it. It helps, for the purposes of understanding Dylan's songs, to get a firm grip on the idea that two or more contradictory realities can and do exist at the same time.

It's a very moving song, full of evident love—neverending love—and real regret. It's sentimental in the best sense; an example of how sometimes the most personal work becomes the most universal, perhaps because it is in those most intimate feelings that we find our common humanity. This is one of the very few places where he mentions his children. All the memories and half-expressed feelings that do tie a man forever to his wife and family are here in this song; and it does make a nice counterpart to the pitiless put-down of "Idiot Wind." Ultimately love is more enduring than anger and frustration, which is not to say that love necessarily wins out on the material plane. In 1977 Sara ("so easy to look at, so hard to define" "sweet virgin angel, sweet love of my life" "don't ever leave me, don't ever go") and Bob Dylan got a divorce and ended their life together—as far as we know—for good.

And as a memento we have—or had; I can't say for sure that it'll ever be shown again—the *tour de force* movie *Renaldo & Clara*. This was shot during the first part of the Rolling Thunder tour, Oct.-Dec. 1975, and edited throughout 1977 (undoubtedly the most sustained effort Dylan ever put into any piece of work), while the divorce proceedings and unpleasantries were going on.

(One more song on *Desire*: "Oh Sister." This one doesn't seem to be for Sara; it's more directed to all of womanhood, collectively and also as represented by any individual woman encountered by any individual man somewhere down the pathways of our tangled lives. What responsibility do we have toward each other; what is our proper relationship in the eyes of God? Just another man trying to justify somehow his desire and need to have a woman's arms around him without recriminations tonight.)

Renaldo & Clara is difficult for me to talk about: I feel like I need to see it again, preferably ten or twelve times (an experience I assure you I would enjoy thoroughly, contrary to what you may have read about the movie elsewhere). I saw the four-hour version twice and the two-hour version (a later release) once; it's been a year since the last time I saw it. It's a wonderful movie, and an important part of Dylan's lifetime achievement.

In terms of what happened to Dylan, one thing that's important to understand up front is that the failure of the movie to attract many viewers or any critical acclaim put Dylan in a difficult position, in more ways than one.

First of all, and most important: when you finally paint your masterpiece, and unveil it, and the people who are paid to look at it spit on it and the rest of the world won't even come and take a look, it's got to hurt a little. In fact, no matter how cool you think you are, it's got to hurt a lot.

The secondary effects of this are many: for one thing, Dylan had planned to do another movie (he talked about it in interviews in early 1978). But the "failure" of *R&C* meant studio financing or distribution for any other project would be almost impossible to obtain. It also meant his own financial position, since I believe he was the sole investor in *R&C* and also had just gone through a divorce involving minor children in a community property state, was a lot worse than it might have been if the film had done okay . . . Which in turn must have provided considerable incentive for the grueling ten-month-long world tour he undertook in 1978, at the age of 37. (Rock stars are like professional athletes—touring is an *extremely* demanding physical activity, and when you're pushing forty years old you're really a trouper. If you're also a heavy drinker, watch out.)

In terms of his work, the abysmal reception given *Renaldo & Clara* must have had a discouraging effect on Dylan's efforts to probe the outer limits of communication, his attempts to not just understand but communicate new perspectives on identity, time, male/female, and the places where myth and reality meet. Or whatever he was trying to do. The point is that if people don't get it—I mean you've got this huge alleged audience and *nobody* seems to get it—then you may not repudiate what you've done but you've got to start feeling like you're barking up a wrong tree. And it gets difficult, suddenly, to find the energy to press on with the next piece of work in the same vein, faced with the certain knowledge that it too will fall on deaf ears. Especially since it's likely to be even more far out than the last thing. Which means your work starts getting taken away from you, at which point you could really begin to feel naked.

A lot of people who are very upset because Dylan isn't working in the secular realm any more ought to think about the fact that they weren't that interested in what he *was* doing before he got religion—it's like they want him to always be there for them, but they're not necessarily willing to give him any attention in return.

But, you say, isn't it possible that *Renaldo & Clara* was a mistake, and Dylan should just accept that and learn from it? Yes . . . except that I've seen the movie, and it's not a mistake, it's another master-piece. And if the public response did cause Dylan to start having doubts—well, you can see how that would also set the stage for some kind of drastic change, reassessment, some kind of new identity that wouldn't be a retreat but would give him a chance—as a person, as an artist—to come back stronger than ever.

Renaldo & Clara is a collage of interrelated materials, each attractive and meaningful in itself, bound together by rhythmic and thematic (melodic) considerations rather than by any kind of linear plot. Dramatic scenes (some scripted, some documentary, most improvised) are interspersed with concert footage from the Rolling Thunder tour—mostly pieces of songs, seldom a complete number, but enough to be musically meaningful and satisfying and in fact tremendously exciting. The timing of the cuts to music and out of music are especially effective. There is also a lot of music on the soundtrack under the non-musical scenes. It all works on a very subtle and sophisticated level. Visual images, musical images, and then spoken and dramatic content: sometimes the camera is absolutely still, as in a number of sequences where David Blue is playing pinball and talking to the camera about the early days in the Village, how he met Dylan and what the scene was like and so on. Many scenes are improvised conversations between two people, usually a man and a woman; many of these scenes, though they're played by many different people, could be conversations between Dylan and Sara at different times in their lives. There's a terrific scene in a bathroom where Ronee Blakely is putting on makeup and fussing over which dress to wear, and Steve Soles is first being nice and then getting impatient and abusive, so that finally (she's nervous about the show she's about to do or something) she explodes, comes at him with a razor, he's saying "I know who you've been fucking," very powerful, one sort of man/woman confronta-tion. In another funny, delightful scene Ronnie Hawkins is trying to pick up a lovely, fresh-faced farm girl (Ruth Tyrangeil, I think), trying to convince her to come on the road with him for a few months while he does a rock 'n' roll tour, and she says I have to ask my Daddy, and she tries to get him to come to the farm instead, the conversation twists and turns and they both have this fascinating series of looks in their eyes. In another scene Ruth Tyrangeil is the angry girlfriend of a young rock musician (Rob Stoner), and they're arguing about his plan to go back on the road, she's saying he loves rock 'n' roll more than her and lots of better lines which I can't remember. In another scene someone is talking to Sara about the power of women, and he says, "I need you because I need your magic to protect me." Another scene: Bob Dylan is in a garage, waiting for a hot car or something, really mythic posturing like James Dean or Jean-Paul Belmondo, he's got his arm around Helena Kallianiotes and is playing a tune on the guitar for her, no talk. And a scene where Sara and Ann Waldman and Joan Baez and others are lounging around in a fancy house, Sara is doing her nails, the talk is existential and comic and just captures the eternity of waiting rooms and time passing slowly when you're lost in a dream. David Mansfield is brought in to the whorehouse by his father Allen Ginsberg to be deflowered, he looks like a Botticelli angel and the girls talk with him . . . A western scene where Dylan, after some long bit with Baez in which he finally won't talk at all, brings Baez on his horse to a saloon and leaves her snuggling with Harry Dean Stanton, while Dylan rides away with Stanton's horse, which upsets Jack Elliott tremendously. And lots and lots of other stuff, but it's the images of women that fascinate me (and seem to fascinate Dylan)—there is this kaleidoscopic dynamic between a man and a woman, wearing all different masks and never quite getting to or away from each other. That, and the tension/release of shifting from a scene to a musical performance and back, are the most powerful images in the movie for me, although it's so cumulative and subtle and such a garden of puzzles and delights that I don't really want to try to nail it down.

It's Dylan's movie, and it's dominated by images of self and images of women—"I think the women in the movie are beautiful," he told an interviewer. "They look like they stepped out of a painting. They're vulnerable, but they're also strong-willed." In a way he's showing us what he sees in woman, women—women and music, motion and silence, these seem to be the elements of Renaldo's life. He doesn't want to be trapped. He's always able to see beauty. He feels, and that puts him in motion. He doesn't think that much, certainly doesn't talk—but he sees the angles of light at the corners of rooms, and the angles of women's cheekbones, the beauty in unusual faces and the patterns of human energy that make this world some kind of big house with many rooms and non-stop activity—people bumping into other people—people trying to escape or get laid or save each other—everywhere you look.

What I take away from the movie is basically another way of looking at reality. And a renewed sense of Dylan's deep silence and extraordinary presence, his invisibility and his energy. And a sense that maybe he's balancing the whole thing on the end of his nose, and if he loses the will to do it it'll just fall and fall until there's nothing left but tiny fragments and dust on the floor of a huge empty hall. Not because the scene is superficial—it isn't, it's full reality, all of life is going on in here somewhere—but because life is illusion, and only will power is holding it together.

In *Renaldo & Clara* Dylan tells us everything there is to know about Bob Dylan; he shows us what we would see if we were the point of light who is singing those songs. ("Ya didn't see it? Here, I'll show ya again.")

The movie is not about pain, or joy, or guilt. It's oddly amoral, a portrait of reality as stasis, ever dynamic within itself, always moving but never going anywhere, an endless party, a dream.

A series of climactic scenes show Renaldo and Clara, played by Bob and Sara Dylan, lying on a bed talking, he's drinking tequila and she's caressing him—it's an apartment in New York City— looks very private like you're seeing inside their life, she's playing with his shirt and it looks like they might be making love pretty soon when the Woman In White, played by Joan Baez, unexpectedly knocks on the door. She starts talking to Renaldo, who's trying to be cool, Clara holds onto him and says, "Renaldo, do you know this woman?" and round it goes, somehow Baez won't go away, Renaldo's not one to make any decisive moves, the dynamic of the situation turns around and turns around again—really it's just magnificent—at one point Clara and the Woman In White are talking about Renaldo as if he isn't there, "Yeah I can never get a straight answer out of him about anything"—and then there's this classic moment where each of them is asking him, "Renaldo, do you love her?" and almost for the first time he opens his mouth wider than a mumble—time stops, like he's trying to figure it out—then he says to each of them, "Do I love her like I love you? No. Do I love you like I love her? No."

Bob Dylan, I think, lives or lived in a world of his own creation, a dream of his own projection. And he played in it and explored it and suffered in it and controlled it and let go to it and did his work and watched endless mysteries like women's faces unfold and dance before him, all the while burning away, pedaling furiously, running the generator, until one day it started to flicker around the edges and then it all went dark. I think he pushed conscious creation to its limit and found that at the next highest level you have to be a servant again.

"You know," he told Jonathan Cott at the end of 1977, "I'll tell you: lately I've been catching myself. I've been in some scenes, and I say, 'I'm not here alone.' I've never had that experience before the past few months. I've felt this strange, eerie feeling that I wasn't all alone, and I'd better know it."

After completing the editing of *Renaldo & Clara,* Dylan began his world tour (Japan, Australia, England, Germany, France, and then 62 cities in the United States), in the middle of which, late spring 1978, he stopped and recorded his last studio album before his conversion, called *Street-Legal.* This album is our final clue to what was happening with Dylan in the months before he gave himself up to God.

*　　*　　*

"If you find it in your heart, can I be forgiven?
Guess I owe you some kind of apology
I've escaped death so many times, I know I'm only living
By the saving grace that's over me."
—Dylan 1979

If we take Dylan at his word, that he was broken and shattered like an empty cup before Jesus came along and "opened up a door that can't be shut," and figuring that Dylan's conversion came no later than the beginning of 1979, we just have to assume that *Street-Legal,* and the concerts I saw in November '78, near the end of that tour, represent Dylan at the breaking point. I didn't notice anything at the concerts—they were excellent, he poured a lot of energy into the songs and their new arrangements, seemed quite on top of what he was doing (as usual, the shows started stiff and got better, with a result that some of the early songs, including "Tambourine Man," were throwaways, while songs that came later in the show like "Masters of War" and "One More Cup of Coffee" were exquisite)—he should have been tired after all the touring he'd been doing, but there was no evidence of it in the shows I saw.

Street-Legal, on the other hand, is an album I've always liked but have never been able to get much of a handle on, and looking at it in retrospect as the work of a man whose perception is getting keener while his reality is coming apart at the seams . . . I have to admit it makes sense. There aren't any songs of love on *Street-Legal.* There are songs about love, of all kinds; it's still topic A. But there's nothing that expresses love the way "Sara" or "If You See Her, Say Hello" or "Covenant Woman" does. There's certainly nothing on there that's as focused and purposeful as "Knockin' on Heaven's Door" or "It's Alright, Ma" or "Slow Train." My favorites when the album came out were "Where Are You Tonight?" and "Changing of the Guards" and "Senor." Today I'd have to give the nod to "We Better Talk This Over"—it seems to me the most fully-realized song on the album, it fits its own rhythm and melody and structure more than the others do. "Changing of the Guards" is wonderful but it leaves me hungry, it promises more than it delivers. "Senor" is just a little bit facile, a little too sure of itself . . . just enough so I can't love it without reservation. I'd sure like to hear the songs on this album get worked and reworked live, but I guess it's not to be.

The most revealing song, in retrospect, is "No Time to Think." (Kind of a partner to "Trouble in Mind.") The song is reminiscent of some of his 1960s songs which were virtual catalogs of perceived reality, long lists that crackled with the ironies of human behavior and the freshness of describing things as they really seem. But "No Time to Think" is more a catalog of the disintegration of a subjective, personal reality, than any kind of prophetic vision of the world we share. Something is catching up with the person singing the song: "But the magician is quicker and his game is much thicker than blood, and blacker than ink; and there's no time to think." "You glance at the mirror and there's eyes staring clear at the back of your head as you drink—" "You know you can't keep her and the water gets deeper, and it's leading you on to the brink . . ." And how about this for alienation: "Stripped of all virtue as you crawl through the dirt you can give but you cannot receive"? Sounds like a terrible fate for anybody, but an artist or performer especially. The song is well-written, but its cocky tone seems at odds with the dark picture it paints. He seems to be saying, hey I'm aware of all this stuff, and that puts me three jumps ahead of anybody else, so how can it touch me?

The same attitude of "I've thought this through already" simply guarantees that he's not going to find love with the woman he's addressing in "Is Your Love in Vain?" Which is okay for her, maybe; she still gets to sleep with Bob Dylan; but it doesn't put him in a position where he's likely to get what he wants.

There's a false self-confidence on this album that keeps it from being as good as it ought to be. It's funny, because what I've always liked best in Dylan has been his conviction, which is sort of like self-confidence, but there's the rub: it only works when you're really being true to something. Conviction means you believe, and you have the courage to show it, and the listener can feel it. False self-confidence means in this case that you think sounding believable is a skill you've learned or a talent you have, something you know how to do. When in fact what you're good at is letting your feelings show through—and standing behind them.

And it only works when you really feel something; and on *Street-Legal* Dylan feels too much and too little both at once. He doesn't have anything to focus on except his own skill and cleverness (". . . till you worship the work of your own hands"), so he reaches out for a little of everything that's around for subject matter. And as a result not only the words but the melodies, the songs, don't quite come together, because just as there isn't anything he really needs to say (anything that takes courage to say) in the words, so also there's nothing he really *needs* to say in the music.

In retrospect, perhaps what he's saying in this album—unconsciously for the most part—is, "Help!" But if so, I didn't hear it when I was listening to *Street-Legal* over and over in summer '78. According to Dylan in his new songs, his friends couldn't hear it either. But the Lord heard, with a woman's help . . .

"True Love Tends to Forget" is a good line about marriage. If we remember that we tend to forget we might learn to be more forgiving of each other. The first two lines are also superb: "I'm getting weary looking in my baby's eyes/When she's near me she's so hard to recognize." (The other side of this is "you were always so close, but still within reach," from "Sara.") The rest of the words in the song, unfortunately, were not so carefully chosen.

"We Better Talk This Over" is good all the way through (neat words, and I like the way they carry the rhythm). If this song isn't about Sara, then it's a good indication that he's repeating the pattern and problems of his marriage in his more short-term affairs. Which is no surprise, but between this song and "Is Your Love in Vain?" one can see why he's having a hard time finding a woman to save him. This character in these songs is setting himself up, over and over—sounds to me like he's looking for a woman just like the one he lost, only when he finds a possibility he says, You won't do, you're just like the last one!

"Where Are You Tonight?" shows how far you can go just faking it—Dylan puts together an impressive string of words and images with a catchy, involving arrangement—and also shows that ultimately you can't go far enough, in the end the song doesn't make it because it's not really about anything. There is no real woman in the song or behind the song, or at least he doesn't convince me there is. His great skill is mixing reality with fantasy, as in "Tangled Up in Blue," but this time there's not enough reality— "Where are you tonight?" is a good concept for a song but he doesn't follow through . . . he's lonely but it's not the penetrating, all-inclusive hunger that would be appropriate here. Two lines are prophetic: "The truth was obscure, too profound and too pure, to live it you had to explode"; and "I fought with my twin, that enemy within, till both of us fell by the way." But the search for love really is no more than vanity when you get hung up searching for what you think you want, instead of simply expressing your need.

These last three *Street-Legal* songs are Dylan's final words on marriage and lovers before *Slow Train Coming* and the shocking renunciation of it all in "Trouble in Mind." They are hopeful songs in that they're upbeat, they show insight, Dylan sees himself as a survivor and wants to survive and go on with the show. But they're also a little scary in that there's what you might call a lack of emotional affect, the further he gets from actually feeling love the more confident he seems to be that he knows all about it, something's out of step here. He says in several of his newest songs that he was "blinded"—what kind of blindness? Lack of awareness of Jesus Christ? (Actually there's a song by Dylan in *Renaldo & Clara*, dating from '76 or '77, called "What Will You Do When Jesus Comes?") I think it was a more pervasive blindness, the kind where you see nothing because you're so sure you see everything—the man became overly impressed with his own vision. On *Street-Legal* that vision is revealed (with the wisdom of hindsight) as being without heart, lacking a center, "thou hast eyes but cannot see." At a time when Dylan believed himself more conscious and more in control than he'd ever been (see the second Jonathan Cott interview, *Rolling Stone*, Nov. 16, 1978) he recorded an album that is actually a portrait of a man suffering from a profound and unconscious alienation.

Which means, I think, that we have reason to take him at his word when he says he was "saved" by the blood of the Lamb. Even though it may make many of us feel separated from Dylan, we can be glad for his sake that it happened.

And once you hear his latest songs, you'll be glad for your own sake too. The man is writing great songs again, and performing them with real conviction, and isn't that what it's all about?

*   *   *

"Was it the real Sara, or the Sara in the dream?
I still don't know."

—Bob Dylan, 1978

What I think happened to Dylan is this: he came to New York an ambitious kid, made the scene, wrote some songs, made some records, became famous, kept on going and did a whole lot of great work and got so famous so fast with so many expectations from all sides that finally it blew up in his face, and through some kind of saving grace there was a woman then to save him, protect him, allow him to go on with his life.

And he completed the work that had been left hanging, then sat around and watched his kids grow and tried to figure out who he was or could be—felt uncomfortable with the limitations of marriage and his isolation from the world (for him with his experience "touring" and "the world" are and always have been synonymous) but too in love and too uncertain of anything else to challenge that. Spent a lot of time working through his fears and rebuilding himself as a human being.

And then with some older version of whatever desire had brought him to New York and performing in the first place, broke out again, went on tour, rediscovered his own genius, dived into it, tried and succeeded for a while but ultimately failed at keeping his marriage together while exploring the outer limits of his own freedom. Swam through the flood, in pain about Sara but exultant about what he could do and who he'd become.

That sense of diminishing returns, when it started coming around again, was not unexpected—he'd known he'd be needing shelter from the storm, it was marked on his calendar, he started looking more closely at the women who crossed his field of vision. Which one would be the new Sara, to offer him the protection he needed so he could go on with his work? Someone with all her strength and grace, but without the flaws that had driven him crazy . . . Well, maybe a few flaws would be okay . . . The women kept coming and somehow he wasn't finding her, something wasn't fitting together, what was wrong with these people that they couldn't make him love them? And then that inner storm that has always driven the man, that restless force that he had ridden like a champ till it threw him the last time, that desperation that is somehow synonymous with his courage and genius and power, grew in intensity and couldn't be placated—"Woman, I need your magic to protect me!", but the magic wasn't there any more.

He hadn't realized it at the time, but in freeing himself from Sara he had, through great struggle, finally overcome the power of all women over him—which meant also they could no longer help him, they wanted to but he'd made himself immune. And thus made himself naked to the greater horror.

And the Devil laughed, we've got you now, you did it to yourself, your own pride and lust, you let it happen. And in this hour of greatest anxiety—all in his mind of course, but where else is there?—someone said, "Take it easy, man, I know where you're at." "You couldn't possibly." "I do—we deal with this all the time. You think you're someone special? Here, let me show you what it says in this Book . . ."

101

And the man who thought he was so alone and so far out in front that no one could help him, discovered with the shock of recognition that signals truth, that indeed Someone had been here before. Or something like that. Anyway, he found a source of help, and a real one, and it humbled him (at least before God) and it turned him around. "And nothing has been the same," as R. Crumb once told us, "since Meatball struck me at last."

Or construct your own scenario. Evidently at least as early as 1977 he felt the presence of someone else with him, a mysterious presence, which suggests that one way or another he did undergo some kind of religious experience—the intellectual decision for Christ, the personal and emotional need for a solid rock to hang onto, were preceded by some kind of event outside his control. I believe such things do happen.

All I'm really saying is this, and I'm just taking it from what I hear in his songs, his movie, his performances: Sara saved him, he rebelled and was reborn creatively, he lost Sara, he still needed saving and thought to find it in another woman, he couldn't, he'd learned too many new tricks that protected him from protection, the need for salvation grew greater and greater and he found the discipline he needed to save himself in an American cultural ritual called giving oneself up to Christ.

So, you ask, what's he going to do now? Try to force Christ on the rest of us? It's a good question.

* * *

> "Mama take this badge off of me
> I can't use it any more
> It's getting dark, too dark to see
> Feel like I'm knockin' on heaven's door."
> —Bob Dylan, 1973

"He used to be so right, and now he's so wrong." That's how one friend of mine summed up the general response among people he knows to the news of Dylan's conversion to fundamentalist Christianity. Some people feel betrayed. Others just don't know what to make of it all. And then of course there are some people—a minority among my friends but possibly a majority among the general population—who are also devout Christians, and to the extent that they're aware of Bob Dylan are pleased to welcome him into the fold.

I had almost forgotten what a powerful and divisive issue religion is. My own beliefs and practices are so private and difficult to articulate that, while they may influence everything I say and do, they almost never come up as a subject of conversation in themselves. And this is true even though the most successful of my books is a collection of thoughts on human nature and human responsibilities towards other humans and towards the universe, a work with considerable "religious" content and implications. Come to think of it, when people try to engage me in conversation on these subjects, I get evasive (unless we're discussing real personal problems and situations, as opposed to abstract ideas). Personal beliefs to me are something quite intimate, not to be discussed casually or in social situations.

And yet, since Sachiko and I went to see seven Dylan concerts last week, and since Dylan has recently shocked the world and people in our age group in particular (we're both 31) by becoming a born-again Christian, the subject comes up everywhere we go. And it's fascinating how many different perspectives I've encountered on this among the people I meet.

Some people see this as a threateningly anti-intellectual move from someone they've always related to on an intense intellectual level. Some people were brought up in an unpleasantly repressive way in the name of Catholicism or one of the stricter Protestant sects, and have very negative associations with Christianity and organized religion. Some people are Jews who are disturbed by Dylan's implicit renunciation of his Jewish heritage. Christians, especially born-again Christians, are hopeful this will bring more people to Christ. Some people (and I'm closest to this last category) feel it's okay for Dylan to be whatever he wants as long as he's honest with himself and as long as he keeps making good music. But then the issue is legitimately raised, why are all his new songs about Christ? Is he on a crusade? Is he lending his fame and his music to a religious movement that is politically reactionary, socially repressive, and fanatically righteous? Has this poet/hero of stalwart individualism joined forces with the enemies of personal and religious freedom?

And (you ask, I ask) if I've identified with Dylan all this time, where have we diverged? Is he wrong, or are we different in some deep way, or does this mean one day I'm going to wake up in love with Jesus too?

Not that I'm necessarily very far from loving Jesus right now. But I'll be damned (ahem) if I'll enter into a monogamous relationship with Him, one that excludes a large part of humankind until or unless they decide to see things my way and express their faith in terms of my language and my historical and cultural referents. This exclusivity—not the love of and personal relationship with God—is the crux of the issue (so to speak) for me.

But I see I'm getting ahead of myself. I do intend to articulate my feelings about all this as clearly and carefully as I can. But first I think it would be worthwhile to take a close look at Dylan's new songs to try to find out what he's saying, what he's thinking and feeling, why he's doing this, where he's coming from.

"Christian" is a big word and, obviously, a loaded word. But what is Dylan actually saying?

Interestingly, there is a fairly sharp distinction that can be made between the songs on *Slow Train Coming* and the eight newer songs that Dylan unveiled at his San Francisco concerts. The newest songs are all expressions of love for God; they are songs of joy, service, gratitude. The songs on *Slow Train Coming*, on the other hand, are more generally directed to the nation of nonbelievers that Dylan presumes is his listening audience; they are more preachy, and the three songs that can be considered transitional—since, like the newer songs, they are essentially devotional—all have significant preachy or "us and them" elements along with their devotional message. (These latter songs are "Precious Angel," "When He Returns," and "I Believe In You." At the live shows these were consistently the best-sung and -performed of the *Slow Train Coming* songs, which suggests that Dylan has already moved beyond where he was when he wrote "Slow Train" and "When You Gonna Wake Up?" and that he isn't completely comfortable with those songs any more.)

So: stage one of Dylan's born-again music was basically his classic rebel stance, this time turned against many of his complacent (unawakened) fans: "Boy have I got news for you! You're up to your noses in garbage and you don't even know it. Watch out—God's coming back and all your petty earthly concerns are going to be so many ashes in the wind." There's more than a little contempt in his tone, which of course is hardly a surprise from the man who wrote "Ballad of a Thin Man" and "Like a Rolling Stone." The trick this time is he's turned around our preconceptions as to who is "us" and who is "them." Suddenly we're "them"—unless we're also born-again Christians—and naturally we don't like it.

But stage one is already in the past, and stage two—which also of course shouldn't be expected to last forever—is a different Dylan, authentically humble, writing songs of devotion so beautiful and heartfelt that if you let down your defenses for a moment they're likely to reduce you to tears. Or cause you to make a joyful noise unto the Lord. I have to admit, when I hear "Hanging on to a Solid Rock" I believe in Dylan's God. I can't help it.

And stage two is real enough and distinct enough from stage one that Dylan can't seem to bring himself to really be passionate with songs like "When You Gonna Wake Up?" and "Slow Train" in concert, even though they're songs that definitely lend themselves to the sort of fire-eating singing and musicianship that Dylan has shown himself to be master of in hundreds of live performances, throwing incredible energy into the likes of "Isis" and "It's Alright, Ma" and "Like a Rolling Stone." There's plenty of energy in his new show at other points, and some nights the "stage one" songs were very good, but he never really breaks loose with them the way I can so easily imagine him doing when I listen to "Wake Up" on record. And it seems to me the reason is that he's afraid, he really doesn't feel right shouting that stuff at us at the top of his lungs, pouring all his passion into it—it's an indulgence—the place where he feels free to let loose his passion is in the songs of devotion and joy.

This is a new "new Dylan" we've got here—and still in motion.

Granted, then, that Dylan has moved on already, let's see what the stage one songs have to tell us. "Gotta Serve Somebody" is the closest he comes to offering an explanation for his new position— you may not know it, he's telling us, but you have to work for somebody—either you do the Lord's work or the Devil's work, which is it gonna be? Only the song is structured so it doesn't come off quite that confrontational; "gotta serve somebody" can be heard as a more general message, plugging the concept of service. That's not really what he says, but it's what it sounds like to the casual listener, so it works pretty well on AM radio. And the simplicity of the verse content, you may be rich or poor, may like caviar may like bread, may sleep on the floor or a king-size bed, is attractive and very effective and again puts a lot of the energy of the song into the suitably secular message: IT DOESN'T MATTER, doesn't matter how powerful or powerless you are, we're all equal and the same when it gets down to the important stuff. Yay! Again, what he's really saying is, we're equal in the eyes of the Lord, but he doesn't make that too intrusive. The song is very cleverly crafted so that it can be powerful and true to its message without necessarily scaring away people who'd be upset at the more explicitly evangelical stuff. Great recording, too—in the later nights of the concerts this song got hot but Dylan never matched the singing he did on the record.

Incidentally, Dylan never sings the "you may call me Zimmy" verse on stage—it seemed to me it was courageous and appropriate on record, but maybe it would have just been embarrassing in concert. He's shy, y'know. Anyway he chose not to do it.

"Slow Train" is a *tour de force*. Mark Knopfler's guitar plays an important role, as does the great production quality (go, Muscle Shoals!) and fine work by the other musicians. A tremendously evocative recording. Gotta mention Tim Drummond's bass-playing, too. But what I want to talk about is the content of this song, starting with the fact that, much as I love it, some of the lines are really unfortunate. "All that foreign oil controlling American soil" is jingoistic. If Dylan had said something about our foolish dependence on foreign oil, our gluttonous and self-destructive appetite for same, I would applaud. But what he does say is silly—and how about the far more extensive American investment in other people's countries? As I say, what makes me embarrassed is our greed and dependence, which perhaps is what this line is really getting at, but only by very generous interpretation. And then "sheiks walking around like kings, wearing fancy jewels and nose-rings" is out-and-out racist, no excuse for it at all. Dylan himself is wearing jewels on the inner sleeve of the album. What kind of nonsense is this? The whole verse is disgraceful.

Having said that, I'll add that I think it's a case of sloppy writing rather than a conscious embracing of racism and jingoism; and Dylan has managed to toss off dumb lines at every stage in his career; nevertheless, if he's going to hang around

106

with fundamentalist Christians, many of whom are ultraconservative simply because they've never been exposed to anything else, he's going to have to be especially responsible about what he says and what views he seems to espouse—in fairness to them, and what he might have to offer them in the way of a broader worldview. That is, assuming Satan is no longer deadening Dylan's conscience. Wake up, kid—you don't have to be political, but if you're going to open your mouth about political subjects you'd better think about what you're saying first.

"I had a woman, down in Alabama . . . she said, 'quit your messing, straighten out; you could die down here, be just another accident statistic' " is one of three places where he mentions the crucial role a woman played in his awakening (the others are "Precious Angel" and "Covenant Woman"). I'm not sure what she meant by "be just another accident statistic"—at first I felt she was telling him to do something meaningful with his life, live and die for a reason. But my whole initial interpretation of this album was overly slanted towards what I hoped and imagined he was into, namely a Catholic Worker kind of activist Christianity, directed towards moral issues, including the environment, corporate responsibility toward the poor, etc. A closer interpretation of these songs, plus the change in direction in the newer songs, suggests this was wishful thinking on my part. If indeed she wanted him to live for a reason, I would now assume that reason is to serve the Lord, period, no embellishment. It's possible of course that she's just giving him the standard warning to get straight with God before you die and it's too late, but that would really be depressing. I don't think much of people whose chief motivation for conversion is to improve their standing in the afterlife.

More "Slow Train" stuff: "Big time negotiators, false healers and woman haters/Masters of the bluff, masters of the proposition" is a great example of Dylan's command of the language. This is absolutely extraordinary cadenced writing; he makes our language come alive like no other living poet I know of. I don't know how these words would work on a page, but that's not the point— they're not on a page, they're in a song, with music, to be sung aloud, that's their proper setting and the context in which their greatness can be felt.

It would be interesting to know who Dylan refers to when he says,

"The enemy I see . . . all nonbelievers and men-stealers (?) talking in the name of religion." Is he crying out against hypocrisy in the church, or is he alas just attacking people whose beliefs are different from his own? We pray it's the former, but nothing seems certain right now.

The start of "Slow Train"—"Sometimes I feel so low down and discouraged"—is important to me in that it shows Dylan and me diverging at a point prior to his embracing Christ. He sees things as looking pretty grim, for him and for the people around him ("so much depression"), and I get the feeling from this album that he thinks his listener will know what he's talking about. But that just isn't how I feel or what I see right now. So it's not just his conclusion (embrace Christ) but his premise (things are real bad) that I can't identify with. I'm not saying he's wrong—it's a simple case of most likely you'll go your way and I'll go mine.

If and when I reach the end of my particular rope, it's fair to say I might see things differently.

(The old thing of all of us being in the same psychic space at the same time listening to the same new record albums just doesn't work anymore. Not that I think Dylan expects it to—but I think that's what a lot of us still expect of Dylan, that he'll bring us the news. And that's why we're so confused and upset about the news he brought us this time. We keep thinking his news is our news, you see.)

Finally there's the line about "My baby went to Illinois" . . . very powerful and effective. Sure does sound personal—could he be talking about Sara? Or her oldest daughter? If you put stuff like this in songs people are just naturally going to speculate. I have to say also that the line about "my loved ones turning into puppets" is effective but it's also arrogant as hell. On the other side of the album he says, "Don't want to judge nobody, don't want to be judged." Hmm.

"When You Gonna Wake Up?" is another great song, great recording, that contains one really unfortunate line: "Adulterers in churches, pornography in the schools." A friend of mine pointed this out to me—she says she couldn't sleep, worrying about why he'd say something like that. "Pornography in the schools"? What is he referring to? Kurt Vonnegut's novels? Bob Dylan's song lyrics? "Adulterers in churches" is pretty stunning too. Now that Dylan has (presumably) knocked off the adultery for a while, is he planning to go around and finger the unrepentant and have them shot by the Ayatollah Khomeini? Incredible. We've got plenty of problems in our schools, but *pornography*? Again, I think this is just sloppy writing, but if Dylan is really thinking like this the only thing I can suggest is that we lock him in a train compartment with Joel Selvin, the newspaper reviewer, and force the two of them to discuss the vast emptiness of our times together on the slow train for the rest of eternity.

The quality of music on this album is superb. The writing, the use of language, is very impressive, even when I have my doubts about the content. I've listened to the album at least a hundred times and I'm ready to hear it a lot more. If he could just avoid those rare lapses into totally mindless righteousness . . . Perhaps we should be optimistic, and take the rareness of the lapses (and the high quality of everything else) as evidence that he hasn't really lost his soul. He just gets distracted . . .

"When You Gonna Wake Up?" does seem to be directed at America, collectively, although some of the verses focus in on the individual who's listening. "Do you ever wonder just what God requires?" is a good line, along with its mate, "Do you think He's just an errand boy to satisfy your wandering desires?" The specific references to Jesus on this album are kept to a minimum, again presumably so as not to scare people away before they get a chance to be turned on by the music, so the last line of this song is notable: "There's a man on the cross, and He be crucified for you; believe in His power, that's about all that you've got to do." For some reason this has been changed in live performances to: "There's a man on the cross, and He be crucified. You know who He is, and you know why He died."

It may be that this song and some of the others were written to make a conscious connection for the public between the early "protest-singer" Dylan (still his best-known image) and the present-day born-again Dylan. If so, something a little more gutsy would be nice: something about Christ throwing the money-lenders out of the temple and how we should do the same to the bankers, maybe?

One thing I don't really understand about evangelical Christianity: given the emphasis on the apocalyptic vision, which Dylan has certainly embraced enthusiastically (not surprisingly, in view of his past work), how much real impetus is there for reform, for improvement of man's behavior on Earth? Does it matter what people do, except in terms of their personal relationship with Christ? Is there any reason for a social conscience within the framework of an apocalyptic vision? Sometimes I think the evangelicals would welcome the next world war, because it'll prove they were right. Nuke the Russians, boys, help us bring on the Kingdom of Christ.

(I do know these are the sort of questions the evangelical movement, born-again movement, is divided over; it would be interesting to find out what Dylan thinks about such questions, if indeed they mean anything to him at all. If he doesn't care, however, he shouldn't sing songs about waking up America. Again: if you're going to be political, do it consciously. Any other approach is hypocrisy and exploitation.)

"Gonna Change My Way of Thinking" is a good concept—there's power in the idea that by an act of will we can see things differently and change our personal behavior. "Gonna stop being influenced by fools"—does he mean that from now on he's only going to be influenced by other true believers? Or only by God? I would think the best path is to let oneself be influenced by everyone, of all beliefs and in any walk of life, but to limit all influence at the point that it impinges on one's personal sense of what's right, one's private relationship with God. To put it another way: is he not a fool himself who believes he has the power to judge who around him is and is not a fool?

When he attacks "doing your own thing," he's pushing buttons, purposely goading the 1960s diehards who believe Dylan was created to speak on their behalf. In this case I agree with him—doing your own thing is a travesty if it's used as an excuse for ignoring the impact what you do has on other people.

"I got a God-fearing woman" is interesting (actually if I understand it right the God of the born-again Christians is not a God to be feared, as in the Old Testament, but a God to be respected, obeyed and loved) because he says he has a woman. The question arises—and this would be an invasion of privacy except that the man has proclaimed himself publicly as a servant of God, and thus has specifically raised the issue of his attitudes towards alcohol, fornication etcetera—is she his lover, and if so are they married?

And if not, does his literal interpretation of the Bible (for there is much evidence in his new songs that he's a fundamentalist in the sense of living by the written words of Christ) allow for the possibility of unsinful lovemaking between unmarried adults? I would hope that it does, as I regard fundamentalist attitudes towards sex as basically unGodly and would feel a lot more friendly towards a devout Christianity that was more enlightened in this regard. (A secret marriage is the more likely possibility, however.)

Also in "Change My Way of Thinking" we have the line, "Jesus said . . . who's not for me is against me." Leaving aside the question of the unaffiliated faithful such as myself, if this line means that Dylan thinks a devout Moslem can never enjoy the personal relationship with God that Dylan has (except by specifically accepting Christ) then Dylan (I believe) is wrong, wrong, wrong, wrong, wrong.

"Do Right to Me, Baby" is a pleasant, minor song about the Golden Rule. Actually, "*If* you do right, then I will" is not the Golden Rule at all, it's a perversion of it, it's the basic misunderstanding that has allowed people to avoid moral behavior towards others for thousands of years. But it's a good song and it gets its message across—he says it wrong but it comes out right anyway.

"Man Gave Names to All the Animals" is vaguely biblical, with its coy reference at the end to the snake, and quite charming. It sounds like it was written to please somebody, which is nice. Perhaps someday we'll see Dylan writing children's songs, as Woody Guthrie did before him.

The three remaining songs from *Slow Train Coming* can be seen, as I noted before, as transitional material, a link between Dylan's initially righteous post-conversion stance ("I've found the truth, and if you had any sense you'd see it too") and the humble and joyous hymns of praise we heard from him at his recent concerts. These are the songs that begin to reveal to us some of the nature of the new relationship between Dylan and his Lord.

"Precious Angel" is a crowd-pleaser—everybody likes it—I certainly like it. The melody and rhythm here are truly infectious; it's very reminiscent of how the Byrds used to remake Dylan songs, particularly the double-time drumming (twice as many beats as usual, creating those meticulously regular circles of music, joyously liberating, what Sandy Pearlman used to call the sound of the Earth turning). Pick Withers' drum-work on the album is superb.

"Precious Angel" is an upbeat song: it sounds happy, it is directed at a woman the singer clearly loves, and the chorus ("shine your light on me") is out-and-out devotional, the sort of religious feeling everyone has felt and anyone can identify with. As in "Covenant Woman," Dylan gets tremendous mileage out of the fact that (in the chorus) he's singing to his woman and to the Lord at the same time, making us feel the strong link between the two kinds of love, enabling the listener to feel Dylan's love for God as an almost physical reality.

But the upbeat tone of the song also serves as a foil for some particularly strong words of warning to the nonbeliever. This is Dylan the evangelist and Biblical prophet, warning of hellfire—not the personal kind but the collective hellfire in this world described in Revelation. "Can they (my so-called friends) imagine the darkness that will fall from on high/When men will beg God to kill them, and they won't be able to die?" And these strange words, which sound to me like resentful criticism of his ex-wife, his previous spiritual guide (Dylan definitely believes that men are incomplete and soulless, and need women to show them the way): "You were telling him about Buddha, and Mohammed in the same breath; never mentioned one time the man who came and died a criminal's death." And this comment, literally true but implicitly threatening: "You either got faith or you got unbelief, and there ain't *no* neutral ground." That of course is the meaning of faith, that it's there or it isn't, but Dylan's voice here sounds like that of a man who thinks he can judge the inherent worth of some other person's beliefs. Actually I applaud Dylan's forceful assault on the fence-straddler in all of us; but I want to make a strong distinction between helping people to search their own hearts versus asking them to stand up and be counted. The pushiness of evangelical Christianity is helpful to some people in finding their faith, but a great hindrance to others. I like it much better in Dylan's newer songs, where he relies entirely on example (seduces us by letting his own strong faith shine through).

"I Believe in You" features an incredibly sweet melody, and is the one song from *Slow Train Coming* that Dylan sings with more energy in concert than on the album. When he cries out his sustained "Don't—" the audience bursts into applause, every time.

This is the song on the album where he speaks most directly to God—it's a pledge of allegiance, and an almost tearful plea to the Lord not to let him doubt or backslide in his faith. It's also the song that crystallizes the theme of "us and them" that runs through this record. In this case Dylan portrays himself in the familiar romantic role of the exile, the man who goes his own way, cast out from society because he won't go along with the crowd. "They . . . they like to drive me from this town, they don't want me around . . . they show me to the door, they say don't come back no more." The twist is that this time what makes him so unpopular is his belief in God. One could wonder how painful is it to be exiled when a fair majority of the American people are right there with you, far more than ever shared Dylan's views before . . . except that real exile is being shut out from home, from the people you're close to. And although I suspect "my friends forsake me" is a considerable exaggeration, it's clear this song is Dylan's effort to protect himself in advance against the hostility of some friends and family and associates and many people who thought of themselves as "his" audience. I get the clear feeling that he's enjoying this stance, it's great to be able to feel righteous again, to be unfashionable, to know that all the misunderstanding aimed at you is just proof that you're in the vanguard of what's really going on.

It's possible Dylan was even disappointed—for a moment—that the persecution anticipated in this song didn't materialize at his recent series of concerts. (In spite of what the newspapers said, there was very little booing or catcalling, none after the first night, and certainly no throwing of vegetables—nothing like the furor that greeted Dylan's switch to rock 'n' roll in 1965. One could say that's because Dylan isn't as important now as he was then, but it's not really true. A lot of his fans seem to accept his conversion, particularly after seeing him perform; there is clearly a significant and fast-growing part of his audience who are themselves born-again Christians; and among those who are dissatisfied, only a few are angry—the others are simply unhappy, or confused.)

"Even on the morning after" and "Oh, when the dawn is nearing, when the night is disappearing, this feeling's still here in my heart" strike me as references to the moment of conversion, the moment of being "born again." He's saying that even though the intoxicating moment of surrender is past, he still feels the same—after a long night of the soul, morning dawns and that feeling's still here, it wasn't an illusion or a momentary enthusiasm, his life is changed forever. There are parallels between this and the Zen experience of satori or enlightenment. But the born-agains put more emphasis on the mystical religious experience as a turning point, a new beginning. It's not hard to see why Dylan chose not to do any older songs in his recent concerts (a decision, however, that could just as well have been made on artistic grounds—Dylan's tour last year centered around fascinating and inventive new arrangements of old material; by 1979, born again or no, it was time for him to get into something altogether new in his live performances).

"When He Returns" is the last song on *Slow Train Coming*, the most profound and heartfelt, a *tour de force*, a recording that will leave some people reaffirmed in their conviction that Dylan can't sing a note, and leaves the rest of us convinced he's the best singer, certainly the best white American singer, in the world today. Barry Beckett's exquisite piano playing on this track has inspired Dylan to new heights of expressiveness.

"When He Returns" is a statement of faith: the only important news of the world, to Dylan or anyone who shares his vision, is that Christ is returning to set up His Kingdom on Earth. Dylan succeeds in making this vision an intensely personal one. There is still a trace of the preacher here, Dylan telling us what he thinks we need to know, but the song leans heavily toward the pure expression of devotion and faith that is characteristic of the newer songs. Dylan singing to and about God is far more moving than Dylan preaching to a nation of sinners and unbelievers (though the songs that fall in the latter category also have considerable power and appeal). It is impossible to listen to "When He Returns" or "What Can I Do for You?" and doubt the sincerity and depth of Dylan's new beliefs.

There are some lines here that cast additional light on who Dylan was, in his own eyes at least, in the time before his awakening. "How long can I stay drunk on fear out in the wilderness?" is a portrait of a man who's faking it, drawing energy ("drunk on fear" is a great image) from his own uncertainty but increasingly uneasy about the fact that he doesn't feel at home in this world. "Can I cast it aside, all this loyalty and this pride?" tells us what were the final barriers to his acceptance of Christ: loyalty to friends, his dead father, all those people who'd never understand; and pride, not wanting to admit he needed such help, the pride that says my own idea-system is enough, I'm not going to submit to yours. Then one of those particularly revealing verses where he says "you" but surely is referring to himself at least as much as anyone else: "How long can you falsify and deny what is real/How long can you hate yourself for the weakness you conceal?" It has long been apparent to me that people of great strength tend to have weaknesses as great as their strengths (because our strengths and our weaknesses are in fact the same things) (look at the private suffering of Churchill and Lincoln, as examples). Dylan retreated from his strength once (the Woodstock years), returned to it because he finally couldn't live without it, saw it build to an intensity that became once again (because of the weakness inside the strength) more than he could bear alone, and then found salvation (he tells us) by putting both his weakness and his strength in the hands of the Lord.

"Surrender your crown on this blood-stained ground; take off your mask" is one of the most powerful lines Dylan has ever written. And I won't argue with the fact that, now that the mask is off, the naked man underneath is more beautiful than ever, because the glory of God shines through him.

* * *

"Lay down your weary tune, lay down
Lay down the song you strum
And rest yourself 'neath the strength of strings
No voice can hope to hum."
—Bob Dylan, 1964

The *Slow Train Coming* songs tell us that Dylan is very, very serious about his faith in Jesus Christ, and that his prophetic vision now runs along the specific and narrow lines described in the Bible in the Book of Revelation. They tell us he sees depression and depravity all around him, that he sees America sliding downhill and he doesn't like it, and that Christ is the only answer. They tell us he believes in the Golden Rule, that he's found a woman who has brought him to God. And they tell us he is impatient with all the fools in the world who have not yet discovered the Truth.

This album also tells us that, quite apart from what he has to say,

115

Dylan has found his Voice again; his music and his use of language are as powerful and as trail-blazing now as at any time in his career. Taking a strong stand and preparing himself in his heart to defend his position against all challengers has done him a lot of good. He seems sure of his own identity again, and that's a critical factor in the ability to create great art.

How do I feel about what happened to Bob Dylan? I'm glad he found religion, glad not just for him but for myself and all of us, because Bob Dylan the artist is an international resource, and I feel that resource has just been renewed. Dylan has been recalled to life; and like John Donne and G. K. Chesterton and so many others before him, he may well produce a finer body of work in the second half of his life—after conversion—than he did in the first half, which would be an extraordinary accomplishment indeed.

The best indication of this is four new songs, first performed at the San Francisco concerts, November 1979, that seem to me to be as good as anything he's ever written. If none of us had ever heard of Bob Dylan, these songs would make it necessary for us to invent his myth right now.

In these new songs, Dylan is no longer impatient. In the songs on the album he seems conscious of his audience at all times, presenting information or ideas or images that will goad them, illumine them, force them to open their eyes to what's going on around them and perhaps help them to find out what he's learned about Jesus Christ. The new songs may or may not have similar effects, but the self-consciousness of "I'm speaking before an audience" is gone. Instead of a three-way relationship, Dylan singing to a listener about God, we get something much more intimate: Dylan expressing his feelings directly, striving only to show his heart, speaking to as well as about God. He is letting us see his inner life now. He lets us look in on emotions he would feel and express in the same way if there were no one listening and no one watching, no mortal that is. He lets us in on his private relationship with his Lord.

These then are songs of intimacy, like his greatest love songs of the past. They are songs that touch on the universal and ultimately personal experience of the individual alone with God. It is not necessary to perceive God as a being or to agree on His name to know the intensity of this experience.

My favorite right now (I should add that we did succeed in seeing Dylan one more time, the 13th concert, Thursday, November 15th) is "What Can I Do for You?" This is a simple song (simple in the sense that "Blowin' in the Wind," "Don't Think Twice," and "Knockin' on Heaven's Door" are simple) whose message is contained in the opening lines: "You have/Given everything to me/What can I do for you?" The singer is thanking God for giving him "eyes to see" and "life to live"—both these qualities are given us at birth; significantly, the words take on new meanings in reference to what is re-given by God at the time of being born again—and is asking, almost begging to know, what he can give in return.

What makes this song so good is the depth of sincerity it manages to convey. The melody is hauntingly subtle and evocative; the words are straightforward and from the heart, and the rhythm and melody of the song give perfect emphasis to everything the man has to say, so that you can just feel his heart—and your own—opening wide as he sings. Dylan's timing has always been impressive, and more so the more deeply he feels what he's singing about. In "What Can I Do for You?" Dylan's pacing is as slow and sure and vibrant as Huddie Ledbetter singing "Fanning Street" or "Goodnight Irene." This is great music.

The drum/organ/vocal ensemble Dylan and his band achieved on this tune, the nights I saw them, is a hallmark of Dylan at his best: this is his sound, a sound that's there in his songs even when the arrangements and instrumentation are very different. To recognize it, listen for that drumbeat cutting through the center of the music, punctuating the vocal and melody as if somehow the drumbeat was the sound of Dylan's mind, and everything else including the words was accompaniment. The organ and guitar (or whatever) and vocals then form an environment around those drum interruptions. This time Dylan adds female harmony voices to the last line of each verse, with terrific results. That last line doubles as chorus, and is preceded by a pause in the words, a short instrumental break, perfectly paced, that gives resonance to the words that come before it and eloquence to the chorus-line that follows. All of which serves as prelude to the real moment of apotheosis: the harmonica solo.

Dylan's harmonica-playing (here accompanied by full band plus

117

backup singers), like the music of Bach, is, at its best, the sound of a human being at one with God.

All this extraordinary music can't help but give the words of the song more poignance, but it works the other way too: the heartfelt quality of the words, what the song has to say, is what inspires the music. "You have/Laid down your life for me/What can I do for you?" The song is well-structured, but when you listen to it you will find that there's nothing clever in it: every sentence is real. "You have/Explained every mystery/What can I do for you?" The way the singing and the accompaniment play against each other is incredible. "Soon as a man is born, the sparks begin to fly/He gets wise in his own eyes, and he's made to believe a lie/Who will deliver him from the death he's bound to die?/You've done it all, and there's no more anyone can do—/ What can I do for you?"

At the last show we saw, Dylan blew my mind by inserting five extra syllables into that penultimate line ("there's no more anyone, or anybody, can do"). Not only did he make it fit perfectly—there's an element of jazz singing about his vocals; every syllable, every phrase, is new and unpredictable and full of the moment in which it is sung—but the addition of those words showed that he is *saying* the words of the song even as he sings them, feeling and speaking from his gut exactly as if the thought had just entered his mind. I've seen him do this with other songs—"Masters of War" in 1978— and it always has blown me away. Right in here somewhere is the quality—conviction? isn't there a bigger word?—that makes him the best performer I've ever seen, in any medium.

What can we learn from this song? That Dylan is in love. When he fell in love with Sara, he was older and more mature than he had been at the time of earlier love affairs, and so the love he felt was deeper and richer and more fulfilling than anything he had felt before. For the same reason, this new love cuts deeper still.

I can't say he'll be any more faithful to the Lord than he was to Sara (though he certainly means to try). But the evidence is already in that this is one heck of a passionate relationship.

And of course there is a difference between sexual love and love for God. This kind of devotion directed at a human being doesn't work. It just makes for impossible misunderstandings. Perhaps that's why some of the most passionate people in history (St.

Francis, for one) have ended up giving themselves over entirely to the love of God.

But Dylan hasn't gone monastic yet, at least as far as we know. The evidence for this (and it is ambiguous) is in another heartbreakingly beautiful new song, "Covenant Woman." Dylan manages, in a very few words, to make us feel at a deep level his love for this woman and, simultaneously, the role the Lord plays in their relationship. It seems clear (and consistent with Dylan's beliefs) that his allegiance to the Lord takes precedence over his commitment to the woman—and that the same is true for her. And, presumably, as long as both stay true to the Lord they will stay happy together in this world with each other.

"Covenant woman/Got a contract with the Lord/Way up yonder/ Great will be her reward." The words are deceptively simple; in conjunction with the music they ring like a bell. There is a feeling of holiness about this song; Dylan makes piety sound like an attractive virtue indeed. "Covenant woman/Shining like a morning star/I know I can trust you/To stay the way you are." At first I thought he wanted her to stay childlike and pure, as perhaps Sara didn't ("You're a Big Girl Now"); but then I realized he's probably saying he can trust her to stay faithful to the Lord. In his present state of mind, this is the only condition on which their earthly love depends (*he* has to stay faithful to Him too, of course; he makes reference to this later on).

So in the chorus (which had different arrangements on different nights; I liked the smooth flowing one much better than the exaggerated, staccato version) he states his intention to "stay closer than a friend"; and goes on to thank her again for "making your prayers known unto Heaven for me." Clearly this is the same woman addressed in "Precious Angel," who showed him he was blinded and brought him to the light.

He goes on to tell us he's a shattered, empty cup, waiting for the Lord to rebuild and fill him. "And I know that he will do it/'Cause he's faithful and he's true./He must have loved me oh so much/To send me someone as fine as you." This last line always brings gasps from the audience—he does know how to turn a girl's head, doesn't he? And see how his love for God and his love for this woman are inextricably mixed—a situation implied in the very title of the song. The first thing he sees when he looks at this woman is her relationship with God.

119

"Covenant woman/Intimate little girl/Who sees the invisible things of Him/That are hidden from the world." Again, he makes her piety a radiant beauty. "And you know that we are strangers/In a land we're passing through/I'll always be right by your side/I've got a covenant too." If he'll always be by her side, surely they are married—or could this just be another reference to the friendship that is greater than a friendship? Again, whatever it is it's a beautiful thing to say.

My dentist, a born-again Christian who discussed his faith with me at my invitation, told me he recently discovered the special meaning of the word "fellowship." "I used to think it just meant Christian friendship," he said. "Then I found out it means a relationship between two or more people in which Christ is also a participant." So instead of discussing the baseball game, you may share your most intimate hopes and fears, as you would if you were alone with Him, in an atmosphere of mutual trust.

This, perhaps, is what is meant by staying "closer than any friend." I must say that, just as institutionalized intolerance is the worst thing, this idea of fellowship—that one has a personal and intimate relationship with God, and that it is something that can at special moments be shared with another person—is the best thing I know about "born-again" Christianity, and I'm very impressed. I have known such moments of closeness with others, rooted in some sort of mutual commitment to and respect for "the force which through the green fuse drives the flower," and I can forgive a lot in a religion that encourages people toward this kind of sharing.

And are they also lovers? Well, they don't necessarily have to be. I think that's important to understand.

Terry Young's piano contributes almost as much to this song's beauty in live performance as Spooner Oldham's organ playing. They should both take a bow.

"The Saving Grace That's Over Me" starts out sweet and personal: "If you find it in your heart can I be forgiven?/Guess I owe you some kind of apology." ("Guess" and "some kind of" are typically Dylan: even when he's being humble he has to equivocate. It's part arrogance and part bashfulness—the man's a born mumbler.) The song has an easy, melodic roll to it; it's relaxing. It's the song of a troubled man who has found grace. The lyrics portray the world as a sinful place, easy to get lost in ("the devil's shining light, it can be so blinding"); when we hear Dylan's shimmering guitar solos we know he really has found some kind of peace in the midst of madness.

There are lines in "Saving Grace" that could sound preachy, but they don't because they come across as personal testimony rather than any kind of finger-pointing. Like "What Can I Do for You?", the dominant emotion in the song is gratitude, the deepest kind of gratitude that contains no resentment at all (this can only be achieved by actually letting go of the self). "Wherever I am welcome," he says, "is where I'll be." Or consider these lines, which on paper sound almost depressed, but which are buoyed by the melody and his singing in a subtle crescendo of emotion that leaves us feeling we've seen the unfailing lantern of hope shining through the darkness: "The wicked know no peace, and you just can't fake it/There's only one road, and it leads to Calvary/It's discouraging at times, but I know I'll make it/By the saving grace that's over me." This is followed by his grace-filled guitar solo (the voice that sings without words). These days I wake up in the morning with this song in my head.

The fourth of the new songs that demonstrate to me that Christ's Dylan is as bold a creative force as any Dylan we've known is "Hanging on to a Solid Rock," which (for a change of pace) just happens to have one of the finer bass-line hooks in the history of rock 'n' roll. (Comparable to "Daytripper," but it rocks harder.) Rock 'n' roll has roots in gospel music—in many ways that's where it all started—and this song helps bring things full circle. Who would have thought a white man could sing the Faith with this much spirit? Hallelujah!

Listening to "Hanging On" is a joyous experience; every moment of the performance pulses with excitement, pulling the audience in like nothing I know of except the last half hour of a Springsteen concert. The musical suspension of time after Dylan sings "I'm hanging on—" is awesome. And the intensity of the musical experience plays into the lyric content perfectly—there can be no doubt in the listener's mind about the solidity of that rock, no question as to where all this energy is coming from. When he shouts "I won't let go and I can't let go!" he's speaking for any one of us who ever believed in anything, and we just have to scream, "Right on!"

With the further result that I have nothing but admiration for lyrics that run contrary, at least by implication, to what I really feel. It's a strange feeling—I don't agree with him, but I have to acknowledge the gut-level power of his language. "It's the ways of the flesh/The war against the spirit/24 hours a day/You can feel it, you can hear it." He's talking about the ways of the flesh as the devil's temptation, and that's not a perspective I can easily relate to. But I know good songwriting when I hear it. Fabulous words. Likewise, "The nations are angry/cursed are some/and everybody's hoping for/A false peace to come./But I'm hanging on . . ." He's definitely turned the power of rock 'n' roll to his advantage here, and all I can do is let go to this joyous feeling and know that I'm hanging on too. The contradictions may iron themselves out somewhere along the line; meanwhile I'm not going to deny that I recognize and identify with this fervor.

The rest of the new songs introduced at the concerts are not quite on a level with the four I've just described, but they're all good, with the possible exception of the first encore, "Blessed Be the Name of the Lord Forever," which doesn't have much to recommend it. It got better the last night we went, mostly because the guitarist and organist asserted themselves more and thus brightened the arrangement. The chorus is repeated endlessly; it consists of the title and one other line, which I think is "Wisdom and might are His" but I can't be sure. The lyrics tell us things like, "He has His own time clock," ". . . and He will not be mocked," and "Like Him there is no other/He's God all by Himself alone." It's an uptempo number, designed for singing and clapping along with, but I'm afraid it leaves me unmoved.

"I've Been Saved," on the other hand, another rocker, while not on a par with "Hanging On," is a moving, effective production number, fun to watch and dance along with. Terry Young gets to really rock out on the piano on this one, and the last night we went I was also quite impressed by the guitar solos. Fred Tackett, lead guitar for these concerts, is technically excellent but seemed to be cowed by Dylan—his playing got more self-confident and louder as the nights passed, but it still lacked the bite that such passionate music deserves.

"I've Been Saved" starts with a fine "Jumping Jack Flash" opening: "I was blinded by the devil" (he sure uses the word "blinded" a lot) "Born already ruined/Stone cold dead as I stepped forth from the womb." Mostly he's telling us he's so glad (to have been saved) and he just wants to "thank you Lord." This "thank you" is a lot more casual than "Saving Grace" or "What Can I Do for You?", but it's a fun song, at least in concert. One rather revealing line: "no one tried to rescue me/Nobody dared." It fits in with my theory that Dylan needed Christ because only a full-blown religion with all the trimmings could offer the discipline necessary to keep him faithful, to restrain his mighty ego from running off on its own trip again. Other situations might also have offered awakening, but only Christ offered Dylan the chance to really surrender himself—which, since it was his ego (sense of his own power) that was torturing him, was the one thing he needed most. Says me.

"When They Came for Him in the Garden" is an exceptional song, probably worthy of inclusion with the four I singled out for special attention. It's particularly effective in performance; in many ways Dylan's show in San Francisco was a stage production, carefully planned and orchestrated (hence the unchanging program night after night), and "When They Came for Him" climaxes the show with a musical enactment of (what else?) scenes from the life of Christ (mostly based on the Gospel according to Saint John). The melody and arrangement are slow and deliberate, almost ponderous—it takes a few moments to realize that they are also extraordinarily beautiful. Dylan's singing on this song is spectacular; drum, organ, and back vocals blend in so perfectly (well, they did after the first few nights of fooling around with it) that the whole mood seems to have been painted with a single brush. (Bass and guitar are in there too, holding it all together.) It all reaches back to the mystery plays of the middle ages, the religious dramas that are the starting point of modern theater. "When they heard him speak in the city, did they hear?/When they heard him speak in the city, did they hear?/Nicodemus came at night so he wouldn't be seen by men/Saying, 'Master tell me why a man must be born again?'/When they heard him speak in the city, did they hear?" This is rare, beautiful music, unlike anything Dylan or anyone else has done (though there might be faint traces of the *John Wesley Harding* album in there). It suggests that even if Dylan chooses never to write another song that isn't about his Faith, the possibilities before us are rich and unpredictable. The man is a well of creativity; as long as he has something to say, he will always find new ways to say it and sing it. For all the battles about his subject matter, he has always been true to song and performance—and I would say he continues today at the top of his form.

This is affirmed by Dylan in the words of his second encore, "Pressing On," a modest but genuine spiritual featuring some wonderful piano playing by Dylan and a catchy refrain to make you feel good inside. Here Dylan is singing self-consciously to his audience again, only for a switch he's being friendly, still talking about people who want to stop him from what he's doing but this time assuming that we're not those people—we're his brothers and sisters who understand. "Many try to stop me/Try to shake me up in my mind/They say, 'Prove to me that He is Lord;/Show me a sign.'/But what kind of sign they need/When it all comes from within/When what's lost has been found/And what's to come has already been?/So, I'm just pressing on/Pressing on/Pressing on to the higher calling of my Lord."

The true artist never stops, never rests on his laurels. He creates only in darkness, and by the time he's turned the darkness to light he's already gone, he's already out there past the edge, working on his next assignment.

* * *

DYLAN: Renaldo's needs are few.
PLAYBOY: What are his needs?
DYLAN: A good guitar and a dark street.
PLAYBOY: The guitar because he loves music, but why the dark street?
DYLAN: Mostly because he needs to hide.
PLAYBOY: From whom?
DYLAN: From the demon within. [*pause*] But what we all know is that you can't hide on a dark street from the demon within. And there's our movie.
PLAYBOY: Renaldo finds that out in the film?
DYLAN: He tries to escape from the demon within, but he discovers that the demon is, in fact, a mirrored reflection of Renaldo himself.

—*Playboy* interview, 1978

Bob Dylan the protest singer. Dylan the mystery poet of a wild generation. Dylan the rock 'n' roll superstar. And now Dylan the musician of Christ.

Actually I think there are two Bob Dylans, the inner man and the outer man, and each of them has a relationship with Christ. The inner man has a deep personal relationship with God, new-found or just rediscovered, and his whole life is focused in on the daily struggle to submit to and serve the will of the Lord. This relationship is sincere and profound, and because he has entered into it the man has a whole lot more to say to us than he probably would have had at this time in his life otherwise. His music is the better for it—not to mention the fact that, in his eyes at least, the alternative was madness and death. So I think those of us who care about Bob Dylan can be grateful for this development, and respect the changes the inner man has gone through.

The outer man, on the other hand, is a chameleon; he sees that the inner man has turned to Christ and so he takes on the intellectual and moral and political attitudes of the "born-again" Christian community, tries them on for size. This man is nothing but the outer shell of Bob Dylan, he's certainly not very important, but he can cause a lot of confusion and therefore I think we should identify him for what he is.

One night, for example, he commented before his second encore, "This concert is brought to you under the authorization of Jesus Christ." Now, that's vanity—and the motivation for it is twofold: to tweak the noses of the nonbelievers, and to show the other evangelical Christians in the audience that he's one of the gang. But he's not one of the gang. Just because people salute the same flag doesn't mean they have a common cause. Dylan knows that, he knows it's not that easy; and he also knows that bragging that your concert is authorized is inviting lightning bolts to strike you dumb. I don't mean to be supercritical—what I am saying is that there's a difference between what God demands of us and what any group of people anywhere may think He demands of us.

As I write this America is in the midst of a "crisis" with Iran, involving Americans held hostage and mounting threats on both sides. The mood of America is frighteningly nationalistic; few people acknowledge the fact that 25 years ago the American CIA caused the overthrow of Iran's rightful ruler and set up a particularly vicious tyrant in his place, and then supported that tyrant to an unprecedented degree throughout the decades to come, while he tortured and oppressed his people. How would we feel if anything remotely similar had been done to us? The question is never asked. Racial hatred is being stirred up by the newspapers, miscalculation and war are real and awful possibilities. And yet the situation could still be defused by a show of humility on our part . . . and has only happened in the first place because of incredible arrogance, the arrogance of letting the Shah come to the United States at this point in the story.

Dylan made reference to this in his introduction to "Slow Train" one night; and predictably, he reflected insular, anti-Iranian American attitudes. He wasn't particularly obnoxious about it, and he did it mostly to lead into an apocalyptic rap ("see how bad everything's getting; the last days are at hand"), but still he added his voice to all the others stupidly contributing to a bad and dangerous situation. He's as smart as I am, or smarter; he could think this thing through. Instead he parrots the nationalism and racism of the news media and the self-absorbed, power-hungry leaders of the Christian (and non-Christian) community in this country.

"We know there's a slow train coming," says Dylan, "but it's picking up speed. We know this world will be destroyed and Christ will set his kingdom up for a thousand years. We *know* this is true." And he goes into the song. I can still hear his rap in my head, I love the sound of his voice. And I know he's talking about what is foretold in the Bible, and that he's committed to believing it all. And I'm still going to say that I consider apocalypse-mongering a cheap shot, and that focusing on it is a reflection of the outer Dylan, the one concerned with his image and getting back at people, and not a reflection of the inner Dylan who is committed to serve the living God.

It's not a question, really, of whether you believe in the apocalypse. It's a question of whether you use the apocalypse to avoid your commitment to the Golden Rule. Whether you use your allegiance to "Christ" as an excuse for thoroughly unChristian behavior. ("But there's one thing I know/Though I'm younger than you/Even Jesus would never forgive what you do."—"Masters of War," 1963)

The emotion of apocalypse is valid, the sense of it all coming

126

down around us is certainly something to be communicated in a song. It may provoke fear, it may provoke joyous nihilism, it may start one searching for a solid rock to hang on to. It's certainly a reflection of a real feeling people have about the world. It's also, I may say, a metaphor for something greater than the imminent destruction of this (perceived) world. It's a vision of one continuing aspect of existence—the world is always coming to an end, it's not the stable place we pretend it to be.

But obsession with apocalypse becomes avoidance of the real work to be done. "Jesus said, 'Be ready, for you know not the hour at which I come.' " That's correct. But what does it mean to "be ready"? It means to live your everyday life and do your work and interact with other people in the context of a constant awareness of one's responsibility towards what is right. Don't be distracted by the apocalypse. One's responsibility in the End Times is the same as at any other time: deal with what's in front of you and try to do what's right.

Why all this preaching from me, suddenly? I guess it's because I think every person is different, and I don't feel comfortable with people who all go around saying the same things. I'm tremendously moved by Bob Dylan's new songs in which he speaks his inner heart and lets us share the experience of his private relationship with God. But there have been some lines in some of the recent songs, and a few comments during his concerts, that indicate that while his inner relationship with God is totally sincere, he's also using the American Christian community as a new dark street to hide on. Under the flag of orthodoxy he may fantasize that all born-again believers will agree with what he says and all nonbelievers will be angered by it and it's all predetermined—us and them—he doesn't have to think about it. But he does have to think about it. He has to think about it twice as carefully as he ever did, because in presuming to serve Jesus he's taken on a greater responsibility.

One thing that is striking about Bob Dylan's conversion is the way that it has brought up the subject of religion, born-again Christianity, the place of God in our lives. Dylan has a power—not merely the superficial power that comes from being a symbol of an era, but a power inherent in the living strength of his art. When Picasso paints "Guernica" we *see* war and the suffering it brings, we see what we thought we already knew and felt but this painting has the power to bring response from us at a deeper level, it cuts through our daily defenses against painful reality and effects a profound awakening. And it moves people collectively as well as individually; ultimately it affects the public consciousness, what people share and talk about. It may not entirely offset the hypnotic drivel of the daily newspapers, but it serves as a vital balancing force, a voice from the heart to cut through the mindlessness of daily chatter.

So also when Dylan plays the harmonica in "What Can I Do for You?" and sings, "Whatever pleases you, tell it to my heart," we are forced at least to realize that the "Is God dead?" controversy is a sick joke a million miles away from our present awareness. I don't personally think of God as a man, or a person, or any kind of physical entity; but I don't object to thinking of Him that way . . . in fact I can see why it's almost necessary. If one needs to anthropomorphize in order to have a personal relationship with the Deity—and most Westerners do—then by all means think of Him as a man, because that personal, moment-to-moment relationship is crucial, without it we have no moral awareness, no hope of direction in our lives. The idea that there is no Purpose and that this whole living universe around us is the result of random factors is as hopelessly passé in the 1980s as the idea that social problems can be solved through legislation and Big Government.

So I am left with this: the important thing to me about Bob Dylan is his art—his records, his songs, his performances. And certainly in terms of what we've seen so far, the impact of Dylan's conversion on his art has been favorable indeed. He seems to have started in on a whole new era of major work, a new outpouring of brilliant songs and great performances.

I am pleased that this event, Dylan's announcement for Christ, is stimulating people to think about and discuss the religious, moral, spiritual side of our lives; and I like to think that this helps open a channel of communication between born-again Christians and the rest of Dylan's past or present audience.

And I can identify with Dylan's experience of entering into a private relationship with God, giving himself over entirely to obeying the will of the Lord. I can relate to his love for Jesus; it speaks to some equivalent emotion in my own heart—less focused, harder to put into words, but just as real.

But I can also relate to the feelings of my many friends who say, "Bob Dylan? Evangelical Christianity? How can *he* have *those* beliefs?" Dylan has said a great deal to us (and for us) over the years about politics and sexual love and the importance of being true to one's own vision. Does he now believe it's a sin to let another person see you naked? Does he believe the United States of America has God on its side? Does he feel comfortable with the idea that most of his fellow humans are eternally damned while he and a few others are saved because they found the one true Faith? By refusing to sing his old songs, is he repudiating everything he once stood for?

These questions do not necessarily go to the heart of the inner man and what he has to offer us in his new role of musician for Christ. But they are important questions to those of us who have cared about Bob Dylan over the years and who have perhaps imagined that we saw our own feelings and experiences reflected in his words and his music and in the roles he has publicly assumed. Dylan has revealed himself to us, through his work, as a man of unusual intelligence and insight, a person capable of great sensitivity and deep compassion, a person willing to make his own decisions as to what is right and what is wrong, and courageous enough to express his views forthrightly in the face of widespread opposition and misunderstanding. More specifically, he spoke out against the moral misdeeds of American government and American society in the early years of the 1960s and helped give voice to a movement for change that many of us identified with and participated in at the time. Now he has or seems to have joined up with the forces of sexual repression, mindless nationalism, and religious intolerance.

It is hard to be lukewarm about a hero figure. One wants to be able either to support him wholeheartedly and defend his actions against all doubters, or if necessary one wants to be able to call him a scoundrel and a traitor for turning against the cause. When heroes change, and that change is ambiguous, it troubles the soul. What we should learn from this of course is that believing in heroes is a risky business at best—don't follow leaders—change your role models regularly like you change your clothes, don't wait for them to start to stink. (It is of course a terrible burden on the living hero figure that other people invest their dreams in him or her. One has to make life decisions for oneself and one's conscience alone; it

129

doesn't help to be carrying the half-formed dreams of millions on your back. Hero-worshippers inevitably expect their hero to be their slave.)

But still, we do believe in heroes, not as many as we used to, but Bob Dylan was one of the few. And he's still a hero to me, because his latest changes reflect the same kind of deep-soul courage and integrity and commitment to personal and artistic growth that I've admired him for from the beginning. So what do I do if he tells me I'm condemning my children to eternal damnation by not baptizing them in Christ?

I turn the other cheek. I shrug it off. And besides, he hasn't said that. Of course I'm interested to know how he feels about sex and nationalism and religious freedom, since he is expressing views that are identical to Bible-belt evangelism in other areas, but he hasn't expressed himself (except in a few places I've already discussed in this essay, none of them conclusive evidence of how he feels or what he's trying to sell apart from the primacy of Christ) and it's probably too early in his relationship with both Christ and Christians to know how this all will develop.

At best, I may hope that Dylan's conscience, combined with the sincerity of his beliefs and his considerable talents as a communicator, will be a force for the good within the Christian community, influencing some of his conservative brethren towards a more enlightened attitude in regard to women's rights, homosexuality, other cultures, nations, races and religions, and so forth. Failing this, if he is not moved to an activist role in these areas, I would hope he would at least keep his mouth shut on social matters and continue to sing and write about the trials of the human heart. What I would do in the worst case—if he starts appearing on the podium with Anita Bryant or urging us to a holy war against the infidels—I really don't know. It's horrible to contemplate. But for now, at least, I intend to give him the benefit of the doubt; nor will I let myself be too bothered by anything he may say while he's still in the first blush of a love affair presumably more intense and intoxicating than anything he's been through before.

Another possibility, of course, is that Dylan will change again, will wander from the arms of Christ and go on to the next thing. I don't really expect this change to happen—I think he's made a lifetime commitment—but the man has a lot of courage, and if he felt he had to do it, or if he couldn't find Christ in his heart any more, I guess he'd move on. In which case he'd probably find himself having to deal with angry fans more crazed and more dangerous than any he's confronted before. Embracing Christ is a controversial move for Dylan to have made; rejecting Him could be catastrophic.

And no doubt Dylan realized this before he made his commitment; he's nothing if not paranoid; we may assume he knew he was walking through a one-way door, and that he considered his decision very carefully indeed.

And then he went ahead and did it anyway.

* * *

"I try my best to be like I am · But everybody wants you to be like them."
—Bob Dylan, 1965

November 23, 1979: I'm finishing up this essay tonight. I've been writing about Dylan for two weeks, and before that I spent a week going to his concerts. We talk about him, we listen to his music, and all our friends want to talk about him too. So much attention directed at this one man! Maybe he turned to Christ so he'd have somewhere to refer all this energy that gets thrown at him. If you don't want to be the messiah, and people keep treating you like one anyway, it makes sense to hook up with somebody who's willing to accept that karma. "No, I ain't the messiah, but let me introduce you to my Friend . . ."

The concerts were wonderful. Dylan doesn't always give you what you want, but he does give, he gives and gives like there's no tomorrow, and where he gets it all from I can't imagine. I've seen him in concert in 1963, 1966, 1968, 1974, 1975, 1978, and now 1979. He was different every time, and yet in a lot of ways he never changes. And he still hasn't changed. You listen to his newest songs, you hear him play harmonica, you see him standing there and you think, he sounds more like Bob Dylan than he ever did. Whatever he's doing, he's not running away from himself. He's getting closer every day.

He's still the same person. He has the same strengths and weaknesses. He may have some new ways of handling those strengths

131

and weaknesses, new truths, new insights, new methods of keeping himself in balance. New friends, new lovers, new shelter. But the same personality, same DNA, same voice, same heart and soul.

There's a lot of things I haven't mentioned, always a lot more to say about Dylan. One of my favorite albums of his is *Hard Rain*—a live album from 1976—all about sex and timelessness and living in the moment, rich in musical ideas that might be 50 years ahead of their time. But if I tried to tell you what I've learned about Dylan from listening to that album we'd be here for months. The subtleties of Dylan's live performances—timing, arrangements, voice, attitude—are the heart of his achievement as an artist; his studio recordings don't tell even half of his story. Someday I'll write an essay about Bob Dylan's music.

But tonight we just want to know what happened, and what's gonna happen. What happened I think is Dylan found a shelter from the storm, the kind of shelter that allows him, in fact requires him, to stay at the center of the storm, and he's very happy about it; he sounds more deeply committed to Jesus in his new songs than he did on *Slow Train Coming*.

What's gonna happen is anyone's guess. Dylan's committed to Christ, but Christ isn't Christianity, and Christianity itself is no monolith. Joan of Arc was burned at the stake for doing what Dylan and other born-again Christians consider the essence of their religious practice: talking to and listening to God. The born-again Christians can be credited with making Christianity a living religion again; and living things can grow, and change. Wait till Dylan starts reading Teilhard de Chardin! There are plenty of surprises still to come . . .

And it is inevitable that some people who might not have considered service to Christ a possible path for them will be influenced by Dylan's example. Dylan might even claim that's the purpose of the new concerts, but I would not take that too seriously. What was the purpose of last year's concerts, and the ones before those? An artist doesn't work for money, or for God, or for the audience, or for personal satisfaction—he works for all of those reasons at once, and for none of them. He sings because he has a voice. He performs because that's the work to be done. Christ loved Judas not because He was infinitely forgiving but because Judas was the one who would help Him do the work He had to do. We are created as instruments, and we do the work we were made to do because we are driven to it by the very shape of our existence. Our choices are few: we can hang back, or we can throw ourselves into our roles.

Dylan does his work extremely well, and I love him for it. He has already given far more than his share, and he shows no sign of slowing down. I must argue with him about the importance of pronouncing the Lord's name a particular way, but that's all right. I admire his courage. I wish him Godspeed.

Paul Williams
Glen Ellen, California
November 1979

12. One Year Later

Dylan's November 1979 shows in San Francisco did turn out to be the beginning of a tour that continued through May 1980. After a five-month break, he returned to the Warfield to start another tour. This year I could only afford to go to six of the shows, but I had a great time. Dylan read What Happened? *at the beginning of 1980 (and had his secretary order 114 copies from me), and apparently because he liked the book he allowed Sachiko and I to spend several hours with him backstage after four of the 11/80 shows. He even read me the lyrics of a new song, "Every Grain of Sand," told me about another song he was proud of ("Caribbean Wind") and performed it at one of the shows at my request.*

I wrote "One Year Later" as a way of answering the huge stack of letters I got from people who'd read my book. I mailed a copy to everyone who wrote to me. I don't talk about my backstage experiences in the piece, but Howard Alk told me Dylan called him up after he read it, and said, "It happens every time—when I meet someone who's written something about me that I like, meeting me spoils them and the next thing they write doesn't work." Or words to that effect. And I agree . . . I think the problem with this piece is that after hanging out with the singer and having him be so friendly, I was too aware of his presence as a likely reader, unconsciously violating my usual approach, which is only to write to and for other listeners like myself.

> "Am I ready to lay down my life for the brethren
> And to take up the cross?
> Have I surrendered to the will of God
> Or am I still acting like the boss?
> Am I ready? I hope I'm ready . . ."
>
> —Bob Dylan, 1980

Bob Dylan's twelve shows at the Warfield Theatre in San Francisco in November 1980 began exactly like his shows here a year ago: three black women do a short solo set starting with "If I've Got My Ticket, Lord, Can I Ride?" Dylan and band come on stage and do "Gotta Serve Somebody," followed by "I Believe in You." And then: "Once upon a time you dressed so fine, threw the bums a dime in your prime, DIDN'T YOU??" God's in His heaven and Bob

134

Dylan's back down on earth singing "Like a Rolling Stone" and—
ask anybody in this audience—all's right with the world.

Dylan's first tour after his conversion (which seems to have taken
place, in the sense of the moment of being born again, towards the
very end of his exhaustive 1978 tour) started in San Francisco in
November 1979 and continued around the U.S. (and Canada a
little) thru May 1980. The album *Saved*, featuring the material he'd
introduced in his San Francisco concerts, was recorded during a
brief stop (five days) in Muscle Shoals, Alabama, in Feb. 1980. More
touring was planned for the summer, but Dylan called it off, reportedly because of the heat wave then roasting the U.S. (concerts were
scheduled for Texas and Oklahoma, I think). *Saved* was released in late
June, just after the end of that series of concerts . . . it almost seemed as
though the release of the album marked the end of that series of
shows, a completion, the word was out. On to the next thing.

So the stage was set, after five months of silence, for what seemed
to be the start of a new tour, and a strange kind of *déjà vu*:
November again, Bob Dylan concerts at the Warfield Theatre
again. Here we go back to Market Street. Can we afford to go to
more than one or two shows this time? What's he gonna do?

There were ads on the radio promising "a retrospective, old songs
and new songs," with what sounded like new rehearsals of bits of
"Tambourine Man" and "Blowin' in the Wind" playing in the background. A lot of people seemed to be hoping that he was off his
"Christian kick," the implication being that the whole idea of Dylan
becoming a committed Christian made them nervous, and they were
looking forward to release and vindication. I still get the impression a
lot of people would like Dylan to plead temporary insanity on this one.

But that's the street, people talking, Dylan the public figure; as
we shall see, the situation inside the concert hall was different.

There was one bad show, the first one. After that, things went
very well. Dylan is a great performer; and his San Francisco stand
turned into one more glorious reaffirmation of that fact. It was a
great success—every audience except the first-nighters went home
very happy indeed. The newspapers wrote up the first night, and
they have their own axes to grind anyway, so word did not get out
through those media and some of the shows didn't sell out. People
are very confused about who Dylan is right now—many seemed to
hope for some reassurance before deciding to spend $15 to see

him. Dylan for his part seems committed to a course of putting his entire self before the public so they can see he is who he's always been, the artist Bob Dylan, and he put on a show that got that message across real well. Surprisingly well. The subject of the concerts was not the rejection of anything, but the rediscovery of self, all parts present at once—continuation of a thread begun in the Rolling Thunder shows, but much more fully-developed, and with a powerful underlying kick: I really am the same Bob Dylan I've always been, all those Dylans are the same person, *including* the one who has found Christ. OK?

And the audience answered back by receiving the religious songs as warmly as all the others—"if you don't underestimate us, we'll do the same for you"—they loved him, all of him, at least while he was singing it. Reconciliation.

But. But it's not so simple a story as it sounds. Not in my weird mind, anyway. Because Dylan is on the move. These concerts, quite unexpectedly after that disastrous first night, turned into real crowd-pleasers. But there is no possible way that these concerts can be anything but a transition, a door into something very different and, uh, quite unpredictable. I'm not sure Dylan knows it yet, but he's got a real tiger by the tail this time.

If any artist can ride this tiger without being eaten alive by it, Dylan's the one. But the theory of countervailing power tells us the bigger the heart, the bigger the challenge it has to meet. And though it all looks easy right now, there's lots of little clues that make me think this reconciliation tour could end up being the greatest challenge of Dylan's career. I hope he's ready.

* * *

"Oh, when your, when your days are numbered
And your nights are long,
You might think you're weak
But I mean to say you're strong.
Yes you are, if that sign on the cross,
If it begins to worry you.
Well, that's all right because sing a song
And all your troubles will pass right on through."
—Bob Dylan, "Sign on the Cross," 1967

Sachiko and I ended up going to six of Dylan's twelve San Francisco concerts, this time around. (For the record, #s 1, 2, 4, 6, 10, & 12.) Last year Dylan was largely silent between songs, occasionally launching into brief monologues about how "These are the end days, and you're gonna need something strong to hang onto." Once, in Tempe, Arizona, he actually preached, haranguing the audience at great length and with much energy. This year Dylan, although he loosened up and got downright talkative (for him) some nights, never once in the six nights we saw said anything from the stage that could be remotely interpreted as being about religion.

Nor was there any indication that Dylan's choices as to which "old songs" to perform were related to his religious concerns. He didn't go for the obviously spiritual stuff, nor did he avoid subject matter that might offend evangelical sensibilities. What he did do was steadfastly open each show with "Serve Somebody" and "I Believe in You," and close each night with "In the Garden." That's a statement, and a strong one. But—even in later nights, when he obviously knew he'd won the audience's confidence—he didn't seem to feel any need, or wish, to add to that statement. He did sing other "religious" songs from his two recent albums—and some (but not all) of his newer songs have religious over- or undertones. But he didn't wear his Faith on his sleeve, this time. He wants us to know he still believes; more than that, he's not saying.

Which is fine, of course. I think I may be somewhat rare among Dylan's fans in that it's okay with me if he talks about Jesus and it's okay with me if he doesn't. Nor is it my intention to get real personal here. But let's face it. Dylan's best songs are unavoidably personal, and more so the more familiar you are with his work and the context his work has created. The extraordinary and shocking and deeply moving statement made by last year's Dylan shows can't help but set the stage, one way or another, for how we feel about what he does this time.

All the contexts that are Dylan's history create the confusion that swirls around him. In that sense his story has remarkable parallels to Picasso's. Mel Lyman once said, "You create a myth, and it turns to stone." Dylan and Picasso almost alone among artists in this century have had the power to move from one self-created myth to another without being totally crippled by public or personal hysteria at the transition. This I suppose is the test of greatness. And it's hardly something that can be consciously planned or manipulated, except in the sense of steadfast courage & clarity & humility as one begins to understand how the process works. One lives one's life and does one's work, stubbornly and good-heartedly and because there's nothing else to do. Keep your hands on that plow; hold on.

Paul and Silas know what I'm talking about.

* * *

"For so long I've been stalled
But I'm saved—"
—Bob Dylan, 1979

"Mostly, I couldn't stay in one place long enough."
—quoted in liner notes, first album, 1962

Saved is a brilliantly-conceived album. The opening and closing songs are perfect. The material in between includes some of the best songs Dylan has ever written. And damn it, the album is a failure.

What happened?

I've been trying to come to terms with my disappointment in this album ever since it was released last June. I kept hoping it would grow on me. I've changed my mind about things often enough— particularly in terms of disliking a record at first, then later coming to appreciate it, maybe even fall in love with it. There's never been any question in my mind that Dylan's performances on this album, particularly of the songs I loved most, can't compare with the best of his San Francisco performances of the same songs a few months earlier. But, I've kept asking myself, suppose I were hearing these songs for the first time? Wouldn't I be enthusiastic about the record if I could hear it with clean ears?

And anyway it's not fair to measure studio performances against songs you saw live (of course "Isis" was better in concert, but it's fine on its album too). So lately I've been listening to *Saved* a lot, just letting it soak in, speak to me in its own language. And I don't have any doubt any more. The album doesn't make it. What should (and could) be heartbreaking is actually boring.

I'm lucky. I heard the songs when they were new and fresh and utterly overpowering. Dylan says something in a new interview (I don't have a copy yet; a friend read me the quote over the phone) about how you can go on stage and perform a song with power but for it really to be great it has to have power and sensitivity, and for that you have to be able to put yourself back into what it felt like when you wrote the song. That's what didn't happen with most of the songs on *Saved*. And it makes me feel sorry, because these songs would mean so much to people—would move them, not necess- arily towards Christ but towards some kind of true awakening—if they could hear them as Dylan sang them when he and the band were fresh and these fragile truths (fragile because it's hard for us to let ourselves hear them) were still naked.

Most of Dylan's studio albums have been recordings of new material, seldom or never performed on stage, and in the majority of cases the musicians who are playing have just been introduced to the song on the spot or in the last few days. Dylan usually records live (as opposed to doing the vocals separate from instrumental tracks), and usually does only a few takes of each song. He's made it clear over the years that this is the technique that works for him, that if he tries to make slicker records he loses interest and the songs lose their punch and it just doesn't happen. So his habit is just to go into the studio and get whatever he has down on tape.

This system has worked extraordinarily well for him, on the whole. There's been a lot of second-guessing by critics and others over the years, of course, but the final evidence is in all the excep- tional work Dylan has managed to produce making studio record- ings his way. It's doubtful that the great records could actually have been any greater; and since the lesser records usually seem the result of lesser material it seems unlikely that some different man- ner of recording would have improved them much.

There is however the fascinating case of the great album (one of Dylan's top five, for sure) that almost wasn't: *Blood on the Tracks*. The first time I heard this album was at the office of Columbia Records several months before release, and it contained different versions of five of the songs: "Tangled Up in Blue," "Idiot Wind," "Lily, Rosemary & the Jack of Hearts," "If You See Her, Say Hello," and "You're a Big Girl Now." (Those versions are now circulating on tapes and bootleg records.) Apparently the album was ready to

139

go, maybe even being pressed, and—as I heard the story—Dylan listened to his copy while visiting Minneapolis near Christmastime ('74) and decided to try again. He went into a studio there with some musicians his brother turned him onto, and the result is the album we know, with its present versions of those five songs. Those recordings are among Dylan's finest; the earlier versions are not just inferior in most cases but actually bad. They're interesting now, of course, but extremely shallow compared with what they became, and certainly in the case of "Lily" few people would have wanted to listen to side two very many times if they'd had to wade through that tedious and interminable arrangement and performance each time. The point is that those new recordings were made on the spur of the moment, less than a month before the album's actual release. And if they hadn't been made and included, *Blood on the Tracks* would have been really a pale shadow of what it turned out to be. I don't think it would have been well received. And I don't think you can say in any sense that the fact that Dylan did rerecord those tracks shows that he really was in control of the situation. He deserves credit for doing the right thing, but it should also be noted that there was an element of luck involved here. He was lucky, and so were we. Whatever happened when Dylan found God, I don't think it's the first time a "saving grace" has been over him and his work. I also should say that I think "being lucky"—whatever that means—is an important factor in the creation of any great work. (Hardly the only factor, of course.)

In the case of *Saved*, Dylan followed his usual practice in the sense of dropping by the studio, laying down some tracks with his band, redoing a few songs, and wrapping the whole thing up in five days. He definitely didn't beat it to death doing repeated takes. But there was something quite atypical about this session, and that is the fact that Dylan and the band he recorded with had been performing these same songs virtually nonstop for more than three months. Dylan has never rehearsed that much before making a recording, and on the evidence of the album, it didn't work. The songs sound tired to me, unconvincing—the arrangements are uninspired—the band plays with obedience rather than fire (the drumming on a number of the cuts is particularly offensive). There are three exceptions, and two of them, interestingly, are songs Dylan and the band had not been performing on tour.

The exceptions prove the rule; one could plead that it was just a bad week, maybe everybody had a cold or Dylan was thinking about something else, except for the fact that the opening track, "Satisfied Mind," is one of the nicest vocals Dylan has ever put on record; the whole performance never fails to send chills down my back, it's magnificent. "Saved" is the next track, and it's just fine, well-performed, exciting, as good as it ever was in concert—it's a simple song, a rave-up, and it fits beautifully in its spot on the album, delivers its message and gets the adrenaline flowing and I like it a lot. Unfortunately, Dylan and the band proceed to butcher all the rest of the songs—"Covenant Woman" is just not what it could be, but "What Can I Do for You?" and "Solid Rock" are downright sad—except the last track, "Are You Ready?", a song they'd only done in concert a couple of times. "Are You Ready?" is a gorgeous performance—it's hot, it's convincing. The arrangement *is* inspired, the song knows it has something to say and it says it. The notion of opening with "Satisfied Mind," following it with "Saved," and closing by asking the listener "Are You Ready?" (keeping in mind the sounds of those tracks as well as the lyric content) is clever and pointed and appropriate and it works. And the other songs would have made a perfect main course if they hadn't been overcooked and undercared-for. Somebody took them for granted. Or else they tried to do 'em right and just couldn't find the handle.

What's particularly interesting to me is that in my opinion—which I admit is getting kind of high-faluting, but I guess I've got to call 'em like I hear 'em—there are various clues in the recorded versions of the *Saved* songs that suggest that Dylan doesn't always remember what the songs mean as he sings them. Of course he's always making his words mean new things, whatever he's feeling at the moment he's performing, and that to me is a large part of his greatness. But in this case I would say in some ways he trivializes these very deep and sensitive and powerful lyrics, which is kind of like turning against his own gift, or you could even say (in terms of the good he might have done by doing it right) playing into the hands of the Enemy.

Greatness is a responsibility, a tough one, and maybe I forgot to say it in my book but that must be an important source of the pain and need that brought Dylan to Christ in the first place.

141

Some examples: it bothers me that in "Covenant Woman," which is about a woman he loves because of her close relationship with the Lord, he originally sang, "Covenant woman/Intimate little girl/Who sees those invisible things of Him/That are hidden from the world," a lovely observation—but on the record it comes out "Who knows those most secret things of me," which changes the whole verse so that it's referring to her intimacy with Dylan rather than her intimacy with God. Bad art. You see what I mean by trivializing. On "What Can I Do for You?", which is either a song of total humility or else it's nothing, an indication of the problem with the whole vocal (the attitude of the vocal) can be found when Dylan sings, "I don't deserve it but I *sure did* make it through." This bit of boasting shifts the focus of the song; the original lyrics and performance here conveyed the subtly (but extremely) different message that "I didn't deserve to survive, but You chose to bring me through and so my life is Yours, please help me find a way to begin to show my devotion." Instead the new vocal almost suggests that Dylan made it because he was smart enough to buy a ticket on the right train. Ouch.

One more example: I have problems with all the arrangements (or really lack of arrangements) of these six songs on *Saved*, but the most subtle and interesting case is that of "Solid Rock." To my ears, there were a couple of nights in San Francisco in November 1979 when Dylan and Tim Drummond and the band really found the heart and soul of "Solid Rock." The audience thought so too— people who'd never heard the song before jumped to their feet to show their enthusiasm at the end of the song, several nights in a row, the only time that happened all evening. As near as I can figure it, Dylan and cohorts saw that the song was a crowd-pleaser and started playing it for excitement, and—with the best of intentions—thereby lost touch with what it was that made the song so exciting. What they did is they sped it up. In doing so they dropped a note from that perfect bass line, so it wasn't perfect any more, and Dylan allowed his approach to the vocal to change with the primary effect that the tension that ruled the song in such extraordinary fashion disappears and instead it becomes another rave-up, look we're playing "solid rock," ha ha.

I know they were just trying to make it better, and I don't mean to be critical about it. What I'm trying to do is throw some light onto those moments when greatness comes and then goes again. Dylan has talked about "learning to do consciously what I used to do unconsciously," mostly I think in the context of songwriting. I think *Saved* demonstrates that the days have passed when divine grace would see to it that he always could capture a song in its prime by randomly running into the studio; but that focusing some of his energies on being able to recognize the moment when it's there & see what form it takes would improve his chances of capturing the moment or (equally valid) recapturing it later. When Dylan's unconscious recording practices of the last twenty years become something he has some conscious creative control over, I think there's a real potential that he'll start turning out albums the likes of which we haven't dreamed of yet.

Getting back to "Solid Rock," and what I said earlier about sometimes forgetting what the songs really mean. The meaning of "Solid Rock" is not "I've got a solid rock to hang onto" or "there is a solid rock one can hang onto," although that's what it's come to mean in its later performances (including the performances this year, on the new tour). But the deeper original meaning has to do with being suspended, dangling as it were, that instant of awareness when one realizes that the only thing attaching us to the earth, to this world, is the will of God. All is illusion, except for this solid rock (of ages) from which I am suspended, on which I depend (*pendere*: to hang) (won't let go and I *can't* let go), the rock that was here long before any of this illusion was created and that will outlast it all. How do I get this out of Dylan's song on those early nights? From the sustained tension, the eerie *calmness* of the performance which they completely lost later, and specifically from the full pause after "I'm hanging on," during which pause (complete with bass line/organ) one could absolutely *feel* oneself and the whole theater hanging on, suspended from a thread, definitely some kind of thread that never could, never would, break. An astonishing musical moment. Here for a few nights, then gone again.

When you can write and perform stuff that fabulous, don't you have some sort of responsibility—to God, to your art, to yourself, to your audience, to *some*body—to make the best possible finished product out of this gift that, after all, isn't yours but is just something you were given to care for? If I were God, I know what Bob

143

Dylan could do for me. Exactly what he's doing, only (here's the turn of the screw) a little bit better all the time.

Eric Anderson once rerecorded an entire album and got his record company to rerelease it as "(same title), Take Two." *Saved* is the album that could have been. Maybe it still could be. (Just don't mess with tracks 1, 2 and 9, okay?)

One way or another, there's a lot of boasting on *Saved* about making it through and being ready to do the work of God and not being stalled any more. The trick is not to have God on your side but to be on God's side, right? It'll be interesting to see what the kid (turning 40 in May) does now.

*   *   *

"You have given all there is to give
What can I give to you?
You have given me life to live
How can I live for you?"
                                        —Bob Dylan, 1979

"I was doing fine. I had come a long way in just the year we were on the road. I was relatively content, but a very close friend of mine mentioned a couple of things to me and one of them was Jesus."
                                —Bob Dylan, 1980 (*L.A. Times* interview)

Who is Bob Dylan to me? He is an artist, and he happens to be the living artist whose work is most important to me; he is someone who has created and is creating a body of work and a thousand individual works that never lose interest for me, constantly and consistently his heart speaks to my ears and my heart and his truth penetrates and challenges and affirms my truth. His colors are colors I see. My reference point recently for understanding Dylan is Picasso: indefatigable, the artist.

Dylan the artist isn't always at work in his most recent concerts. Sometimes he's just coasting. That sits well with much of his audience—gives them a chance to catch up with him, which is something that's been needed—but it doesn't really satisfy me, and what's more important is I don't think it's likely to satisfy Dylan. Not for long. He's clearing up some old business right now—

hence the newspaper interview acknowledging his Christianity, for example—but that work is going smoothly (deceptively smoothly), and won't provide stimulation much longer. A considerable part of Dylan's greatness is that he can't be bought cheap. He's always hungry for something real.

Picasso in his paintings is transparent; all the generalities and specifics of what he feels are there for the eye to see. Dylan in his songs is the same way. When he says, "I would have done anything for that woman/If she just would have made me feel obligated," I know he's not talking about some incident that never happened or some woman who never existed. (The line is from a new song called "The Groom's Still Waiting at the Altar.") When he sings "Covenant Woman" without any conviction other than his desire to sing a song he knows is a good one, I know something's changed since a year ago. When, on the other hand, he sings "I Believe in You" with real joy and shapes it into an anthem powerful and appropriate enough to join to his signature anthem "Like a Rolling Stone," I know the man's got something to say and feels a real satisfaction in the saying, full conscious of all the nuance and reverberation created on many levels by his brushstroke. He always performs best when he's got something to communicate, something that by definition can't be said easily, something felt passionately and truly a part of the cutting edge of his moment.

What has he been doing in his shows? He's done a lot of preconversion songs: chestnuts like "Rolling Stone" and "Blowin' in the Wind" and "Just Like a Woman," and less obvious choices like "Girl from the North Country" (fine arrangement, gorgeous piano playing—as good as the singing, and that's saying something—Willie Smith on keyboards is definitely MVP of Dylan's current series), "Simple Twist of Fate" (another fine arrangement—keyboard & guitar—and excellent vocal; you can always tell when Dylan feels real affection for the song he's singing), and "Senor." Other "old songs" have surfaced once or twice: "To Ramona" (great), "All Along the Watchtower," "Hard Rain," "Just Like Tom Thumb's Blues" (I missed that one, damn it), a magnificent "Tambourine Man" on closing night with Roger McGuinn, "Knockin' on Heaven's Door," "Love Minus Zero" acoustic with harmonica as a final solo encore, "It Ain't Me Babe" and "It's All

145

Over Now, Baby Blue" in the same slot on other nights. He does other people's songs: Dion's "Abraham, Martin, and John" every night as a duet with Clydie King, Dave Mason's "We Just Disagree," a contemporary Christian item called "Rise Again," and in one of the true high points of these shows for me, a knock-em-dead rock rendition of Little Willie John's "Fever."

He does a few new songs: "I Ain't Gonna Go to Hell for Any-body," which first surfaced last spring; "Let's Keep It Between Us," great performance (bluesy singing at the piano *à la* "Ballad of a Thin Man"), another high point and strangely another of those songs that reached a peak of arrangement and performance mid-way through the shows and then started losing its edge, unraveling; "The Groom's Still Waiting at the Altar," one night featuring Mike Bloomfield unrehearsed and hotter than hot; "City of Gold," fine encore, a spiritual that sounds like it might have been around for hundreds of years. And one night he did a song he said he wrote a year or two ago called "Caribbean Wind," which sounded on first listen like it could join the ranks of Dylan all-time classics; he sang it with tremendous feeling and energy despite frustration at the band's inability to follow him. As far as I know he didn't attempt it on any subsequent nights.

And he does some of the songs he was doing last year, the songs from *Slow Train Coming* and *Saved*. The "religious" songs, the ones the public calls his gospel songs even though few of them fit that description. This show is, or started as, an evolution of that earlier show—in theory it's the same show with earlier songs added in for variety. (The band is the same as last year except for keyboards.) In fact, as I said, it's in motion, evolving into something else altogether, and largely I think because none of last year's songs are really clicking except "Serve Somebody," "I Believe in You," and "In the Garden." And it's not a question of the audience being unreceptive. It seems rather that Dylan can't get fired up about those songs right now, he seems mostly to be doing them because if he didn't do them you'd misunderstand.

The songs in question are "Solid Rock," "Slow Train," "Covenant Woman" (which he didn't play the last night), and several that I only heard once or twice during the shows: "Precious Angel" (he started working out a fresh and interesting arrangement of this one night, which I liked quite a bit, but then he didn't perform it again), "When You Gonna Wake Up?," "Saved," and "What Can I Do for You?" (He also does "Man Gave Names to All the Animals" every night—I like the arrangement—a song from his *Slow Train* period with less direct religious content than any of the others.)

"Solid Rock" is still overplayed, and has devolved into a good rocker that seems emptier of content with each performance. Dylan plays it as though he mostly just wants us to know that Christians got rhythm too. "Slow Train" is a subtler case—it sounds good, well played and rather well sung except to me he's just singing the words and remembering the right inflections. Something's missing. I don't know why—think it has to do with his ideas about his audience, or maybe there's some deeper uncertainty—but Dylan was sleepwalking through most of his Christian material (much more so than any of his other material) the six nights we saw him. The sensitivity (except on the three songs mentioned above) wasn't there.

I see I left one song out of my rapid-fire survey of what Dylan performed this time, and maybe that's good because it gives me a chance to say something about what was best about these recent shows, their frequent spontaneity and generosity of spirit, friendliness, a willingness to experiment and open up sides of himself he hasn't acknowledged or shared for quite a while. The song in question is an old ballad called "The Wind on the Moor," a folkie number Dylan introduces by saying here's a real "old song"—a song he used to do before he ever wrote any songs. He does it as a duet with Regina McCreary, and she plays autoharp while Dylan strums an acoustic guitar (Fred Tackett plays mandolin). It's a good number—good performance—it seems to represent some obstruction that's been overcome, and in a modest, appropriate way it definitely sends out the message that Bob Dylan is the same Bob Dylan who started singing songs for people more than twenty years ago, and that's still what he does and that's what it's about for him. The night he first did it—the same night he attempted "Caribbean Wind"—was just an incredibly giving evening, the idea of an audience really liking his show is something he hasn't necessarily gotten a surfeit of in the last year or more, and he seemed very pleased at all the positive response. (Opening night, by contrast, Dylan and the audience seemed very much at odds

147

with each other. Dylan turned it around the next evening, but there was a time there when he must have wondered if he was going to be able to go on with his tour. So naturally he was happy on the rebound.)

For most of the audience, I'm sure, the best symbol of Dylan's new openness and of his acknowledgment of his past came in the nightly encore that started with a spontaneous performance the second night—opening night he'd done "Blowin' in the Wind" as an encore and that was it. Second night the audience authentically wanted and put out the enthusiasm appropriate to a second encore, and Dylan finally came out and did "City of Gold" on acoustic guitar with his lady vocalists. The audience cheered a lot and he gestured his thanks and tried to end the evening gracefully, blushed, waved his guitar as if in salute, turned to leave and then shrugged and came back and did "Love Minus Zero" alone with his folk guitar and—the ultimate crowd-pleaser—his harmonica and its legendary holder. Sounded great. Hearts melted all over the theater.

After that he did the same three encores each night, sometimes varying the last acoustic song—one night it was "Baby Blue," a real thrill for most of us I'm sure, certainly for me, ending with a harmonica solo that must have seemed not quite enough to him because he kept going past the end and suddenly he was just playing completely from the heart, naked out there, a moment of showing how much he really cared. Whew.

The audience loved the shows. That's a fact. And Dylan got a definite jolt of energy and some kind of renewed confidence or even cockiness from it all. And now he's in Tucson, or I guess San Diego tonight, with more shows scheduled in other cities this weekend and probably on into the new year. Old songs, new songs, odds and ends, mixed together and served up hot, always in the framework of "Serve Somebody"/"Believe in You"/"Like a Rolling Stone" . . . "In the Garden." Sounds fine. So why don't I think he'll just go on happily working and developing this vein? Why this talk about grabbing a tiger by the tail?

The answer has to do with reconciliation. The kid's got some things to reconcile, and it's not all together yet. He can't be happy with doing lackluster performances of his "Jesus" songs just to keep them in the show. And the side of him that is committed to surrendering to the will of God must be a little uneasy at how readily Dylan the performer and star falls back into the routine of having his ego stroked. I *know* Dylan in his heart has a more radical vision of living for Jesus than just traveling around filling halls and being a good old boy. He's learned that hanging a "buy Jesus" sign on his music isn't necessarily his current task. But the "regular guy" pose he strikes in his recent interview won't sustain him long, either.

Dylan may say now that he was doing great in '78 and Jesus was just the natural culmination of a good year. But that's not what the songs he wrote for *Slow Train* and *Saved* say. Those songs speak musically just as much as lyrically of a difficult and painful struggle, of a man recalled to life. Dylan's voice on those songs back when they were fresh tells us the whole story with excruciating honesty. Art is tricky. But Dylan's art doesn't lie.

Reconciliation. Dylan may win back his audience. But in the process he's going to have to reconcile his commitment to Jesus with his commitment to his art. The failure of *Saved*—that album cover almost makes you wonder if something in him *wanted* to throw the album away—and the ambivalence I hear in Dylan's performances at his latest concerts are signals that this struggle is not necessarily behind him yet.

The problem is the relationship between the art and the ego. Dylan's ambition, Dylan's pride, Dylan's self-confidence, Dylan's arrogance, are the cornerstones on which he has built his extraordinary oeuvre, all those incomparable songs and unbeatable performances. Will power. Dylan is will personified. And since I don't hear Christ in Dylan's new performances anywhere near as much as I did a year ago—and I'm not talking about any kind of superficialities here, not talking about surface trappings—and I do hear will flexing its familiar muscles and feeling good about itself . . . well, I can't help but wonder how long it will be before spirit starts telling will that it feels shut out of this picture.

To be born again in Christ means submission of the will in total service. It's not an easy thing; it's seldom accomplished overnight. Among movers and shakers—the performers, the businessmen, the politicians, the (alas) most visible and noisy members of the Christian community—it's seldom accomplished at all. It's easier for a camel to pass through the eye of a needle, than for a powerful and successful man . . .

Dylan's new concerts, his reaching out to his audience, his

attempts to clear away the confusion from around his public persona, are all right on. He's moving; that's the most exciting news there could be about a great artist, that he's visibly in motion again, going somewhere, and by definition that somewhere will be a place neither he nor we have ever been to before.

Dylan tells us in his 1970s music (and his movie) that the greatest tragedy of his life was that his commitment to his woman and his commitment to his art could not be reconciled. In this sense he differs from Picasso, who I think never entertained the notion that anything but his art could win out. Dylan, the record shows, didn't discard his lady quickly or easily. Instead, for year after year, he dived into the struggle. I believe his commitment to Christ is as deep or deeper than his earlier passionate commitment; and with the help of his God this time I think reconciliation will be his. But I don't see it as having happened already. And I don't see it as coming easy.

I do believe Dylan's artistic will is going to end up in enthusiastic and total service to his higher spiritual consciousness; and in terms of the art that results this won't really be something new, *this has happened before.* But to keep happening, it has to keep moving, and that means this time the stakes are higher and the potential achievements greater than ever before. It is incredible, as Dylan himself has pointed out, that he is still alive, still moving. I long to hear the art that will be born of this struggle. And I empathize deeply with the burden this man has taken on: "I don't care how rough the road is; show me where to start."

Where to start seems to have been San Francisco in 1979, and again San Francisco in 1980. But it is still only the beginning.

Will and understanding. I don't think it's easy for them to learn to work together. I don't think the struggle is ever completely behind us, while we live and serve. I do think Dylan is, half consciously, half unconsciously, taking the first small steps towards living his faith and letting his rekindled fire shine through his art. I hope he can remember that as we grow more conscious, simultaneously we must also grow more unconscious—because our whole being is bigger, and that new larger unconscious is our greater submission to God. So conscious creation must go hand in hand with an equal or greater surrendering of control to the unknowable higher power. Unknowable or utterly knowable . . .

One year later, "what happened?" no longer matters. Dylan in his new, open concerts has set us free from that one. "What happens next?" is the question now. There aren't any old songs in Dylan's current concerts after all. Dylan like all of us is just doing his best to surrender to and work with the force that makes all things new.

13. The Endless Road—Highway '86

I went on the road in June 1986 to follow a Dylan tour around the United States, 29 shows and 12,000 miles in six weeks (and a 30th show in early August). It was something I'd wanted to do for years, and now I had the excuse that I had a contract to write a book about Bob Dylan's music (Performing Artist, *which I started writing in September '86) and I thought this would further my education as well as be fun. On the road I met John Bauldie, editor of the wonderful "Dylan information magazine"* The Telegraph, *and he asked me to write something for his magazine about the tour. I got around my tongue-tiedness by writing my article in the form of a letter.*

August 12, 1986

Dear John,

I love the photo of you and Christian and me in Hartford, it gives me a warm feeling, thanks. I do want to write something for *The Telegraph*, and I imagine I will, but it's a challenge. On the one hand I'm thinking my problem is I'm searching right now for the hook, the note, the rhythm, whatever, to hang my book on, and talking about the tour for *The Telegraph* doesn't fit into the process. (Just as I have this fear of meeting Dylan now lest I end up writing the book to him, I'm also sure it would be a big mistake to end up writing for the fans, preaching to the converted.) On the other hand, it feels as though the challenge of saying something about my experiences on the road for your fine publication is plunging me precipitously and right on time into exactly the tangled mysteries I have to confront: what I want to say? Where to fucking begin?

I just read Scaduto [a 1971 Dylan biography] for the first time, believe it or not—I've read little pieces of it before, but never was attracted to sit down with it; this time I did and I like the first half or two-thirds much more than I expected. Anyway I'm sort of in a

152

stage of flooding myself with information. I'm reading little bits and pieces of everything. My attention span is weird, I'm just letting it direct me. I like *Knocked out Loaded* a lot, I think it has a sound that goes deep, speaks from and to the unconscious, the once-was and about-to-be. It's all one piece to me, a very clever bit of work. I love the Dylan character in the *Rolling Stone* article, who starts by dropping the jaw of and rocking the socks off the journalist with the sessions at the beginning of the piece—here I am at the making of history, ma!—and ends by confounding journalist and Petty and readers by putting together a whole different album, one song from those sessions and the rest from the grab bag of the last few years—quick, decisive, contrary, on his own trip, not caught even by last week's model or the hopes and aspirations of current friends and companions—he's got other considerations to follow, what they are we'll never know but we do get the product, the records, the concerts, the outtakes, the interviews . . . Who was that masked man, anyway?

Apart from *Knocked out Loaded*, I find myself listening to a bootleg from the Rolling Thunder tour—*The Night The Revue Came To Boston*—sounds great to me for some reason, just what I want to hear right now. And tonight I'm playing side two of *Street-Legal* over and over. I have a tape of Berkeley, 14 June 1986, which was a great show, and it sounds terrific to me when I listen to it—and different from what the shows sounded like sitting in the audience, different sound, different qualities, different feeling—but I find I can't listen to more than a few songs at a time. My heart is somewhere else right now.

Now I'm using this letter as a kind of build-up to possibly writing something. What would it be? After thirty shows I sometimes feel like I wasn't at those concerts at all. I can't think of anything to say that wouldn't be evaluation (was it good? how does it compare with . . .? oh yawn) or information (like I could tell you about John Lee Hooker and Al Kooper each singing a song at Shoreline August 5th, and Petty's mysterious disappearance just before he would have done "Refugee"—instead, Petty's set ended abruptly, Kooper did "Caress Me Baby," Petty didn't come back till four songs later and in the meantime Dylan slipped in a *fabulous* performance of "Gotta Serve Somebody"! Petty's walk-off came as an obvious surprise to his band and to Kooper . . .

perhaps he was sick, although he was in good voice a moment earlier. Weird. Doesn't seem like he'd step on his own climactic number if there'd been any way around it . . . anyway, that's the news from Shoreline, a good show overall, one of those that might have seemed utterly transcendent if you happened to be sitting in one of the front rows, or if it caught you in the right mood, no surprises except the ones I mentioned, but that was enough . . . see what I mean by information? I could go on like this about any or all of the shows I think, and it would have its uses, but the thing is I don't wanna).

"I feel displaced, I've got a lowdown feeling . . ." So what I wanna know, John, is, what is the question? I know I have the answer—not necessarily the right answer, and never of course the complete answer you would have wished for, but still half a million words of answer easy ready to be cut down to a hundred thousand or so as I stick 'em on the screen under the pressure of an April deadline, and really I just want to jump into it. Going on the road following the tour was completely satisfying, no regrets and I hope he does more concerts soon, I'll go—but just as I've been telling people, it was for me like background, like soaking it in, maybe someday (listening to the tapes, or just when enough years have passed) I'll be able to really get in touch with the wonder of what occurred, for now it's too close or something, too familiar. And always this slight tinge of regret that it isn't Rolling Thunder summer '76 or Dylan with The Band spring of '66, some imagined time when everything was at risk and on the edge every moment. Which isn't even how those shows seemed to me when I did see 'em. I mean the two shows I caught in Philly winter '66 I was very excited because I'd got to meet Dylan, but I was basically frustrated—I liked the *idea* of the rock & roll set but I couldn't pick out the words or much of the melody or anything to hang my hat on most of the time, the show seemed to be getting away from me even as I watched and listened, I was thinking: "if only I could go back and hear that verse, this song, again, I might connect with it . . ." In hindsight though it seems like such an attractive place to be, I can even use it to distract myself from the shows I'm seeing now, why isn't it crazier, more improvisational, angrier, louder, more outrageous? Why didn't you paint the stripes on her blouse purple instead of green?

154

There were moments to die for. "Hattie Carroll" in Dallas. Performance of a lifetime, or so it seemed to me then. "All Along the Watchtower" in Philadelphia totally blew me away. "St. Augustine" was more of a surprise and a fine performance but something about "Watchtower" just made that evening extraordinary for me, gave me the energy for my three-thousand-mile drive home. I liked watching Dylan in Akron trying to come to terms with the Deadhead audience ("Okay, I think I got a line on you now," he said, quietly and with a little laugh, after "When the Night Comes Falling from the Sky"). "In The Garden" reached unexpected and unequaled heights in Buffalo, spontaneous, hard as nails and twice as holy. That was the period in the tour where "One Too Many Mornings" was obviously his favorite song, especially the guitar part, it said everything he wanted to say that week. "We Had It All" was the most heartfelt a week or two before that. I agree with Christian that "Union Sundown" in Houston was a high point— even better in Dallas two nights later according to my notes—and as good or better still at Saratoga, where, I'm sure, he played it specifically because Christian had requested it when he met him on the street in Hartford. Amazing, because I don't like the words or the sound of that song on *Infidels* (the outtake is more to my taste); and the new arrangement and the new words, even though I couldn't really hear what he was saying, left me certain that now the song was saying everything I and perhaps Dylan had always wanted it to say, and more. "Greed got, in the way." Yeah.

But it's in my nature as a fan, and somebody seeing so many shows, to seize on the anomalies, the songs done only once or only a few times, or the unusual arrangements that seemed to break the mold and transcend the very context of the show. Listening to the Berkeley tape, I realize that I probably didn't appreciate "Positively 4th Street" a lot of the time, though it sounds incredible to me now. But again my mind races back to the anomaly, the night in Austin where "Positively 4th Street" put my hair on end, I'd never heard him so angry, I just knew as I listened that he was singing to people writing about him, and I squirmed in my seat—it was like I was hearing a new level to it—and then later in the evening he specifically confirmed what I'd intuitively known, as he rapped at length about critics (complaining bitterly) before singing "Ballad of a Thin Man," and, still not complete, continued his rap (making some corrections, he'd been thinking about it) as an intro to "Seeing the Real You at Last." The tapes, I want to hear the tapes. But you know, once I do I'll no longer have any hope of knowing what I heard and felt and how it sounded to me before I heard it as a recording, when I was just out there having it go by once, in the flesh, from wherever I happened to be sitting and in the context of whatever thoughts and emotions and external distractions were assaulting me at that particular show.

Are we drifting too far from the shore yet? Let me say one thing, just one small thing, about *Knocked out Loaded*, and then I'll shut up and leave you to contemplate whether this letter could pass for a *Telegraph* piece, and if not, what would you like from me? Write back, give a clue, point a direction. Anyway, what I wanna say is I like the moment in "Brownsville Girl" when he says "You know it's funny how things never turn out . . ." and the girls and the sax and all the joyous noise disappears with a twist of the mixing board dial as he says it. It's a great moment, and I suggest it's an example of Dylan-as-engineer expressing himself with the kind of crude genius that characterizes Dylan the guitar player and Dylan the harmonicat. The whole song, and maybe the whole album, works with sound in ways that break the rules every bit as much as Dylan's harmonica playing always has—so emphatic, so simple-minded, so boorish and yet so magical. Listening to this album I'm beginning to understand why Dylan has had these female voices behind him on every tour and album for the last eight years, I mean I'm not saying I can or want to explain it but I'm beginning to get a glimmer, and in some ways it's possibly more central to his music than his entire interest in and relationship with Jesus. Not that it's separate from that, but it's almost like what comes first is that sound one hears in the back of the mind or the corner of the heart, and everything else is what occurs in one's life and art as one reaches for it. And there is no purpose bigger than or even other than letting it come out. And somewhere in here is also the answer to how come the guy who was infuriated at having to play the same tune twice for Harry Belafonte can sing "The Borderline" and twenty other tunes every night for thirty or forty shows and be loving it, just obviously having a ball. I don't think it has anything to do with growing up or selling out or even changing direction. Dylan has never changed direction. The problem is you or I imagining we know what his direction is. What I can say is after twelve thousand miles and thirty shows and *Knocked out Loaded* my faith is restored one more time; this guy's going all the way, till the wheels fall off and burn. I'd see him in anything. So what? I'll stand in line.

Thanks for letting me rave—

All best,

Paul Williams

14. Bob Dylan and Death

I wrote this piece for The Telegraph *after seeing the first four concerts of Dylan's 1988 tour. They turned out to be the first shows of what is still referred to as the Never Ending Tour; but something in the singer's voice on a couple of songs made me think about endings . . .*

In the autumn of 1980 I visited Dylan backstage at the Warfield Theatre in San Francisco, and at one point he gave me the number of his friend Howard Alk, who he said had really liked my book, *Dylan—What Happened?*, and urged me to get in touch with him. I talked with Howard on the phone, and some months later when I was in Southern California, visited him and his wife in Malibu. They were living next door to Dylan's property and, I think, caretaking it for him to a certain extent. They were used to dealing with Dylan pilgrims, joked about our breakfast eggs (from Dylan's chickens) and about the obsessive in each of us.

When I first arrived, Howard's wife told me he was up on the ridge in back of the house, and I went up to meet him. We were sitting on canvas chairs, looking at the ocean, and he said some nice things about my book, but what he really wanted to talk about (I was startled by his seriousness) was the fact that I had over-looked, in his opinion, a major possible factor in Dylan's conversion to Christianity: awareness of and fear of death.

I don't remember much of our conversation—I may have argued that I did call attention to lines like "By this time I'd've thought that I'd be sleeping/In a pine box for all eternity," but if so it was a weak argument, because certainly the text of my book focuses on loneliness, guilt, the search for something to fill the hole left by loss of marriage and family. As soon as Howard spoke, I knew he was right—like any commentator I'd focused on the reasons, the parts of the story, that I identified with, and fear of death was not one of them at the time. In hindsight, and in light of comments

Dylan has made since, Elvis Presley's death in August 1977 must have had a subtle but very powerful effect on Dylan, particularly in light of Elvis's age and the fact that Dylan in 1977 was 36 and closing fast on the big 40. Forty is mid-life for a lot of us, but for one who identifies himself with other rock stars and culture heroes it can look like the end of the line.

What I didn't know, of course, was that Howard Alk, like all of us, was focusing on the part of the story he identified with. He died, reportedly by his own hand, a year later. I liked him a lot, and am sorry I didn't get to know him better.

Death is a major theme on Dylan's first album, a common obsession of the young, perhaps because leaving home and the loss of childhood confronts us with our own mortality. Thereafter it's a theme that's present throughout his work, as one would expect with any artist, but seldom as a central concern. The *Saved* songs do seem to be about being saved from death ("You have given me life to live") as much or more than from damnation. "Trouble in Mind" and "Slow Train" also refer directly to death as the danger that awakened him ("she sure was realistic").

The songs about death on Dylan's first album are cover songs, not ones he wrote himself. In 1986, Dylan toured with Tom Petty and the Heartbreakers, and included an unusual number of cover songs in his standard set. Two of the songs he did almost every night are striking in their similarities: "Lonesome Town" ("There's a place where lovers go . . .") and "Across the Borderline" ("There's a place, so I've been told . . ."). So what is this lonesome town across the borderline that Dylan is so interested in? What kind of "place" is he singing about? For me, a clear sense of what Dylan is feeling often can be heard in his voice more than his words, and there were moments on the '86 tour when the emotional significance of these two songs came across with particular power. (Tape collectors might want to listen to June 14 and July 17, 1986 to check this out further.)

I need to acknowledge another moment from that extraordinary June 14, 1986 concert in Berkeley before I get to the performances that are most on my mind right now and that forced me to write this article. Dylan sang another cover, "Lucky Old Sun," with real gospel fervor, wonderful relaxed penetrating joy: ". . . take me to Paradise!/Show me that river, take me across, wash all my troubles

159

away/'Cos that lucky old sun give me nothing to do, but roll around heaven all day." When I heard this in 1986 (and I have to say it sounds even better today—what a fabulous performance) I couldn't help thinking there was something in Dylan (as in all of us, but a little closer to the surface in some) that longed for and looked forward to release from this vale of suffering. ("This time I'm asking for freedom/Freedom from a world which you deny...")

The image is of a physical place, of a body of water to be crossed and a "shore" on the other side and, sometimes, of lost friends waiting on that shore. I wasn't completely surprised to hear Dylan sing "Man of Constant Sorrow" at the Concord Pavillion on the first night of his 1988 tour, because "Rank Strangers to Me" is the Dylan performance that speaks most powerfully to my heart this year, and every time I hear the lines, "They've all moved away, said the voice of a stranger/To that beautiful shore by the bright crystal sea," I think of "Man of Constant Sorrow":

> Your mother says I'm a stranger
> My face you'll never see no more
> But there's one promise darling
> I'll see you on God's golden shore.

Dylan sang "Man of Constant Sorrow" twice in his first four 1988 concerts, at Concord and again at Mountain View, June 11. Both performances are exquisite; I'd say Mountain View has the edge, partly because of the spirit with which Dylan leans into the first word of each verse. He garbles a line, and several are unintelligible, but the depth of feeling is so great here, the quality of the singing so amazing, I believe in time this could be regarded as one of Dylan's finer performances. It's a heartbreaker, a real treasure.

An incredible sadness overtook me, a flood of empathy (reminiscent somehow of the mood of the poems in Kerouac's *Mexico City Blues*), the second or third time I heard "Rank Strangers to Me" (recorded 1987?). What an unhappy story this song tells (some kind of a bad dream, "I ain't got no home in this world any more" to the nth level), and how astonishingly penetrating Dylan's vocal performance is here. It just had to be the last song on the album; and I've found myself praying it's not the last song on the last album.

Dylan's 1988 "Man of Constant Sorrow" is different lyrically from his 1961 recording of the song. He sings six verses instead of four (the last a repeat of the first). The "golden shore" verse is almost unchanged (he sings "friends" instead of "mother," but then it seems likely that the word "mother" and the last verse about going back to Colorado were spontaneous additions during the recording of the first album, related to a fight with this girlfriend's mom). The new verses, which sound like they're traditional (every old ballad has a thousand verses if you do the research) but could have been written by Dylan, contain further references to death:

> You may bury me in some deep valley
> Where many years I may lay
> Then you might learn to love another
> When I am sleeping in my grave.

And then there's this astonishing, heart-chilling quatrain:

> For six long years I've been in trouble
> No pleasure here on Earth I've found
> I'm bound to ride that open highway
> I have no friend to help me now.

What are we hearing? Not fear of death, certainly—more like acceptance of it, a welcoming. This does not mean, of course, that our hero is going to leave us soon; but it seems reasonable to guess that the possibility is on his mind. And as always I can only acknowledge him, thank him for sharing his feelings so openly, for letting it all through into his art. I pray as I write this that he survives this tour and keeps going, singing, recording, performing, writing, or just quietly living. But if that's not to be, I guess there's something to be said for dying in the saddle:

> Faretheewell my own true lover
> I never expect to see again
> I'm bound to ride that morning railroad
> Perhaps I'll die on that train.

161

15. Those Talking Crazy, Spilling My Buttermilk, Not One More Kiss Blues

This review of Under the Red Sky *(written for* The Telegraph *in 1990) was such an immediate response that I didn't have the lyric sheet that came with the album, just an advance tape. So my friends and I listened carefully and guessed wildly and compared notes. And had fun.*

"Songs and words are not always the same. They do not always say the same things. Sometimes words lie—but the song is always true. If you listen to Oogruk's words, sometimes they don't make sense. But if you listen to his song, there is much to learn from Oogruk."

—Gary Paulsen, *Dogsong*

What do I think of *Under the Red Sky?* Is that what you wanna know, pal? OK, I'll tell you. I fucking love it.

It's a triumph. Dylan, after putting together a phenomenally good (and unexpected) studio album of new songs in 1989, has come up with an album that may or may not be as memorable (if it's not, it certainly comes close) and that has almost nothing in common with the sound(s) or style(s) or intentions or achievements of last year's effort. Indeed, *Under the Red Sky* is like *Oh Mercy* in that it is only superficially related to anything Dylan has ever written or performed before. What an artist! Thirty years on and he's still breaking new ground, with all the imagination and hunger and intelligence and humor he's drawn on and shared with us at past moments of inspired creativity. It's unbelievable. What's most unbelievable is that there's nothing interchangeable about it. Some familiar elements, yes; the Voice especially, and the personality behind the Voice. And it's just possible that "Where Teardrops Fall" or "I'll Be Your Baby Tonight" or "Yea Heavy and a Bottle of Bread" could have been slipped onto *Under the Red Sky* (if we'd never heard

162

'em before) and wouldn't seem entirely out of place. But the fact remains that *Under the Red Sky* sounds no more like another Dylan album than *John Wesley Harding* does. What's also true is that like *John Wesley Harding*, it is stunningly, almost mysteriously successful at being what it wants and intends to be.

There's been some stuff in the press about how this record was made, different people coming in for different sessions and the producers (Don Was, David Was, Jack Frost) keeping Dylan uninformed about who and when so as to keep an edge on things (nice turnaround on how Dylan keeps his bands spontaneous). At this point I have no idea who plays on what tracks (I'm listening to the advance promo tape), or whether there are any surprises on the songwriting credits, but the great thing is, it doesn't matter, the album is so consistent, all its variety somehow the expression of a single idea, a moment of inspiration, something we've heard Dylan reaching towards as he's tried out various obscure R&B covers on recent tours—a sound, a feeling—*Under the Red Sky* is one of those albums you play over and over, till you find yourself living inside it and ascribing to it all sorts of meanings that are really yours alone but have gotten stuck to the walls somewhere along the way.

It's a deep (but light-hearted) journey inside one person's mind and spirit, and I think I can tell you how this is done: you (the songwriter/performer) reach for the feelings, reach for that back-of-the-mind sound and chatter and try to pull it forward, and just keep putting aside everything that comes up that might distract from the process. It's all about what you don't say. What you do say may seem mighty mysterious—"the little boy and the little girl were baked in a pie"—but you know the real reason you said that is that everything else you thought of, every other sort of thing, wasn't right, took things off in a wrong direction, just wasn't true, until by process of elimination the "nonsense" that wasn't false won out over all other possible sense and nonsense and became the cornerstone non-message of this evening's entertainment. Say what? Exactly. Or perhaps for us insiders "Say 'WHAAAT?' " would be the appropriate comment.

"Wiggle Wiggle," don't know if I'd even like it in any other position (ahem), but as the starting song it's magnificent. Bam! Bam! Bam! Bam! Bam! Bam! Bam! Bam! (Dave Clark Five, right?)

What is this? Well, it's a command, an invitation, incitation, invocation. Here we go. Humor. Childishness. Sexuality. Confidence. Friendliness. (Where's old sourpuss tonight? Aw, he wasn't invited to the session.) Let's dance. Nothing complicated, two-step'll do. In fact, you dance, I'll watch. Egg you on. Come on, we're going to enjoy this. Play it again. What a great sound! There, you see, you're feeling better already . . . (Can a leer be sweet? "Dirty World" didn't make it, but "Wiggle Wiggle" is a whole higher level of creation, c'mon, you gotta love it.)

It's a real wonderful beginning, but it's the transition to the next song that lets us know (even as our conscious minds are going crazy, confronted with all this silliness) that we've got a great record here. A few listens, and you're hearing that "Red Sky" intro in your mind already as the first track fades, delicious anticipation. And it would sound just as romantic and tantalizing if we didn't have the opening figure of "Queen Jane Approximately" dancing through our deep memories, it's not so much that this recalls that but that both of them recall for us some larger something we can't begin to give a name to. This is a great song. The words do what they have to do, no more, no less. The tune, the sound, and the vocal absolutely blow us away. (Speak for yourself! say the doubters. No, no, I say, you speak to five other selves, and four of 'em will tell you how they've been in a trance since the first time they heard this and can't and won't and don't wanna wake up no more.)

Fairy tale. Nursery rhyme. It's the moon album (wiggle till the moon sees you—man in the moon went home—something in the moonlight still hounds him . . .). Sky album. Reaches back to adolescence (the rhythms) and to earliest childhood (Mother Goose lyrics and images, skip rope song structures) both at once, like a dream, time is suspended, we're inside it. Remember clasping your hands and twisting a certain way (grandfathers know it), wiggling fingers, this is the church, this is the steeple . . .? "This is the key to the kingdom, and this is the town" (oh that bridge, Dylan mesmerized as in '65 and sharing with us his sense of wonder at what happens when you push certain keys on the piano in a certain order: spirit bursts out of itself), "this is the blind horse that leads you around . . ."

Wow. Extraordinary colors and composition, Mr. Picasso. But why are the figures so childlike . . .?

"Unbelievable." Reportedly the first single—dunno if it'll get any play, but too bad if it don't, because this is just the sort of thing that could come over the airwaves and change the life of some kid who's never heard anything like this before. (Not because of what it says, you dummy; it's the sound—including the sound of the words— that tells us we're not alone.) Cooking combo. Evokes the '50s not by copying but by getting inside that musical reality and taking the next logical step—hey, let's try it like this! And of course the so clever off-the-wall lyrics efficiently and hilariously evoke the end of the go-go '80s: "Turn your back, wash your hands . . ." There's a lot going on here. The more I listen, the more it tickles me.

"Born in Time" was my favorite at first. Probably still is. (Funny how the big question about *Oh Mercy* was, 'What's your favorite song?', and how as you go on listening the answer to that question changes and changes and changes.) Some say it sounds like it's from another album, but I think that's just because it's so self-contained (whereas "Under the Red Sky" and "Handy Dandy" both have a fascinating incompleteness about them—unanswered, unanswerable questions—that makes 'em reach out to each other and helps hold the album together). Nice guitar playing, wow. And the vocal performance—49 years old, singing with what's left of his voice, and he can come up with something like this! It's indescribable, it could drive you to drink. Could break your heart. Could bring romance back into your life. Watch out.

This is what we live for, isn't it? And this is why we read *The Telegraph*—in hopes of hearing someone else say that they felt it too.

Bob Dylan has written some great love songs; this is certainly one of them. From those opening "Sukiyaki" chords to that exquisite instrumental fade (whoever plays that last piano bit was speaking straight from the singer's heart at that moment) it just cuts me open: "You were snow/you were rain/you were striped/you were plain . . ." (But why does he sing "hung the flay" instead of "hugged the flame"? It's gotta be "hugged the flame," doesn't it?)

"TV Talkin' Song," neatly complex though it is, may suffer a little by being the most decipherable song on the album—no ambiguity, just a damnably clever bit of storytelling, framing a marvelous tirade against the true opiate of the masses. The narrator's dead-pan performance is reminiscent of "Bob Dylan's 115th Dream" and the punchline, though predictable, is deeply satisfying. What splendidly witty lines trip off this poet's tongue: "Don't let an egg get laid in there." "It's all been designed he said to make you lose your mind/And when you go back to find it there's nothing there to find . . ." Once again the small combo performance is just perfect. Slick.

"10,000 Men" on the other hand is anything but decipherable. Great Howlin' Wolf riff, urbanized, sweetened (what a swell keyboard album this is), and arguably a lot closer to the R&B Dylan hears in his head than, say, "Obviously Five Believers." (That's what makes it worthwhile to keep making records; there's still something to reach towards, stories untold, sounds heard in memory or imagination or back of the mind at midnight, challenging you to try to bring them forward somehow. And then the deep satisfaction when you get something like "Unbelievable" or "10,000 Men" down on tape, promises kept to the child inside who once heard Jimmy Reed records on the radio.) As for the words, hey, I can't even remember most of my dreams, let alone explain them. But they still affect me. "None of them doing nothing that your mama wouldn't disapprove" is a heck of a phrase, isn't it? As for all those men moving by and all those women standing around, I don't know who they are, but I got to admit I can feel their presence. This song is fun. It's also more than a little spooky (with a charming last verse that serves to keep a sort of you-and-me romantic thread running through all this).

"2×2" has a great intro, like so many of these tracks, and a captivating, almost Beatleish melodic structure. Oh we're deep into childhood and dreamland now. Lines jump out and can seem very meaningful ("They step into the ark"), but they're not meant for consumption by the conscious mind. Gotta give yourself up to the sing-song, just let it wash over you. And the less you try to understand, the more there is here to feel.

"God Knows" is a piano riff, got the album data now, it's definitely Dylan on piano, OK I'll use that information: notice how he pokes at the thing, never quite got over the thrill of "Chopsticks," did he? It's a rhythm instrument, mother of rhythm, producing melody as some kind of natural gorgeous by-product, and of course the other truth about the piano is how easy it is to sing with it, words and voice just springing into the air off those

166

taut strings. Language riff too, partner to "it's unbelievable," take an everyday phrase and repeat it, explore the feeling of it, what people mean when they say it and all the phrases that follow from it, riff on it, scat it, and look listen see how the world the phrase comes from (our world) opens up and reveals itself to the singer as a result. It's fun. To be specific: "God knows" sometimes means, "no one knows"; sometimes means Someone knows; sometimes only means the speaker doesn't know, or doesn't want to say. Dylan has it all these different ways, often at the same time, which is the advantage of not being all too specific, isn't it? It's funny. Ha ha. And, typical of this album, the instrumental lead-in (intro) is the very best part of the song. (Although if you like words, "God knows the secrets of your heart, He'll tell them to you when you're asleep" is pretty bloody splendid too.)

And "Handy Dandy" is "Like a Rolling Stone." Now this is a good trick. Dylan has often commented on "Rolling Stone's" debt to "La Bamba"; here he sets out consciously to write a different song based rather more overtly on the "La Bamba" progression, writes something that doesn't lean on "Rolling Stone" at all in terms of subject matter, mood, verse structure etc., and then performs it as much like "Like a Rolling Stone" as he can, given that it's a very different song, including great overdubbed "Like a Rolling Stone" organ intro and accompaniment (by Al Kooper, no less! Al also did the "Queen Jane" variation on "Red Sky"). My friend Robin points out that the phrasing on "If every bone in his body was broken he would never admit it" is precisely the phrasing (delivery, bite, attack, method of spitting out words) of "You've gone to the finest school all right Miss Lonely but you know you only used to get juiced in it." Jeez. So what's it all mean? Well, it means he's exploring something, getting inside something, having to do with performance and content and communication and the component pieces that make up his (and any true performer's) art . . . exploring it not to provide an answer but with the joy that comes from discovering a new question (or maybe discovering a way to ask a question that's been in him unvoiced for decades). I can't think of anything in rock 'n' roll/modern music that is comparable to this (in terms of conscious exploration; unconscious reworking of old motifs and effects is of course the very life blood of rock creativity), but it does seem rather similar in its implications to some of Picasso's later work, for example his 1955 series *Women of Algiers, after Delacroix,* which not only reinvents the work of an earlier painter (suggesting in the process that Delacroix must have known Picasso's present wife in some earlier incarnation) but also I think re-examines and re-creates Picasso's own oppressively famous 1907 breakthrough *Les Demoiselles d'Avignon.* Well, so what? you ask. Quite right. Controversy surrounds him. I'll say, have I gone past the point when I should have gotten out of this paragraph? John'll say, "you got all the time in the world honey." Mmm.

It's a very good song. It's a very good song (and performance; is there a difference any more?) and it is extremely well-placed on this surprisingly clever construction of an album. Oh that bridge ("They'll say, 'what are you made of?' "), what a delightful change, this musical moment is precisely where the song departs from and truly adds to "Like a Rolling Stone," making a graceful leap that's possibly been building up in the man for 25 years of playing and singing these chords, it's nothing, you know, just a nice little musical/rhythmic/melodic change but, you see, it expresses the heart. Meaning follows music, not the other way around. Let's open this door and see what's in the next room. In Victoria last week (August 19, 1990) Dylan grabbed his harmonica during "Like a Rolling Stone" and did something he clearly had been wanting to do the night before at the concert in George, something I've never actually seen or heard him do before, an expression through the harmonica of a feeling that builds up in him as he sings the song; in Victoria he grabbed for it and broke through, an extraordinary moment, it looked to me like he wanted to keep going but the band didn't pick up his cue, no matter, the statement was made, the door opened and looked through. I was surprised he didn't follow up on it the next night but it doesn't always work that way, the important thing is that the song is alive and the performer is alive and he's in a relationship not just with the audience but also with this living thing called the performance. He talks to it, it talks to him. They dance. They enter new realities together. We watch, astonished. We come back for more.

And you still wanna know what the song's about, don't you? ("Please. Spare me.") It's about this guy, you know, he's sort of mythical and he sort of creates his own myth even in the act of making fun of his own alleged myth-making powers, he's like a Jack of Hearts in the corner face up but you still don't see anything but you like the feeling of it, he got a basket of flowers and a bag full of sorrow (a man of constant sorrow, yes indeed), he finishes his drink he gets up from the table . . . It's real, the glimpse of a fragment of a part stands for the whole and it works, that's the power of performed art, some tiny gesture catches your attention and is burned indelibly into your brain.

Meaning nothing and charming our socks off is the bottom line with this album, and it is underscored exquisitely in the closing track, "Cat's in the Well." For those of you (you corner me everywhere) who just have to believe every song and album is "about" something, let's take a look at the first verse here:

> The cat's in the well, the world is looking down
> The cat's in the well, the world is looking down
> He got a big bushy tail dragging all over the ground.

Mother Goose again, but OK let's look at it literally. Two images. One is a sort of humorous disaster, like Humpty Dumpty, like that little girl in a well in Texas a few years ago—not that that was humorous, but it does provide a basis for "the world is looking down." Anyway, this is a cat, OK? The image: cat down the (wishing) well, wet or dry we don't know, the world (I see a Herblock cartoon-type world, on spindly legs) inspecting the situation with fascination and concern. Second image: "He (the cat—can't be the world, can it?, although that's a good joke and not I think an unconscious one) got a big bushy tail dragging all over the ground." This can be taken literally as confirming that the well is dry, but I don't hear it that way, partly because "all over the ground" is hardly consistent with the limited space down there and mainly because something in Dylan's singing of the word "big" conveys to me an image of BIG, and so what I see is a sudden inversion, that bushy tail coming down from the sky somehow, as if the world's in the well and the cat is looking down. I can't justify this interpretation, rather my intention is to report on the effect (one possible effect) of this sort of wordplay. My personal feeling is that these words come out, spontaneously, and then Dylan keeps 'em because they fit the tune, just right for the sort of "jump" he's up to here (I keep thinking of Morris Zollar, and the endpapers in *Writings And Drawings*), and because he likes exactly the sort of effect I'm talking

169

about, images that contradict themselves and turn the listener upside down, pictures that don't quite fit, words that sound like something but aren't exactly that something, harmless cleverness with the hint of an edge, nonsense with a twist in its bushy tail.

OK [paragraph inserted a month later by a flustered writer], the album's out, he printed the goddamn words and my cloth ears and convoluted reasoning stand naked before you. "The wolf is looking down." Hold on, I'll have a new theory worked out in just a moment . . .

An even more unjustified example of how I convert this stuff as I hear it: third verse, "The cat's in the well, and grease (Greece?) is showing its face." That's what he sings, but I just have to hear it as a verbal erasure, the word was "greed" and that was too overt, too specific, had to muddy it a little. [Again, a month later: The word turns out to be "grief," which admittedly is a lot better than whatever I thought I was hearing.] See, he doesn't want these songs to be limited to interpretable meanings, he specifically wants to stimulate the unconscious, to prod us into dreamlike associations more suited to the sort of spirit openings created by these ancient memory playthings, these rhythms and images and sounds. Another example I'm not so sure of: at the end of "God Knows," it seems reasonable that the verse is "God knows there's a heaven, God knows it's out of sight, God knows you can get all the way from here to there but you have to walk a million miles by candlelight . . ." This is absolutely delightful, and maybe it is what he's singing, but the first line is obscured—sounds a lot like "heavy". Maybe my ears are shot. But maybe he just sings it that way to make sure we can't be too confident of any single message . . .

The ending of "Cat's in the Well" ("Goodnight my love" and the sound of that guitar-drum crash) is as perfect an ending to this album as could possibly have been come up with; just makes me want to go back and hear it all again.

In any event. Hope this is helpful. I could have said a lot more about those early songs, but I just wasn't wound up enough yet (lucky you). If Don Was says he discovered Dylan's voice sounding like it does on "Born In Time" when he took off the snare drum and the lead guitar ("they were playing in the same tonal range where the warmth in his voice was. I thought, that's what's been going on in these records"), I say, two gold stars and a place in the

170

Dylan hall of fame to you, boy, and to anyone else who can find something to remove that may be blocking our view of the magic, even if I don't know what you're talking about. (Three gold stars and a certificate of honor, our highest award, is reserved for the man who isn't on this album, G. E. Smith, who has served Dylan longer and done more to encourage and support the man in being the great performer he is than any guitarist ever, including Robbie Robertson. Take a bow, G.E., and thank you.)

One last thing. Comparisons are odious, but they do tend to help us make some sense of the inevitable subjectivity of a "record review." I love this album to pieces, you got that, but just how do I rate it? Well, looking back over the past ten years, and leaving out *Biograph* 'cos it's a compilation (if I didn't leave it out I'd probably put it first, but it's tricky to know what that means 'cos it is you see a compilation), I would rate *Oh Mercy* the best Dylan album of 1980–1990. Easily. (This needs to be said, considering certain aspersions in *RTS* and Roy Kelly's astonishing failure (in his *Telegraph* 34 article) to recognize the deep expression of spiritual purpose that is "What Good Am I?"; go back my man and listen again, you've shut yourself off from the heart and soul of the critter.) Number 2: *Shot of Love*. 3: *Under the Red Sky*. 4: *Empire Burlesque*. 5: *Infidels*. *Infidels* is a distant 5th (OK, I'm weird), but 2, 3, and 4 are so close together that this rating is arbitrary, you could just as well call it a three-way tie for second place. Just so you know where I'm coming from.

Romance, sexuality, ambiguity, freewheelin' inebriation, profound slapstick humor-in-language, and full-out up from the depths over the top unself-conscious R&B rock 'n' roll unique Bob Dylan sound are back. There's even some whispered secrets here and there. And amazing, great singing. Praise be. It's an OK record. You can dance to it.

> "When you don't allow yourself an adjective
> You can't report to the stockholders"
> —Bob Dylan, 1973 or earlier

> "('This makes perfect sense, Morris')"
> —likewise

16. *Good As I Been to You*

At the beginning of 1993 I started Crawdaddy! *again, as a subscription-only newsletter, and the first issue consisted of a huge essay "reviewing" six albums I found myself listening to, notably R.E.M.'s* Automatic for the People, *plus new stuff from Bruce Cockburn, Television, Neil Young, Sonya Hunter, and finally this review of a brand new Dylan album.*

Good As I Been to You is Bob Dylan's 40th album (including the two with the Traveling Wilburys). It's also, remarkably, the first solo acoustic album he's made in 28 years. Why so long? Probably (ask Neil Young) because he just didn't want to do what people wanted him to do.

And he hasn't. He's found a new way instead. New old way. He's playing acoustic guitar and harmonica and he's singing songs he never wrote. An album of covers, not goofy and detached like *Self Portrait* or quirky and wildly uneven like *Down in the Groove*, but affectionate, modest, intimate, and committed. My friend Jonathan nailed it: "There are no grand gestures on this album." That's right. I love the grand gestures Dylan performed in his solo cover spots on tour in 1988: showstoppers all, the climax of each evening, "Barbara Allen," "Trail of the Buffalo," "Eileen Aroon," "The Lakes of Ponchartrain." But this isn't that. This is something new, again. A new way of being with a song, of speaking through performance.

In a different way from *Blood on the Tracks*, in a different way from *The Basement Tapes*, it is an intimate album. I think indeed it may be the most intimate album Bob Dylan has ever recorded.

Secrets of the heart.

Singers love songs. It's a simple truth, but not always remembered in this day and age. They love 'em, they love to mess with them, they love to hang out with them, they love to sing them. Bob Dylan successfully uses his voice and his guitar playing to express and explore his great affection and respect for every one of the thirteen songs on this record.

This is an astonishing accomplishment, and I know I'm not the only listener who finds his thoughts turning to something Dylan said to Nat Hentoff in 1962, quoted on the back cover of *Freewheelin'* : "I don't carry myself yet the way Big Joe Williams, Woody Guthrie, Leadbelly and Lightnin' Hopkins have carried themselves. I hope to be able to someday, but they're older people."

We know a friend is sharing a secret of the heart, a privacy, when he tells us straight out about his pain and longing, as Dylan does on "You're a Big Girl Now" or the less obviously confessional "Most of the Time." But we also feel our friends' hearts' truths when they speak of them indirectly, speak of them through tone of voice, through posture while sitting or walking, through movements of hands and shoulders and facial muscles, through a fleeting look in the eyes. Often this is inadvertent, but there are also moments when we know a friend is consciously, purposefully communicating with us in this fashion, asking us to receive something that cannot be put in words. This album's like that, I think. You can come real close on this one.

At the risk of repeating myself: intimacy is not the same as confession. Our confusion on this point is a reflection of our *People Magazine* culture. Intimacy is closeness, mutual sharing. Dylan's embarrassing and/or incomprehensible performances on national television in recent years are expressions of his inability to pretend to be communing with another person (his listener) in a context which in fact he experiences as extremely uncomfortable, dishonest, and humiliating. "One should never be where one does not belong." The converse of this statement is that when one is where he belongs—as determined by the heart, not the intellect— then one enjoys a certain freedom from prosecution, from the pressures of outward censure or inner guilt. It is in this personal oasis that intimacy exists. Time out from the universe. You and me in this room.

Stories have drifted down through the years, of Dylan playing songs for the other musicians before or during a recording session, or sitting around with friends in a hotel room, folk songs, rock-abilly, country, blues, pop standards, even "White Christmas"—

amazing snatches of performance that are often incomplete, that come and go in a moment, but that are remembered with awe by the people who happened to be there. This album, recorded rather spontaneously (Dylan had done a lot of recording for a completely different record, involving various other musicians, when he suddenly went in the studio for a day or two and did this one instead), seems to me to be the official opportunity for a public peek at the backstage Dylan, not what he says or does but what songs he sings, and how he sings and plays them, when he's by himself or with one or two other people.

All of the songs on *Good As I Been to You* are traditional, with the exception of "Hard Times" by Stephen Foster, "Tomorrow Night" by Coslow and Grosz (a huge hit record for Lonnie Johnson in 1948), "Sittin' on Top of the World," which was written and recorded by Jacobs and Chatman of the Mississippi Sheiks in 1930, and "You're Gonna Quit Me," recorded and probably written by Blind Blake in 1927.

The range of source material is fascinating, and reveals a side of Dylan few people are aware of: he is, in his own way, a song scholar, and throughout his career has learned many more songs than he has ever performed publicly. He likes oddball sources, though he's not a showoff about it; he doesn't hesitate to include very familiar songs—"Frankie and Albert," "Blackjack Davey," "Froggie Went A Courtin' "—alongside more unusual choices. He has not gone out of his way to rework these songs—rather each is to some extent a tribute to the source he learned it from, and it comes out sounding similar to or different from that source depending on Dylan's mood as he sings it, what feels good to his fingers or his voice, what key he's comfortable playing it in, and so forth. Dylan apparently learned "Arthur McBride," an Irish song from the 18th century, from Paul Brady's 1976 recording; and his appreciation of Brady is there in the performance even though Dylan's assumption of the personality of the narrator is so complete you'd swear the cousin in question just told you the story himself.

It's a virtuoso performance. Dylan's ability to identify with victims of injustice and members of the underclass fills this story— about a couple of punks who verbally and then physically resist the predations of His Majesty's recruiters—with an immediacy that is riveting. The subtlety of the singing and the guitar playing is

174

characteristic of this album, and very much the work of a mature artist. His voice is amazing—it reminds me of what a peculiar and brilliant creation Dylan's original assumed vocal persona was, that hybrid Okie accent, not measurable against any standard because it was *sui generis*, a "Bob Dylan" accent, his private vehicle. This Irish accent of Dylan's is not Irish nor American but is born rather of the song itself, its key and chords and musical texture, its ironies and understatements and emphases. It is an accent created spontaneously by an inspired, hard-working artist who is looking for the right vehicle to transverse the space between this singer and this song at this moment of performance, a place where the feelings he gets from the song can become sounds, a place where the sounds of the words can become music and the colors and textures in the melody can become narrative. A voice. Every song on this album has its own voice, each a unique creation and not for show but for the specific purpose of honoring and getting across the song. Each performance full of respect for history, and for the human feeling and experience that is back of that history. "Christmas morning." When he sings the words he is not Bob Dylan. He is Arthur McBride's cousin. We've met him, and unlike the sergeant in the story our lives have been enriched by the experience. New messages. As great artists mature, their work often becomes simpler and more deeply felt. Dylan—Dylan the performer, not Dylan the songwriter, who's semi-retired despite the genius displayed at the *Oh Mercy* sessions—is no exception.

This is not an album for all moods and moments. It's a thrilling musical and emotional expedition better suited to regular rediscovery than to saturation repeat listenings. Not a pop record, in other words, though it is certainly capable of speaking directly to many different sorts of listeners.

"Jim Jones," an early 19th century song about a prisoner's boat trip to the penal colony in Australia, is an exquisite example of the beauty Dylan's ravaged voice is capable of when it finds a melody that delights it. This is a song about the dignity of the human spirit; Dylan's portrait of Jim Jones is compassionate, unsentimental, uncompromising, and extraordinarily lucid—his voice is a paintbrush, wielded by a free and confident hand, subtle, supple, exulting in the finest detail work while never losing the sweep and character of the performance as a whole. The guitar's support is

175

invaluable, full of imagination, intelligence, consciousness. Listen to him sing this couplet: "With the storms raging round us and the winds of blowing gales/I'd rather have drowned in misery than gone to New South Wales." Maybe you're still looking for some other Bob Dylan, voice of some great remembered collective moment. That's okay. But are you missing, through the single-mindedness of your search, the ongoing work of a great artist alive and actively working among us now?

Every song a painting. Every painting filled with light, and full of details that become visible at different moments, on different listenings. The first four songs on the album are classic narratives, their purpose is to tell a linear story; this is also true of "Arthur McBride" and "Froggie Went A Courtin'" (though in the latter we're not so much interested in the story as in the chain of images the storyteller conjures up, lightly of course, almost a parody of narrative, but still your basic "series of pictures" song in a tradition that Dylan reinvented for much of his most distinctive work, from "Hard Rain" to "Chimes of Freedom" to "Series of Dreams"). Other songs here are what I might call "implied narratives," where there's clearly a story behind the song but we aren't told it directly or in sequence—"Little Maggie," "You're Gonna Quit Me," "Diamond Joe." We know the singer of "You're Gonna Quit Me" is going to jail, but we don't know why, and the song's not intended to tell that story. Rather, it speaks of the situation, a man speaking to his woman whom he believes is abandoning him (presumably because he's no good to her in prison). A song like "Tomorrow Night" is pure situation; no story except, tonight you're here with me but I wonder how you'll feel tomorrow. And yet it is still Dylan's character as a performer to imbue the song with an astonishing narrative moment. He sings, "Your lips are so tender/ Your heart is beating fast/And you willingly surrender/[long pause] to me, but Darling will it last?" That pause is so rich in sexuality (I imagine Dylan heard the song as a young teenager and thought it very daring, which it is), and more than that: the dominance of the male, he who is surrendered to, is immediately transformed into vulnerability; the singer feels helpless in the face of his desire for this moment to be repeated, and his knowledge that his fate is now entirely in her hands. The narrative quality I refer to is the feeling we get, largely because of that pause, that he has just described

176

their actual lovemaking, that we are there as it's happening. We also feel the shift take place as confident lover becomes uncertain supplicant. It's a sweet song. Dylan's voice, to my tastes, is gorgeous here; his harmonica playing full of compassion, appreciation of beauty, and resignation. And other things. No simple answers. Rich complexities of the human heart.

I also love the texture of his voice on "Hard Times." This is purely a matter of taste (no accounting for it), I think, the way one is drawn to a particular color in a painting or finds beauty in a particular body and face. I hear the sound of his voice here and I get chills, I get all sorts of feelings, there's a quality to it that pulls me, ear candy, someone else might hear it as nails on a blackboard and how could I argue or explain? I can praise however the uniqueness of the sound here created, another new message, new creature. I am intrigued by Dylan's ability to convey to me both the guilt and compassion of the narrator, who is part of a more privileged class ("While we seek mirth and beauty . . ."), and also the feelings of the sufferers themselves—when he sings the chorus he is not the narrator quoting the miserable ones, he is himself one of them, feeling and living the pain, hope, hunger, and despair of the situation and again deeply communicating the dignity of the human spirit at the same time. (This dual role of the singer can be expressed also in the question, is it the hard times that are lingering "all around my cabin door," or is it the poor themselves, or the song they sing that plucks at the conscience? I suppose it is probably all three.) Obviously a timely and well-chosen song, and far from simple in its implications and reverberations. But it is a vehicle for feelings first; thoughts and politics are strictly secondary, or more accurately, the singer believes they appropriately arise from feelings.

The album is full of moments. When Dylan sings, in "Blackjack Davey," "She answered him with a loving smile," I can see and feel that smile. It's the inflection in his voice, the way he's inside the song, the charm and conviction of the storyteller. Lust in his voice—the girl's lust, not the gypsy's. How does he do that? And how about that guitar playing? My God. I don't think he practiced for months in preparation for making this album, but the difference between what he does here and on the other songs and what he's been doing on stage (as a guitar player) for the last many years, is staggering. It seems clear that the gift is in him, as great as ever or more so, needing only an occasion it's willing and inspired to rise to. The seducer, the charmer, the gypsy poet guitarist comedian rock and roll star, has resources he'll always be able to call on if so moved. It's the sweetness of the lady that's the variable, from his point of view—is there an audience I care to charm, after all these years, can you somehow make me want to strut my stuff?Evidently someone was able to.

Maybe Bob just woke up in love with his audience one week, and moved quickly to execute this project before the feeling passed.

(Actually, this happens all the time at his live shows—I mean affection for and openness to his listeners, expressed in the performance of a song. But it's not such a consistent occurrence in the studio. And I can think of only a few occasions—certain concerts or segments of concerts over the years—when he has shared himself so openly and unself-consciously.)

"Step It Up and Go" is in some ways a key to the album: it reminds us that the guitar is a rhythmic instrument as much as a melodic one, and that there is a strong rhythmic element in the performance of all these songs, even if this is the only real rock and roller in the bunch. It's an old jug band song, often called "Bottle Up and Go," and among other things it tells us that Bob Dylan understands the history of American music in the 20th century, knows where rock and roll came from and maybe where it's going to. Certain feeling, makes you want to get up and dance. Listen to that voice! His fingers are a complete band. "Everybody's gonna have a wonderful time tonight." He doesn't sing that but we can hear it. I can also hear, for example, "Silvio," but this is a much better song (or is transformed into one by a much better performance). 28 years ago I used to listen to "Snaker" Dave Ray sing "Go My Bail" accompanied by himself on 12-string and wonder why I loved it so much and what was the difference between that and rock and roll? I'm still trying to work it out.

Rhythms. How come he plays the same "Sittin' on Top of the World" he helped Big Joe Williams record 31 years ago, and yet it sounds like Rev. Gary Davis (and the Stones) doing "You Got to Move"? Just something his fingers got into, I guess. Rhythms. They float freely between songs and performers and eras and styles of music just like melodies do, recurring over and over in new forms and permutations. With melodies it's called "the folk process" (steal everything) (it ain't theft if it never was private property to begin with). Anyway. I appreciate that none of these songs are primarily nostalgic in content or effect. The point is just the opposite, really: they are alive now, have as much or more to say about our present condition as any new stuff that's being written.

And I like the album title, too. Very funny. Certainly Bob Dylan has been good to us. But certainly he hasn't done it because we wanted him to. No chance. He just happened to notice that we were walking in the same direction, and thought he might offer to entertain us while we walk along. "Hey I know a love song, and a dance tune, and a story about a girl who disguised herself as a tar and shipped out on a Navy boat. You wanta hear them?" And he tapes a list of songs to his guitar strap. And starts singing them to us.

And we can't get him to stop.

17. You've Got to Hear This Tape!

A new Dylan magazine, On the Tracks *(based in Colorado, whereas* The Telegraph *hails from Essex, England) asked me to write a column. What I wanted to do, since most of the Dylan fans I know listen obsessively to concert tapes (or bootleg CDs of same), was write about tapes as if they were new albums, an opportunity to dive deeply into the artist's current work and state of mind, and the impact of that work on us listeners. Tapes are almost always traded between listeners, as opposed to bootlegs which are sold. It's hard to write about live concert experiences, because all you have are your memories, but tapes like albums can be played again and again, allowing listeners to become intimate with the performances, like the lasting works of art that they are and can be. The recording process, since it's done by audience members, is outside the artist's control; but the performance is always his own creation (remarkably, a new creation every night, often a hundred nights a year). This piece was written in spring '93.*

The news, first of all (I try to keep up with the Dylan magazines to some extent, but if this has been talked about it certainly hasn't been given the banner headlines I think the event deserves), is the fanciest fretwork we've seen from Mr. Bob Dylan in roughly thirty years . . . not just on the thoroughly delightful *Good As I Been to You* but in live performance (solo *and* with band) as well. There've been hints here and there over the years, of course, but these recent performances—it's like, Johnny, we hardly knew ye! (That's Johnny Be Good to you, Lucky listeners . . .) Even the fine (but unvarying, and therefore technically cautious) performances of "Little Moses" and "Love Minus Zero" at those lovely spring '92 shows gave little foreshadowing of the eloquence and the startling, sometimes breathtaking virtuosity of Dylan's autumn '92 guitar playing. (The old harmonica's in great form as well.)

These comments are based largely on my enthusiastic recent discovery of a concert tape a reader sent me some months ago, of the November 1, 1992 show at Wilkes-Barre, Pennsylvania (John

Green's intelligent and valuable "Magnetic Movements" column in *Isis* assures me that this performance was not a fluke but rather is representative of the high quality of many of the postBobfest {October/November 1992} U.S. concerts). Writing about live performances, as I've said before, is a slippery task at best . . . but obviously a necessary one if one is even to begin to discuss the oeuvre of an artist like Bob Dylan or Van Morrison or the Grateful Dead. One pitfall is that by discussing anything as arcane as a particular concert on a particular night, one of forty in a row or 100+ in a year, one that the commentator wasn't even present at, the impression is given of a vast expertise. This is false, at least in my case. I haven't heard any other concerts from fall '92, and I have only a minimal experience of the tour segments that came just before (Europe/Canada summer '92) and after (Europe winter '93). I am certainly proud of having attended 17 concerts during Dylan's exceptional west coast U.S. tour in spring '92, but in many ways this experience is more of a hindrance than an aid when it comes to hearing what Dylan is doing in these fall shows. I loved the west coast shows I saw, and almost none of the magic of those shows—exquisitely delicate heartfelt vocals on the acoustic numbers; passionate, epic performances of "Idiot Wind" and "Every Grain of Sand" and "Desolation Row"; marvelous humor and timing on the likes of "Cat's in the Well" and "Absolutely Sweet Marie," etc.—is represented on this fall tape. One could feel a sense of loss. But one would be a damn fool, of the kind that we've all been when love for one record or concert deafens us to the fresh virtues of the performances that follow. (Greil Marcus, last I heard, was still complaining that Dylan no longer sings like he used to on *Blood on the Tracks.*) There's new magic, astonishing stuff, on this November 1 tape. And certainly this is Dylan's great accomplishment, the reason for my frequent comparison of his output with Picasso's: this ceaseless flow of new magic, never standing still, constantly throwing out the baby with the bath water and giving birth all over again in each new day's work. Constantly finding new ways to do this, in what one might have wrongly supposed was essentially a limited medium. Not to these wacked-out geniuses. Tour without end, amen.

Let's talk about the show. It starts like a bolt from the blue with "West L.A. Fadeaway." Say what? It's a Grateful Dead song—

presumably Dylan figures, since they perform so many of his copyrights, he'll return the favor (at other times in the past year he's covered "Friend of the Devil," "Deal," and "Black Muddy River"). People with a limited view (any of a dozen limited views) of Bob Dylan's purpose or identity will probably have difficulty imagining what value there could be in such a performance—it's not a song he wrote, it's not some well-worn folk or blues or even rockabilly song that might serve to remind us where he comes from and show off his love for the great old tunes. It's not a song that invites a particular vocal expressiveness from Dylan (by contrast with "Little Moses," say). And finally it's not hip, in the sense that Dylan fans may be charmed by his covers of contemporary works by Van Morrison or Leonard Cohen. It was evident in 1986 and 1987, and I imagine is still true today, that there are more Deadheads who can appreciate Dylan (even the "shambling, mumbling" 1990s Dylan) than there are Dylan fans who dig what the Dead are all about. Too bad. Because the genius of this 11/1/92 Wilkes-Barre tape, for me, is focused in the first five songs, all of them examples of Dylan's recent (and oft-complained-of) "long endings" style of performing, exploration of an extremely sophisticated musical language that up until now has been almost exclusively the province (for the last three decades) of the Grateful Dead.

Why should Dylan pretend to be the Grateful Dead? The question is as silly as when we asked in 1965, "Why is he trying to be the Rolling Stones?" Because he wants to! Why, for that matter, emulate Woody Guthrie or Little Richard? Dylan is the kind of musician who reaches out towards whatever attracts him; this in no way creates a loss of self, because what attracts him is any musical approach that seems to articulate and give form to the strong feelings already present in his heart. This articulation can be verbal, melodic, rhythmic. It can be achieved through vocal phrasing, or through manipulation of chords and melody to obtain very specific sound-colors and emotions. It can also be achieved by creating a certain musical dynamic on stage (or in the studio). Dylan loves to do this. For 28 years he has refused to perform without a band. Music for him is clearly an interrelationship. He likes to get a groove going as well as the next guy (or gal). And then he works with that groove, employs it, leans into it, to tell us everything he knows, everything he feels, everything he still

182

wonders about—uses it to express his humor, his horniness, his curiosity, his affection, his boredom, his anger, his spirituality, his aliveness. There are weeks on the road when he doesn't seem to connect with his fellow band-members at all, no matter how much he and they want to. And then there are weeks like these when everything clicks, taking new forms every evening, and you can see and hear that he's just having a wonderful time.

He's having a wonderful time, and so are we. One of the cornerstones of the Grateful Dead approach to music-making is that the audience is a band-member, a major component of and contributor to the composite sound and mood of any given performance. Failure to engage the audience—whether the fault lies with the band, the circumstances (sound system, etc.), or the audience doesn't matter—guarantees that the music will lose its momentum and integrity somewhere far short of critical mass. The audience contributes not a sound but an emotion, and so this is a hard concept to get across to skeptics—at best, they understand this to mean that when the crowd feels good, the musicians feel good. Yes, but the actual creative and emotional interaction is so much richer (and more musical) than that. Think of the way one soloist (or a member of the rhythm section) inspires another during a particularly hot jazz improvisation. Something is *felt* by each musician that makes a palpable, substantive difference in the quality and nature of the performance that results. In the same way, the Grateful Dead soloists trade licks with the crowd, or ride on the rhythmic pulse of all those bodies and faces and heartbeats. This is not a metaphor—it's *felt*, and it shapes the music to a very significant degree, often taking things into subtle and surprising spaces the musicians would never have arrived at by themselves.

The audience is important in jazz, too, as in any live musical performance; but the specific concept of a collective improvisation in which the audience is a primary participant is perhaps unique to the Grateful Dead—or at least they've run with the concept in a direction all their own, so that the particular thing they do is not rock and roll, not jazz, not folk, not country, but *Grateful Dead music*, improvisatory musical compositions for two drummers, three amplified fretted instruments, keyboards, a vocalist, and a live audience. Omit the keyboard, and you have Dylan's fall '92 ensemble. Not a coincidence.

And isn't that Bob himself, on some songs, playing those liquid Jerry-Garcia-like looping lead guitar figures? Wow. And this is no Grateful Dead tribute band. This is a fellow musician of comparable experience and stature, a fellow who's been just as far out on the edge for just as long (or maybe a little further, and longer), a listener/sponge who even listens to his co-bill partners, and who now for his own purposes has *broken the code*, rewriting his own history in the process, so that we can retroactively recognize his fall '87 and spring '76 and spring '66 ensemble performances as part of the same continuing effort to explore a particular musical language (and technique, but it's the language that is primary, that requires the technique to be invented).

"West L.A. Fadeaway," shortest song of the first five at six and a half minutes, is brilliantly successful in its attempt to engage the crowd in a musical act of collective creation. Dylan when he's hot gets wonderful performances from his bass players, and he does it with the timing and inflection of his voice and guitar, the specific angle and velocity with which he as leader and spokesperson throws himself into the rhythmic, percussive center of the group performance. A singer who can do this plays a group of musicians like they were his private drum set, and the impact on a live audience is immediate and electrifying. We're up and dancing, feeling the pulse of it in every part of our bodies. Dylan's voice achieves a creative, emotive intensity possible only to a great singer, though what it is that's so effective in his vocalizing ("running errands for the Mob/Ain't this pathetic?/It's a shame those bastards ain't more copacetic") is not easy to describe. Not easy except that the song—as words, as music, as story, as pulse of performance—totally comes alive as we hear it. "West L.A. Fadeaway" is a modern blues shuffle about a part of the world and a state of mind Dylan presumably knows very well—and on November 1st he and his band (and their audience) get into a groove with it that won't quit, and then use this groove to kick off a nonstop (each song segueing into the next as if they were written together) Dead-like run of five-songs-and-44-minutes of often incandescent musicianship, a jam, an improvisation, a catharsis, a statement, an inspired and inspiring moment.

"Pretty Peggy-O", second song in the series, is the sort of performance that tape collectors live for. This is the reason we give this

184

guy such an unreasonable amount of attention. He repays it. What a gorgeous piece of music! This is also, certainly, what Dylan lives for. It's worth going out on stage, night after night, for hardly enough money to keep the entourage going, just because, on one more dark stage in another dim city, you may run into moments like this one, moments of pure collective inspired sacred music-making. Thrilling and humbling. Worth hitting the boards for.

What is Dylan doing? Well, he's singing a song he likes, in an arrangement he and his band worked out, more or less, in rehearsal. It's a song from his first album, seldom performed. And Dylan is just giving his heart to it, through his voice, through his guitar, and through his band. Seldom has he been so articulate. This is a performance of astonishing beauty and clarity.

It's much, much more of a song than the version of 31 years ago. That was all goofiness and charm, less a song than a bit of showing off. Dylan redeems himself now by resorting the song's power-ful narrative line, and by celebrating joyously the richness of its melody and tone at the same time that he sings and performs a funny, honest, harrowing story of men and women and war. As "Drifter's Escape" ("stop that cursed jury") and occasionally "Hattie Carroll" were brought out in response to the L.A. riots during the spring shows, so this song, first played in Italy in July, could be intended as commentary on the news from Yugoslavia. It's a Civil War story, Scottish or American or what-have-you, of an officer falling for an enemy gal, being rejected by her, threatening to come back and destroy her town and all the women there because of his anger at her (as he earlier promised to protect and spare them when he was courting her), and instead dying himself, probably in battle, probably due to carelessness or headstrongness brought on by a broken heart.

What drives young men? Older men know, and that's what this song/performance is about. Dylan sings in a voice that is tender and strong and full of ancient rhythms and deep awareness of and compassion for the humanity of his characters, his listeners and himself. And he interweaves this exquisite vocal performance with another kind of singing, heart singing through fingers on guitar strings, audience cheering as he steps out to take an obvious solo after the climactic verse (amazing how he makes "Come trip-ping down the stairs!" the hair-raising climax of the song) but in fact he's leading the band (on acoustic guitar) throughout this performance, and particularly on the almost four minutes of instrumental coda after the closing verse of the vocal.

This instrumental excursion takes all the emotions raised during the narrative part of the song and soars with them far beyond the limits of verbal communication. Its meaning (and it is rich with meaning—message, intelligence, emotional and spiritual information) is as much a gift from audience to Dylan as it is a gift from Dylan and band to audience. Something comes into being here. It's an odyssey, a deep, far-ranging, powerful journey of the soul. In my book *Rock and Roll: The 100 Best Singles* I attempted to sum up the Grateful Dead in four words: "In music we travel." Dylan too is a traveler in music (roaming gypsy boy with something to sell you in his caravan), a traveler for music, a traveler through music. Feel him dancing with spirit here, spirit that for us is personified by the rhythm of his guitar playing and the melodic figures he and the band spew forth, each following and commenting on and wrapping itself around the one before, ascending towards the infinite . . . but for him the spirit is in the earth and the audience that stands on and is the visible extension of the earth. He says three words to the crowd tonight, after the third song; it's probably, "Is everybody ready?", but it sounds to me like, "Is everybody here?" And he asks because he already knows and feels the answer.

We're here. Dylan's atypical full-force assault on the evening in these opening songs (audible words, unmistakable sense of purpose, powerful presence as bandleader and rhythm-and-melody guitar ace) catches us off guard (along with two songs the audience hardly expected but can't help being moved by), and we let go of preconceptions and just get into it. The groove. No time to think about the maelstrom of feelings stirred up by Dylan's passionate re-creation of "Pretty Peggy-O," no time to ponder the rich musical tapestry (opening notes sounding like "Ring Them Bells," sublime surprising-but-inevitable (in hindsight it was all moving inexorably toward this) ending chords sounding like *Desire*, journey across a thousand musical/emotional landscapes for audience and singer both, but no time to think because rattle shudder crash we're immediately off into a tour-de-force new 1992 version of "All Along the Watchtower," taking those loose ends of emotion and energy and running with them, lighting up the sky, not by rote as was often the case with the previous Never Ending Tour "Watchtower" rave-up but with real passion and spontaneity and fury and love. No brakes. Dylan's rhythmic groove and sense of connectedness with the band (Winnie rules okay) move us forward like a wheel on fire, listen to the way he leans into the words (leans the words into the music), listen to his guitar, and now the harmonica inserts itself like some kind of intimate higher authority, and listen to the rest of the band respond, wow, building, building, replaced by extraordinary Dylan guitar playing (he's the weird broken brilliant one), obligatory *Sturm-und-Drang* ending almost anti-climactic, but no pause as he shouts his three-word-greeting and moves on to the stately warm (and as John Green noted, strangely affectionate) 1992 arrangement of "Positively 4th Street." The groove leans back a little here, but the richness of the music compensates, we're turning in another direction, still circling the Mystery. "Do you take me for such a fool, do you think I'd try to make contact?" Maybe. Fools rush in, and angels sometimes can only drop their jaws (and haloes) and follow. A good night on the Eastern Seaboard circuit. Leaving pretentious star-studded televised tribute evenings far behind him. Back on the prowl.

"Positively 4th Street" noodles brilliantly (if that's not a contradiction in terms) as its jam gets going (especially just before "I wish that for just one time"), bandleader finding new aspects of the endlessly wondrous world of music to explore with each song, each riff and progression. I remember Dylan in '86 with Heartbreakers fooling around with the ending of "Like a Rolling Stone," and the long instrumental transitions in 1989 that always seemed to trail off into the ethers. There was an itch he wanted to scratch, and it hasn't gone away. Many Dylan fans and commentators would like to police the man, and tell him how to do a better, more consistent job of whatever it is he does, but happily he doesn't listen. He listens to some far-off whisper, some grungy set of obscure impulses and resistances, instead. And gets the most interesting results!

The five-song 11/1/92 run that delights me so much climaxes (not that anything could equal that version of "Pretty Peggy-O," but dramatically it climaxes) in a glorious driving rhythmic life-affirming performance of "Tangled Up in Blue." What a great song this is to sing and perform. Here it gives Dylan and the band a chance to recapture the crowd-pleasing intensity of "All Along the

Watchtower" with an openness and looseness that seems to gather us all back from all the many different places the music has taken us. The effect is a sense of community. Dylan's voice is a different kind of instrument here, not the intimate intense narrator of the first two songs nor the gnomic voice of music and mystery of the next two. What is it? Square dance caller, maybe, rapper, circus barker, shaking his voice like a set of maracas, and still throwing his heart into it too. This fast-talk narration is still totally real to him, listen to the explosion of feeling in the final verse ("... point of view!!"). Verse ends and harmonica comes in, light, lively, earnest, soulful, straining at something, harmonica exits and John Jackson plays those patented Garcia guitar licks, plucking at that familiar place somewhere deep in our consciousness where it all makes sense, feels like home or something, and meanwhile Dylan as rhythmic bandleader drives the music on, bouncing towards the inevitable sloppy cosmically ordinary conclusion, last remnants of groove still pulsing through us, happy, exhausted, bewildered, amazed, hey we just went somewhere together. Yeah.

And for me, I rewind the tape and start over, but the concert goes on, with the usually soporific '92 arrangement of "She Belongs to Me" (but you might love it, and certainly the singing is terrific— I just don't feel any gestalt in the performance as a whole, meaning the band, including Dylan as instrumentalist, just never come to life here). The rest of the set is "Silvio" (Dylan having great fun on lead guitar), a very pretty "Mama You Been on My Mind" (acoustic), a totally lifeless "Boots of Spanish Leather," a bright acoustic "John Brown" with some daring and dazzling guitar acrobatics, "Don't Think Twice," a draggy "Cat's in the Well" (it's become a standard shuffle number like "Broken"), imperfect but still very lovely "Under the Red Sky" (fine arrangement), dull "Times They Are A-Changin'," good but not great "Maggie's Farm" and "Ballad of a Thin Man," "Highway 61 Revisited," and alas the tape I have is missing the final song, an acoustic "It Ain't Me Babe" (absolutely marvelous a few months later as the closing song in Paris, February 23, '93).

Thanks to Lex for the fine recording (but leave your kid at home next time). Thanks to Bob for still being on the road. I've praised the band as a whole without giving them much credit for their specific contributions—Bucky Baxter's pedal steel does a lot for

"Pretty Peggy-O," he also pays mandolin and guitar I think, John Jackson plays lead guitar when Dylan isn't hogging the limelight (hey I'm not complaining), Tony Garnier on bass, Ian Wallace and the recently arrived Winston Watson on drums. Someday people will play their officially released CDs (or whatever) of the best shows of fall '92 and these guys will all be remembered as heroes. Thanks to Mick for twisting my arm to write this, and thank you for your patience in reading this far—I basically feel that talking about live performance is an almost impossible task, but for most of us these tapes and the music on them are the reason we're Dylan fans, and damn, the tapes, the concerts, the nature of what Dylan is doing musically and artistically, change so much from year to year and tour to tour and even night to night, we just have to try to talk about it anyway. Negative reactions are inevitable and often easy to articulate ("those bloody endless endings"); talking about what we like, especially when it's new and different and we haven't got words for it yet, is a struggle. I like the long endings. I like their daringness, originality, freshness, I like the fact that as so many times before Dylan is finding ways to make the music live for him, he's reaching for something that really matters to the music-lover inside him, and on a good night he grabs a chunk of it. I don't think anyone could listen to "Pretty Peggy-O" from Wilkes-Barre and fail to recognize the value of the long instrumental passage that makes up the latter part of the performance. So, um, it all comes down to the title of this column. That's all I want to say. Listen to the tape. See what you hear from it. (But don't ask me for a copy, please; I've got to go write an equally long and enthusiastic ramble about Arrested Development.) Come tripping down the stairs, okay? See you next issue.

18. *World Gone Wrong*

This review was written for Crawdaddy! *in December 1993, as part of a larger essay that also talked about Nirvana, the Velvet Underground, Zap Mama and Prince.*

Bob Dylan's been telling friends how enthusiastic he is about his new album. That's unusual; and so is *World Gone Wrong*. In one respect, however, it fits the classic concept of a new Dylan album: it's a Rorschach test. A gorgeous rich heartfelt splatter. Be careful. What you hear is what you've got.

I hear death, desire, compassion, humor, integrity, fascination with the simple deep lives and emotions of human beings, love of music, and an older person's awareness of the complex patterns of work, suffering, loneliness, failed ambitions, and small pleasures that life is mostly made of. I hear presence, depths of feeling, and subtleties of feeling. I hear intense concentration on performance, and I feel a friendship or camaraderie that that concentration somehow implies. This singer/player cares passionately about getting something across to me. The record overflows with warmth. I am moved.

World Gone Wrong is so warm, in fact, that it makes Dylan's previous album (*Good As I Been to You,* which I praised at the time for its unusual intimacy) seem cold and distant. It wasn't, but it is an indication of the extraordinary power of this new set of performances that they set a standard that, unfairly but inevitably, diminishes prior efforts in the same direction. Of course, the creative process is a working-out, involving a great variety of internal and external considerations. *WGW* very probably could not have come into existence without the personal and public breakthrough that *Good As I Been to You* embodies, and one can further speculate, from the comfortable perspective of hindsight, that that album was the fruit of a variety of frustrated earlier efforts, including the relatively unsuccessful (personally, aesthetically) *Down in the Groove*. Perhaps Dylan's inability in the early '80s to get or create record company support for such projects as his collaboration with Clydie King also laid the slow groundwork for this 1992–1993 reassertion of self.

For that is what it is. Reaching back 23 years to a still earlier attempt at recording an album made up mostly of cover versions, we can recognize *World Gone Wrong* as the *real Self Portrait*, the one Dylan wasn't willing, able, or ready to perform and share until now.

Being literal won't get you anywhere. What Dylan was trying to say in 1970, and what he succeeds in saying now, is that a self portrait moves from the inside out, not the other way around. It's not a peep show. This album does not reveal that Dylan killed a lover, was killed by one, patronizes prostitutes or died of the plague on the way to a Crusade. All the songs about death on his first album did seem to indicate that, like most 20-year-old kids, the singer was scared of and fascinated by the idea of dying; but all the songs about death this time out don't even tell us that. There's more personal fear, it seems to me, in the chorus line from "Delia" ("All the friends I ever had are gone") than in any of the death stories told here, even though "Two Soldiers" does capture the terror and despair of the two protagonists with astonishing immediacy. What comes across instead is that death for the singer is a narrative focal point, awakening him as listener (the self he's portraying here is, in every case, the listener in him awakened by hearing these songs) to the poignance and humanness of these life stories, murderess mocked by a parrot (if she could eliminate all witnesses, her vanity assures her, the event would never have happened), murderer haunted by his victim (Stack A Lee, whose bullet created rather than destroyed his tormentor, and Cutty, who still yearns pathetically for Delia's attention even after he's done the one thing he could think of to prove his own existence). Dylan shares with us his empathy for these characters (and for the characters he inhabits as first person narrator, ragged, hungry, bloody-eyed, broke down, abandoned and yet mysteriously enduring, even indomitable), not to boast of anything (he ain't philosophizing disgrace here) but I think to confess and share his humanness, which is ultimately no more or less than ours, or

191

theirs. "What good am I?" That 1989 song asked the bones of a question: "If my hands are tied/Must I not wonder within/Who tied them and why/And where must I have been?" This album puts flesh on the bones.

You can hear it in his voice.

And of course you can also hear it in his guitar playing. The two, voice, guitar, work together so closely it seems inappropriate to speak of one as accompanying the other. They are inseparable partners in the act of articulating the mood of the performer, a mood as multifaceted and full of subtle intricacies as a tidepool at sunset, half moon rising over the observer's shoulder.

My notions about the primacy of performance in Dylan's art are well-known at this point. Ben Edmonds, in a recent review in Detroit's *Metro News*, sums them up efficiently: "Dylan's genius is, Williams contends, as a performer. The act of composing the song is only preparation for the moment of its performance. At that moment, the artist is telling us everything we need to know about his art and his life." Everything we need to know. That's a lot. The point is, a great artist is one whom we experience as being almost inexplicably articulate. A measly brushstroke speaks volumes. And speaks them not just to the critic/scholar who has some grasp of the technique involved, if there is such a person, but direct to you and me as we look at the painting, ignorant perhaps of painterly technique but one with the artist in terms of human experience. We've seen and felt the movement of a man's shoulders as he receives news of a great disappointment and pretends it makes no difference to him. We know, even if we could never describe or paint it, the look in a woman's eye as she persuades whomsoever stands in her way ("it would not make me tremble . . .") to let her go to the aid of a loved one. And when we hear or see the artist's representation of this truth, we *recognize* it. Magic word. We know it to be true, not through persuasion but because it matches our experience. Indeed, the moment of recognition is a moment of re-experiencing. Art would have no power if life itself did not open our hearts at times (more times, perhaps, than we care to remember or admit). Art reopens our hearts, and the greater the art, the more simple and mysterious the process. Why does Delia's song turn out to be about Cutty? Because it is. Because that's the way Dylan *heard* it. In 1963, in Cambridge, Mass., I fell hopelessly in love with Jackie Washington's performance of a version of this song, different melody, different words, all I remember or ever heard is the incredible chorus, I could sing it for you if this weren't print: "Delia gone, one more round/Delia gone, *one more round* /Delia gone . . ." Maybe that song was about Cutty too. It was certainly about someone not gone, about his feelings of pain and loss and something regretted and inescapable. Thinking about it, intimations of my own response as a 15-year-old to—something. words? chords?—stir deeply in me. And this new (to me) version hits me almost as hard, but somewhere different. New story. No end to them. No limit to the power of performance.

But some of my friends feel cheated that Dylan hasn't written any great songs lately.

He obviously hasn't needed to. But that doesn't matter, if you're a fan you just want what you want, and Dylan understands that, and so—a further expression of his enthusiasm for *World Gone Wrong*— he reaches in his pack and plays a trump he's been saving so long it's grown whiskers: liner notes, genuine 1965-style liner notes, funny and crazed and rhythmic and earnest, and on top of that an absolutely gorgeous cover photo, those colors! that angle!, evocative of and satisfying as *Bringing It All Back Home.* Is that his own painting? The placement of the title is impeccable. Latest rumor is he played a club in Manhattan and the *New York Times* gushed and Sony got it all on film. It just doesn't sound like the recalcitrant (mumbling, shambling) public Bob-face we've grown so accustomed to. (Not that anything he does, however welcome, is likely to make the album sell any better than any other disc he's put out in the last ten years—one week at number 30, then off to oblivion. But you can look at it another way, which is that this will almost surely be the bestselling collection of traditional blues and ballads released this year by any American artist.)

World Gone Wrong sounded good to me on first listen ("Blood in My Eyes" jumped out) but took a little getting used to—the rawness of some of the recording, the succession of violent deaths in the story songs. Two months and many listenings later, I can fairly confidently guarantee that it will amply repay as much time and attention as you choose to give it. It has legs. It passes the one real test: it gives pleasure, and goes on giving (still fresh, in other words) on listen after listen after listen. Of course, I can't tell you now if I'll lose interest next week, but I suspect not, and anyway it's been a great ride so far.

So much for evaluation. But what is the story he's telling? What is the story I hear? Well, first of all, of course, the world's gone wrong. This is not a suddden occurrence. We've heard this report from this particular weatherman before—and it's always been correct. But what a delightfully off-kilter song, written well before Bob Dylan was born, and as timely and up-to-date as Pearl Jam or the poems of Rumi. Strictly a relationship song, but with Implications (roughly the inverse of "Everything Is Broken," now that I think of it, which is ostensibly about the state of the world but sneaks in a couplet suggesting it could be about a relationship after all). There's a nice pronoun confusion, B Dylan specialty: *who* is it who can't be good no more, who's gonna quit whom anyway, and why? If her, then is he being all sarcastic about her "world gone wrong" excuse? Well maybe. But it's surely gone wrong for him. Way I hear it, she's given him walking papers, probably because world's gone w. in the sense of money tight and she can't afford to house the bum like on previous occasions. Wounded pride, he responds that she can't throw him out, he's just leaving before he does something nasty, and "No use to ask me baby 'cause I'll never be back." By way of bonus, we get this memorable & highly useful bit of advice (women substitute the word "man" please): "If you have a woman, and she don't treat you kind/Pray to the good Lord to get her off your mind." I love the sandpaper sweet texture of his voice throughout, the easy beat and that astonishing little melodic hook on "world gone wrong," vocal first and then the guitar goes on to twist the endpieces and leave you with this indefinable physical feeling that includes among other things gratification and regret. Opening guitar strum and notes and first words of song/album are pretty devastating too, how does he do that? Expressive. We got a master at work here. "These are just as good as it's possible for me to play them," he told an interviewer recently, and yes I believe it's true.

"Love Henry." Notice how there's a very successful unity of sound on this album and yet the guitar playing and vocal approach are so different on each song. We can listen again and again because so much more is communicated than meets the conscious mind. This gal is arguably the only unsympathetic female on an album full of

194

men beseeching women for something (and frequently getting turned down), but, as Dylan's notes suggest, Love Henry himself is one of only two wholly unsympathetic male characters on the record, the other being the wealthy merchant father in "Jack-A-Roe." Dylan the liner note writer doesn't like men with power and money. Okay. Incidentally, there was a murder trial recently in northern California where the defense attempted to introduce, indirectly, the testimony of a parrot ("No no, Richard!") who was at the murder scene. (Richard was not the name of the defendant.) The judge was not amused.

"Ragged & Dirty." I find this one strangely attractive, even though there doesn't seem to be much to it. Must be the riff. The right blues riff at the right moment has a totally mysterious, hypnotic impact on me. That little lick he plays, combined with the sound of his voice, tells me everything about the mood of the narrator, everything he feels about the way his life is at the moment. And the low notes that drive the song along. Rhythm section. Pulls me in. "I'm broke and hungry, ragged and dirty too." That says it all, and the meter (Dylan's phrasing) is irresistible. "If I clean up, sweet mama, can I stay all night with you?" Rest of the song's a lyric blur, she won't let him stay (this is "make me a pallet on your floor" territory) but he still threatens that he's "leaving in the morning." She's got a man, he's got a woman, maybe he's singing to two different women in different (alternating) verses, they both mistreat him, everyone mistreats him, he's outta here. Bye.

"Blood in My Eyes." Early favorite, and still intoxicating. Dylan is one of the few contemporary male singers who can sing about desire without trivializing it. (Prince is another; his poses on the subject get tiresome, but his performances remain the real McCoy.) A more devastating or sympathetic portrait of a dirty old man would be difficult to imagine. Dylan captures the shabby dignity of the narrator with great relish: "I tell you something, tell you the facts/You don't want me, give my money back." The story of the power women have over men is told four times in a row on this album, without rancor—on the part of the singer. The persona he inhabits in "Ragged & Dirty" is definitely peeved, and Cutty's anger at Delia has turned into a nightmare for himself and every other character in that narrative. But Dylan never suggests, at least to this listener, that the women in these songs are deserving of criticism or judgment. They are human beings, dealing with life as it is, and with the evident imperfections of these men they're involved with. To the men, however, they are almost forces of nature—certainly they hold their fates in their hands. Sexual power—not societal, but personal—is the subject here. Or one of the subjects. The singer in "Blood" has at least a little money (and a room to keep his tie in), the singer in "Ragged" has none, but they are equal in their powerlessness. Cutty, who makes the greatest show of power (shoots her down), is not coincidentally the most powerless of all (the woman in this song, Delia, is least like a force of nature and most like a character in her own right—she even has a name—this is presumably because it is the one song of the four told in the third person).

Conversely, the one character in the four songs who does not in any sense blame a woman for his troubles, the narrator of "Broke Down Engine," is easily the strongest, most attractive, most manly and vibrant of the lot, even as he begs on his knees for the Lord to bring him his woman back, even as he pounds futilely (but oh so musically) on her door. This song today strikes me as the hidden *tour de force* of the album (maybe I warmed to it slowly because I so love Dave Ray's very different 1965 version—don't even know Blind Willie McTell's original but will seek it out, box set coming soon). This man has no money and he tells us why—lost it gambling—takes responsibility, ain't necessarily feeling sorry for himself. Neediness don't have to be wimpiness, or self-pity. Listen to that guitar talking! "Feel like a broke down engine, ain't got no whistle or bell." Dylan tells us in his essay it's a song about trains, but that's misdirection—beyond the title simile, repeated several times, there's no trains here. It's not about variations of human longing, either, sweet though the phrase may turn, or dupes of commerce (which of course we all are), or Ambiguity, but somewhere in there he nails it okay, song and performance are most certainly and precisely about "revival, getting a new lease on life, not just posing there" (in the bare mattress room I envision the "Blood" narrator living in). This hero (he is a hero, him and Jack-A-Roe might be the only ones on the album, oh and the lone pilgrim I guess) embodies the reawakening human spirit, viscerally not intellectually, I mean listen to that guitar talking, listen to

196

that singer singing, "Lordy Lord, Lordy Lordity Lord, Lordy Lord, Lordy Lordy Lord." Feel like I ain't got no drive at all, and that surely is how he's been feeling, but in the very announcing of it exactly the reverse becomes true. Lordy Lord. What an extraordinary performance. She don't open that door, half the other women in the neighborhood will, 'cause authenticity rules. In the praying is the answer to the prayer.

I've said a lot about "Delia" already. Its sweet sadness is the heart of this album. The gentleness that's there in the first strummed notes of the performance, and never lets up for almost six minutes. New voice. New voice for every song. Same uncanny vocalist. He makes me care about people and situations I'd rather not even think about.

Dylan suggests in the liner notes, and I don't think it's misdirection, that "Stack A Lee" is about reputation. "All about that John B. Stetson hat" is gently ironic, Billy in any version of this song didn't care about the hat, he was a compulsive (gambler, cheater, thief, whatever), and "Stack A Lee" was "bound to" take his life because his treasured rep as a "bad man" was at stake, plain and simple. After you make a fool of a man, don't walk into his favorite barroom. Dylan calling this a "monumental epic" is also ironic, it's the least of the performances on the album, which I think is why the harmonica's brought in to add some color. Nonetheless it's well worth while, full of little riddles ("Harlan Alley"? "On an alley"?) and bursts of humor and pathos. If only these guys *were* dupes of commerce their fates might make more sense, but life was less simple once.

"Two Soldiers" is the longest tune on the record, and even so it's all compacted like a New York School poem or a *Readers Digest* novel. You have to fill in the part where the tall guy gives the Boston boy a message for his girlfriend; the climactic nondelivery of both messages presses them up against each other so close that if you're careless you might think it a song about incest instead of about war and loss and duty and bad luck. Over apple wine in Sacksenhausen last Frankfurt Book Fair, I watched the advance tape and the Walkman being passed back and forth amongst the cream of European intelligentsia, and I had to ask what part it was everyone kept rewinding to. It was the end of the vocal of this song, without a name or any knowledge of subject matter, just something in the sound of his voice that transfixed even those who weren't sure how they felt about the album as a whole. Months later I've decided that this was unconscious fascination (on the part of true fans) at the arrival of Dylan's *old man* voice, previewed perhaps on some of the Basement Tapes tracks but now here it is in the flesh, on the tape, in our present reality. Scarily beautiful (de gustibus non est disputandum).

In the notes to "Jack-A-Roe" we find what may be taken (indeed, may be intended) as an epigraph for this album: "Are you any good at what you do? Submerge your personality." Is Dylan boasting? Certainly the persona and personality of the songwriter is sub-merged on *World Gone Wrong*, no easy thread of autobiography may be found at all; instead the storyteller's professional, theoreti-cally impersonal selection of good stories to tell (picked to get a response). And yet this submersion leads paradoxically to a suffu-sion of personality, in which the performer might feel, at least for the moment, that no album he ever made has come closer to telling the truth about his private world. Self portrait. I like the tense strumming in this song, always suggesting that something exciting's going to happen (he strums more quietly when import-ant events are actually taking place), and the abstract moodiness of Dylan's voice with extra reverb on it ("My kind of sound is very simple, with a little bit of echo, and that's about all that's required to record it"—Dylan to Greg Kot, 1993). Speaking of echo, how about that great third line in each verse of this song, always starting "Ohhh . . ." and then repeating the last half of line two? Simple, and full of mystery. Singers are drawn to songs by such curlicues, and rightly so. Hints of the inner structure of the universe. Wonder why Dylan likes songs in which a woman passes herself off as a male (ask Lou Reed if the phrase sounds familiar to him) sailor? In addition to "Jack-A-Roe" and last album's "Canadee-I-O," he did a song in concert last year called "Female Rambling Sailor." His own answer is the "submerge your personality" line (oh, and tradition-ally in American lit we go to sea for discipline and freedom). Maybe it has something to do with his relationship with the Muse.

I see from reading other reviews that disagreements might arise as to which songs on *WGW* are third person or first person. I think of "World Gone Wrong," "Blood in My Eyes," "Ragged & Dirty," and "Broke Down Engine" as true first person, the form Dylan most often writes in. (Of these, "R&D" is directly addressed to another person, or maybe two of 'em. "Broke Down Engine" is a kind of soliloquy, sometimes addressed to the man's woman and sometimes to God or us or whoever's presumed to be listening. The two Mississippi Sheiks songs are addressed to a collective audience, with choruses that quote a line said by one person to another.) "Love Henry" is third person, omniscient narrator, told largely in dialogue. Interesting form. "Delia" is a third person narrative with a change of protagonists partway through. (The first person chorus phrase might throw people off. The narrator is quoting it. This is also true of the last two verses, in which the narrator seems to become the protagonist. Fascinating form.) "Two Soldiers" is third person, omniscient narrator, with some dialogue. "Jack-A-Roe" is a narrative told in the third person by a first person narrator—the singer takes on the persona of a storyteller, as opposed to just telling a story. This is communicated in the first verse—"The truth to you I'll tell"—and pays off in the last verse, with its bizarre, unexpected moral, a sort of advertisement, albeit an unconvincing one. Dylan definitely likes eccentricity in songs. Hence a version of "Stack-A-Lee" that omits gambling and seems to focus on the hat. Speaking of "Stack-A-Lee," it's the same as "Jack-A-Roe," although the first person narrator is extremely unobtrusive—I think I hear him refer to his own existence in the line "I heard a bulldog bark," but Dylan's diction in this song is elusive. It's also possible (but unlikely) that there's a reference to "our police."

Finally, "Lone Pilgrim" is a first person narrative (first verse) that quotes a first person monologue (the other three verses). This actually is closer to the third person narrative form, in my opinion, than it is to the first person songs listed above, in which the story being told is a personal one to the character the singer inhabits. But the point is quite arguable. I guess I'm saying the first person narrator of "Lone Pilgrim" is just a framing device, related therefore to the form of "Jack-A-Roe."

(I like examining such matters because they point, ultimately, to the question of who the person singing the album is, or claims to be. Who is he, anyway?)

I like "Lone Pilgrim" a lot. It's different, as a good last song should be. A country spiritual, while everything else on the album's a blues (the "first person" songs on my list, hmm) or a ballad (all the third person narratives). It's beautiful and eerie, like "Rank Strangers to Me" on *Down in the Groove* —always a good trick for an older artist to end an album with a song that could be about his own death ("weep not for me now I'm gone"). But "Rank Strangers to Me"s eerie beauty was bleak (loss of friends, as in "Delia"), whereas "Lone Pilgrim" is ecstatically serene. And how fitting, after all these songs of murder and death and guilt and haunting, to close with a character speaking of his own death with an acceptance beyond forgiveness ("the lunacy of trying to fool the self is set aside") and a simple need to pass on to those he's left behind the news that all is truly well with him. Great adverb images in this song: "pensively stood." "sweetly sleep." "kindly assisted." The guitar playing and lyrics and vocal communicate an extraordinary stillness, filled with comfort and deep insight. You could say, though obviously it's just a reviewer's conceit, that the album progresses from the implied atheism of "World Gone Wrong" through the fierce agnosticism of "Broke Down Engine" to the simple faith of "Lone Pilgrim." You could say all kinds of things. It's an album that allows you to have this kind of fun.

Just two more comments, then. One: it's a classic Dylan album, listenable and quotable. If I were writing a book about the effect that big money dominance of the news media and the entertainment industry has on individual writers and reporters and artists, I'd certainly call it *The Doors to Your Cage Shall Be Decked with Gold*. (The phrase is from "Love Henry.") And two: Dylan, by ending his liner note rant/essay with talk about "the Never Ending Tour chatter" (delightful!) makes a rare and welcome (if implicit) acknowledgment that Bob Dylan fans exist and make up a significant segment of his record-buying, concert-going audience. Who else would hear chatter about the Never Ending Tour? Who else would have access to playlists? (His dates are off a little, but what the hell. New Rising Sun Tour, anybody?)

19. The Supper Club Shows

An installment of my "You've Got to Hear This Tape!" column in On the Tracks, *written early in '94.*

"Suppers 1st & Last" is what my friend Blair cleverly scrawled on the label and is the subject of my sermon this evening. *Why only two?* some of you ask immediately, while the others want to know, *how can I get ahold of this?* Very few of you are unaware of the instant mystique that this venue name "The Supper Club" has acquired in our particular circle of hell, thanks to Bob Dylan's four performances there in two nights, November 16 and 17, 1993, 240 West 47th Street, Manhattan, Earth. (The Earth in which that archduke got assassinated in 1914, you know, the one with the fax machines.)

The answer to the latter question of course is, "Wait patiently for Bob and Sony to make it available to you through proper commercial channels, if ever," and the answer to the first question is, two is all I've got so far, and it's way past time to write this column. And anyway I hardly have space or time enough to talk about all the wonderful performances included in just these two sets. This is superb music, reminiscent in its generosity of Rolling Thunder in the early days (something about going back to New York City?) or the second Warfield stand (San Francisco, late 1980). You bet I want the other two shows, and I'd also like to be able to listen to all four "Queen Jane"s in a row, or all four "Ring Them Bells." Meanwhile here are a few notes on the incredible cornucopia of heart and creativity and musical warmth and vocal fire to be found in the ten songs of supper the first (audience about 400 people, plus camera and audio crew), 8 pm Tuesday, and the eleven songs of sup the fourth, 11 pm Wednesday. 1993 was a very good year for Bob Dylan fans, was it not? No, I didn't get to the NYC shows, and this time I really do envy Ian and Glen and John H and other friends and strangers who actually sat in on those "free concerts" and provided such a supportive audience. But hey, tapes will get you through times of no memory better than memories will get you through times of no tapes, I always say, mutter mutter . . .

The simple truth is, these performances represent yet another breakthrough for Bob Dylan. On his latest album he sings and plays old blues and ballads with more feeling and presence and musical sensitivity than on any other recorded session (i.e. a set of performances, not just one song) from throughout his career, with the possible exception of the 1962 Gaslight tape. Pretty amazing, and then here in these small-club New York City acoustic band performances (similar to the last two albums in that the underlying concept and context is intimacy, intimacy between performer and audience), Dylan comes very close to what must have been, quietly, another life-long goal: to return to something like the small-combo musical "feel" he achieved on his three 1965–66 albums, which he has famously described as "that thin, that wild mercury sound . . . the closest I ever got to the sound I hear in my mind."

Arguably all of Dylan's greatest live performances over the years (of which there have been many, quite a few of them in the last decade) achieve some kind of pure white-hot articulation and realization of "the sound he hears in his mind." That is what makes them great, that feeling of *arrival.* And I'm not even prepared to argue (yet) that these Supper Club shows are among his best performances. (Certainly I can imagine that they were among the best of all his performances to actually be present at, because of the smallness of the room, the unusual choice of songs, the quality of the singing, and that remarkable feeling of being part of a— positive, joyous—historical moment.)

But the breakthrough I think I hear on these tapes is related to the fact that this is not precisely a live show but a cross between a public performance and a studio recording. There is something very conscious and deliberate about the choice of material and the preparation of the band (symbolized perhaps by the identical "double-breasted suits with burgundy shirts" they're reportedly wearing). Dylan prepared this two-night stand with confidence and clarity and even a kind of vision. Dylan's vision is essential to his accomplishments as an artist—it was his vision, for example, that left him unsatisfied with the recordings he and The Band did for *Blonde on Blonde,* and led him ultimately to Ken Buttrey and the unique sound of those Nashville sessions. He was after something, and he intended to get it. This applies to his last-minute revisions of *Blood on the Tracks* as well. In the case of the Supper Club shows Dylan has recorded an entire album, with lots of outtakes, right in front of our eyes (or our ears, not to mention our hidden tape recorders). And the point is that he seems to have succeeded in these two days of performances in creating a fresh, sparkling group sound that has magic in it, a sort of perfect setting for the present-day Bob Dylan to sing in, one that naturally supports and echoes and amplifies the subtle nuances of his mood, how he feels today, the musical and emotional intentions he brings to this moment's performance. The thin metallic wild mercury sound is this plus a certain rhythmic groove and vocal texture, or more probably a set of grooves and textures, defined by the 1966 recording of "I Want You" or the 1965 recording of "Queen Jane Approximately" or (perhaps?) the 1993 recordings of both those songs and "My Back Pages" and "Weeping Willow Blues" and "Jack-A-Roe." A very Bob Dylan sound, indeed. And to achieve it consistently, in a loose-but-controlled recording situation, consciously but not overly self-consciously, is a breakthrough I believe Dylan has been reaching for (or running away from) for a long time.

The instrumental sound of this "album" is basically a chorus of strings with a beat in it, fretted strings, a little like an old-timey band, and lots of pedal steel guitar (frequently taking the place of a keyboard). Dylan's guitar is often the defining instrument, playing lead or sharing lead or leading the rhythm section. The vocals throughout are very open-throated, giving his voice an unusual texture (guttural but well-articulated; you can hear every word, and lots of great singing on the extended vowels; almost no mumbling). The music sounds like itself, no other category—maybe somewhere between country swing and rock and roll as the term was understood in the mid-1950s. Dylan the singer sounds like he's been listening to Jimmie Rodgers and Bing Crosby. Maybe even Sinatra at times. He likes the idea of being a singer of songs. Every one of the nineteen songs he sings over the course of these four shows seems to be here because the singer considers it a well-made song—good structure, strong message, distinctive melody, and highly singable. Thirteen of the songs were written by the singer, but he doesn't handle them like personal property (this is certainly not any kind of career retrospective). Instead, he treats all the songs with the affection and respect (and healthy disrespect) of a crooner, an old songplugger, just a guy with a band who never says a word but sings his heart out, happy to be here and playing for you tonight. (This is an act—"happy to be here" "just a guy with a band"—and a very charming one, climaxing with Dylan's delicious and startling "Aw shucks!" in "Weeping Willow Blues.")

The final show is extraordinary, "Weeping Willow," "Delia," "Jim Jones," "Queen Jane Approximately," "Jack-A-Roe" . . . but the opening show is no slouch, with definitive performances of "Tight Connection" and "Ring Them Bells," and a stunning "Disease of Conceit." (Joe I-Used-to-Be-a-Big-Dylan-Fan, if he reads this magazine, is scratching his head saying, "I've only heard of one of these songs." You don't know what you're missing, Joe. But at least Dylan isn't catering to you this time around.)

Even the lesser performances are full of pleasures. "Absolutely Sweet Marie," first song first night, suffers from a poor vocal mix, but there's lots of attractive phrasing if you listen for it, and the band is cooking, just raring to go from the first moment. "Lay Lady Lay" is unconvincing at both the first and fourth shows, but the *Nashville-Skyline*-like arrangement (taking advantage of the pedal steel) and vocal approach is striking, after all these years, and there are moments when Dylan's vocal gymnastics are most gratifying, particularly at the last show, when he is "mugging outrageously," as Ian Woodward reports, "bending and leaning and with exaggerated facial expressions." Somehow all this silliness makes the sleepy song come alive, and it's good to be reminded, as we wonder why Dylan chooses to perform so much, so tirelessly, that there's a lot of ham in the old boy yet. "Let me see me make you smile," he could be singing.

"Blood in My Eyes" can't match the humor and poignance of the *World Gone Wrong* vocal, but it successfully takes off in another direction; the band finds a honky tonk groove and milks it lovingly. Dylan's good-time-music ensemble is up and flying, and you can hear the bandleader relax about that and give his attention to his vocals instead, as the first set catches fire with an incandescent "Queen Jane."

Suddenly we're in a whole new world. I imagine each listener is thinking that he or she has always wanted to hear Dylan sing like this. There's a magical quality in his voice that seems to have everything to do with the *sound* of the song as performed by this band in this room. Voice and sound get together and reflect off each other with great delicacy and passion. The obvious high points of the performance are those exuberant howls on "pain" and "remain" and (sometimes) "Jane"; but the full emotional impact of the singing sinks in deepest as the melody is restated in the instrumental passages, between and after the verses. Now the sweet melancholy in the voice (reminiscent of the original recording of the song, and of "Born in Time"—*that* voice) can be fully absorbed and felt by the listener, as it echoes in this loose shimmering crescendo of melody and rhythm, Dylan on 6-string guitar, John Jackson on 12-string, Bucky Baxter on pedal steel, and Tony Garnier on stand-up bass, with Winnie Watson whacking away behind them. It's a painting. Dylan as Cezanne. The Tuesday 8 pm version is magnificent, as is Wednesday 11 pm, but this is one worth hearing in all permutations, because it can't come out the same way twice. If forced to choose, I might favor the first show version, for overall soulfulness and because of Dylan's haunting guitar solo (really a duet with Baxter) at the end. A sound painting. Dylan's instant confidence when he finds his musical footing, right song, right sound, right moment, is unmistakable. "Queen Jane"—finally, as sung tonight, a song of welcome, accepting and embracing the prodigal, whether lover, family member, audience, or oneself—is the centerpiece of these performances. It demonstrates that what Dylan can do with traditional songs on *World Gone Wrong*, he can do with his own songs too, if he likes them enough, if they happen to be the right song for this moment.

"Tight Connection to My Heart" (without the girl chorus the title is never mentioned, so Ian Woodward suggests it should be renamed "Has Anybody Seen My Love?") rates similar superlatives, except that this time the version from the first show leaves the later version in the dust. Indeed, the two together provide a perfect example of the difference between finding a groove and just going through the motions. When band and singer locate that groove, miracles happen. This November 16 "Tight Connection" is to me a defining performance, in which Dylan tells us everything we need to know about who he is as a singer and performer and songwriter, and why he continues to pursue his muse in this manner. Listen to the harmonica at start and end and tell me he hasn't recaptured wild mercury. Listen to the simplistic guitar riff (simple until you try to duplicate it) that runs all through this performance, insistent as a mountain creek in the rainy season. Listen to the singer's voice, not at all the gorgeous specific texture of "Queen Jane" but a whole other animal, and just as compelling. In some ways it interests me more because, of the quintessential Bob Dylans, this is one that many listeners have not yet encountered or opened their hearts to. Listen to how his voice opens up as he sings this song, filled with spirit like a room filled with sunshine and fresh air when shades and windows are opened. Every time I listen to the performance I am more excited by it, and more moved by its subtle beauty. Truly a springtime song, in its Supper Club interpretation, new flowering of the relationship between artist and muse. If this version doesn't make the "official album," I'll be heartbroken.

"Disease of Conceit," one of Dylan's best spiritual songs from the last ten years, here receives the interpretation it's been waiting for, far better than the album version. Again the band is spot-on, and there's an awesome confidence and power in Dylan's voice from the first moments. I could listen to him preach like this all night. His voice is filled with heart, and it breathes magic into the instruments that accompany it and carry on its work—most obviously the harmonica solo at the end, but every instrument in the band is aching with its need to successfully serve as a vehicle for this performance. Loving sensitivity to the melodic mood of the song is the secret this time (rhythm does play a part in this, in a subtle way). What a sound these players achieve! Maybe it has something to do with Dylan being willing to be a bandleader again, at least for this two-night stand.

Okay, "I Want You" is short of a masterpiece at this first show, but it sure is fun to listen to. Charming rhythmic groove (Dylan has always thrived on this kind of loose-as-a-goose ensemble approach), delicious breathless phrasing, neat musical swoops and time changes between verses (love that stand-up bass), he sings *all* the words (including the great impromptu line "and because I lied"), and finally that swell harmonica playfulness, and dramatic flamenco finale on top of it. You gotta smile.

And "Ring Them Bells." Now Dylan is really hamming it up, and he's entitled. Where'd that sweet fierce liquid vocal come from? It's fascinating to me that this is a piano song, like "Queen Jane Approximately," and in both cases Dylan sings with the confidence and exuberance of a man in a shower, a songwriter alone at his piano. He and his band (no keyboard player; he hasn't toured with one for six years) sound like they've *become a piano*, all those struck strings vibrating in orderly but free progressions, and Dylan's voice resonating with all of them. His confidence is understandable—he knows this crowd loves him, and he knows they're going to be thrilled that he's doing this song. It's like he's been saving it for such a moment, saving it to sing in cabaret. And he sings it so well. I'm particularly taken with the first show, where he repeats the bridge and the last verse. It's a very pretty, very generous performance.

And then "My Back Pages" and "Forever Young." "Ring Them Bells" is the climax of each set, I think, and seems to be performed almost as a pure celebration of singing; but these last two selections are about something, I mean something this singer wants to say on this particular evening. As a result, when I listen to the tape I often find these performances more moving than the show-stopper. I like the way Dylan sings when he's got a message to get across. He's not coy about it. In the first of these two songs he's singing about himself ("I'm younger than that now"). In the second he offers blessing and benediction ("may you stay forever young") to his listeners. And in both cases you can hear in his voice that he's speaking from his heart.

"My Back Pages" is as good a performance of the song as I can remember hearing. It rocks like an outtake from *Highway 61* yet aches with the beauty of the Rolling Thunder Tour version of "Hattie Carroll," from which this arrangement is partly borrowed. The band sounds great. Dylan sounds like he's singing autobiography, which he is.

And "Forever Young" is just really tender. I haven't always liked this song. I sure do tonight. Lots of great singing, and those long guitar passages—well, they're as soulful as, and really quite similar to, a Dylan harmonica solo on the right song on a good night. I like the music this man hears in his mind. And I love the way he puts it together out of the instruments that are available.

The last "supper" starts with "Ragged & Dirty." It's a perfunctory performance, a warm-up, Dylan doesn't take on the persona of the character but just sings the words, and the band flails away in generic fashion, and yet I have to admit there's something I like about it, the sound of Dylan's voice doing this kind of Saturday-night-rent-party uptempo easy blues singing is appealing, it tickles me. The set gets off to a slow start, pleasant "Lay Lady Lay" and ho-hum "Tight Connection," and then suddenly Dylan wakes up with a vengeance as he tackles the one completely unfamiliar song of the stand, apparently a Blind Boy Fuller tune called "Weeping Willow Blues."

The easy tempo of the song belies the incredible intensity of the singing. This time Dylan totally becomes the person in the song. In one sense it's like he has a closet full of voices, and he's been waiting decades for the opportunity to use this one; and at the same time this is the same Dylan voice we've always known, so alive and unmistakable, so personal, so thickly-textured . . . it's just that we've never heard it quite like this before. Like if you keep creating, keep performing, you keep getting down to deeper levels of self, and the funny thing is they can be so new and so familiar both at once. "You're gonna want my love, mama, some old lonesome day . . ." Like "Moonshiner" so many years ago, this is a unique, unsettling, unforgettable performance.

Just as it is tiring to hear certain songs over and over on recent Dylan tours ("All Along the Watchtower," "Memphis Blues Again," and "Tangled Up in Blue" have all outworn their welcome), so it is thrilling to hear Dylan attempt a song he has never (or seldom) sung in concert before. I like his November 17 performance of "Delia" a lot—it can't match the extraordinary beauty and sensitivity of the solo album version, but it doesn't need to. This is a new song, new version, performed with the band (I like the loudness of the drumming); Dylan respecting the song enough to take it on the road with him, try it on in front of an audience, see where it might take him. This is part of why I use the word "generosity" to describe this set of performances—Dylan, having already given us a near-perfect solo studio "Delia," now parts the curtain in effect to give us an alternate take, a look at him and the song going on with their relationship. More "Delia," more Dylan—both very welcome. Another side of . . . The band sounds so sweet. The live arrangement features all the verses of the recorded version, but grouped in threes with guitar breaks intervening, three sets of three verses and then two verses at the end ("Delia oh Delia," what the French call the *envoi*, hail and farewell). This structure actually makes the song more accessible, since each of the groups has a different set of characters (Delia and her parents in the first, Cutty and his pursuers in the second, Cutty and the judge and the jailhouse in the third) (always a judge somewhere on every Dylan album), and dividing them this way makes it easier to grasp the story. I wouldn't trade this version in for the album one (though if there was a fifth show, I'd like to hear where they could have gone with this), but I wouldn't want to live without it either.

Dylan on a roll follows "Weeping Willow" and "Delia" with yet another song not heard before at the Supper Club shows, "Jim Jones" from 1992's *Good As I Been to You*. This one, which did get regular airings on Dylan's spring/summer 1993 tour, is quite amazing; I daresay four out of five would call it an improvement on the excellent album version. You try these songs out, and sometimes they really come alive with the band and in front of an audience. Or they die one night, and achieve immortality another. What is it that makes this song about the hard life of an unrepentant convict (judge cameo in this one too) so appealing? Melody, lyrics (so visual, so immediate), Dylan's voice (that funny accent he takes on, probably straight from the record he learned this from), rhythm, narrative, but what all this adds up to (and it adds up so fabulously this particular evening) is the portrait of a life, not the events of the life but the immediate feeling of *being* this person, identifying with his situation. He's totally trapped, they've got him, it's been this way for years and he hates it ("I'd rather have died in misery") and yet on the evidence of this story/song/performance his spirit is unbroken. A joyous hymn of survival and defiance—getting inside the skin of someone so many miles and years and circumstances away from us can sometimes provide uncanny insight into our here and now.

And then "Queen Jane Approximately." Whichever version I'm listening to at the moment is my favorite, I think. Winston Watson sounds great. Reality is pierced (veil torn asunder) when Dylan screams "complain." Wow. "Ring Them Bells" a knockout again, fine showcase for Bucky Baxter on pedal steel. And I like the way the band plays the riff from 1992's "Pretty Peggy-O" at the end of the song.

The previous five performances are a hard act to follow, but "Jack-A-Roe" meets the challenge gleeflully. Dylan's having so much fun with this, and John Jackson's banjo playing is like a beacon in the wilderness, you can never get lost, just follow this note. This song about a powerful woman ("jackaroo" is Australian slang for new chum or novice, says the Oxford Dictionary; of course, she's also making a pun on her boyfriend's name) is just made for live performance. "This body you may imprison, this heart you'll never confine." Defiance again. And love conquers all.

"Forever Young" is the show-closer again, and then for the first time in four shows, Dylan comes back for an encore, "I Shall Be Released." Hopefully this won't be the last song of the video (done that already), but it's a better rendition than we've been used to in recent years. The band sound like they'd like to play all night. Dylan sounds relieved that he got through this, and maybe even a little pleased with himself.

There are shouts from the audience of "Thank you, Bob!" What else is there to say? For me it's a real keeping of the promise to see an artist retain his power and his daring and his sense of purpose and his imagination and his keen love for music year after year, decade after decade. Sets a good example. "Climb on every rung." Words to live by, til we sup again.

20. Live and in Person

After the Supper Club shows Dylan took his usual December break from touring. By February, he and his band were launching another year of touring, with eleven shows in Japan. A Japanese periodical called Music Magazine *asked me to write something for a special issue marking the tour. I wrote this piece in early February after a friend in Japan had phoned to tell me what songs were played at the first show.*

1986, 1987, 1988, 1989, 1990, 1991, 1992, 1993, 1994 . . . Bob Dylan's recent series of concerts in Japan marks the beginning of his *ninth* straight year of almost nonstop touring. He's made a few excellent albums during this time period (*Oh Mercy, World Gone Wrong*), but he's also made it abundantly clear in interviews and by his actions that making records is not so important to him. His real work is on stage.

This makes him a throwback, an anachronism. He's not comfortable on television, he's not a media personality, not an "entertainer," he doesn't even talk to his audience—but he's extraordinarily serious about the work, the creative artistry, of performing. For his February 1994 tour of Japan he reached into his songbook—easily the finest body of work of any American songwriter—and brought out two major songs that he has not performed for more than ten years: "Jokerman" (from 1983's *Infidels*) and "If You See Her, Say Hello" (from his 1975 masterpiece *Blood on the Tracks*). He didn't need to do this to impress the audience—a "greatest hit" like "Like a Rolling Stone," no matter how familiar, is a safer bet with any big-venue audience anywhere in the world. I assume he chose these as his opening songs for his new tour to challenge and stimulate himself—and thus give the audience a better overall show as a result. Because when Bob Dylan can get himself excited about the music he's making on a particular evening, he is one of the world's greatest living performing artists, comparable for example to the Pakistani Sufi vocalist Nusrat Fateh Ali Khan.

An example of Dylan at his finest occurred just a few months ago in New York City, at a tiny (400-seater) venue called the Supper Club, located close to the heart of Manhattan's old jazz district, at 240 West 47th Street.

He had just completed a relatively short tour (31 shows in 50 days) co-billed with Santana. He had a new album coming out that he was known to be very pleased with, and so perhaps he considered the benefits in terms of publicity, but mostly he seems to have been setting up an opportunity to make a live film, for broadcast or videotape, of himself and his band performing an acoustic set in a small-club environment, in front of a real (i.e. not television studio) audience. The result was four shows in two nights, November 16 and 17, 1993, at the Supper Club, all caught on film. The tickets were distributed free at a New York record store. I wasn't there, but have had the pleasure of listening to audiotapes made by a fan in the audience. (Audio recordings I believe are the best medium for appreciating musical performances—other than being there, of course. A video recording can be fun to watch and hear once or twice, but in the long run audio offers a much fuller musical experience. More information does not necessarily mean better art.)

From the point of view of those familiar with Dylan's work, his choice of material for these shows was just as thrilling as the intimacy of the setting. Another artist, hoping to sell the video footage to TV networks in the U.S. or overseas (which was supposedly Dylan's plan), might have opted for songs he was more used to performing or that would be recognized by a broader audience. But instead Dylan offered songs he rarely (if ever) sings in concert: his great 1989 anthem "Ring Them Bells," four traditional songs from his new album *World Gone Wrong* (including the magnificent "Delia"), "Jim Jones" from 1992's *Good As I Been to You*, and his 1973 hymn to his children, "Forever Young." Dylan's performances of "Queen Jane Approximately" (1965) were a high point of every set, arguably the most moving version of the song he's ever done. The relatively obscure "Tight Connection to My Heart" (1985) is an absolute delight at the first of these shows, Dylan and band falling into an irresistible rhythmic groove that climaxes with a little harmonica ecstacy. On songs like this we can hear the jazz singer in Dylan. Elsewhere (a marvelous, unexpected

"Aw shucks!" in the middle of "Weeping Willow Blues," a Blind Boy Fuller tune Dylan's never performed in public before), he reveals his love for country-and-western phrasing. As David Hinckley noted in his review of these shows for the *New York Daily News,* "Dylan has incorporated more styles into his own music than any other living artist."

My friends who were lucky enough to be present at the Supper Club shows report that Dylan was in unusually good spirits, clowning and making faces, obviously enjoying himself. The contrast between this New York City appearance and the Madison Square Garden extravangaza Sony Records put on for him in 1992 is striking. That 30th Anniversary Concert featured a lot of stars but not a lot of first-rate music. Dylan's own brief performance was adequate, dignified, forgettable. A "big event" that will mean nothing when people look back on the accomplishments of Dylan's career.

The Supper Club shows, on the other hand, are an artistic triumph, Dylan breaking new ground once again at age 52. They will be remembered along with so many other great Dylan moments: the Rolling Thunder Tour in 1975, the 1966 tour with The Band, his week of shows at the Hammersmith Theater in London in 1990. The musicians who played with Dylan at the Supper Club (the same band he brought with him to Japan except that in New York they played only acoustic instruments—Bucky Baxter on pedal steel guitar, Winston Watson on drums, Tony Garnier on bass and John Jackson on guitar and banjo) will forever carry a bit of glory for having been part of this moment.

But do not hold your breath waiting for the video to be released. The same Dylan who played and sang so joyfully in November, reportedly turned sour when he saw the footage, and declared the project dead. No Supper Club movie. It's a heartbreaker, but Dylan fans have been through this before. Dylan refused to release his greatest song of the 1980s, "Blind Willie McTell," for eight years— it didn't sound right to him. Dylan the critic does not always appreciate the genius of Dylan the performer.

The performer takes the criticism in stride, however. He's already getting ready for another tour . . .

21. "Hard Rain" in Japan

A "You've Got to Hear This Tape!" column from summer 1994.

"There's always new things to discover when you're playing live. No two shows are the same. It might be the same song, but you find different things to do within that song which you didn't think about the night before. It depends on how your brain is hooked up to your hand and how your mind is hooked up to your mouth."

—Bob Dylan, to Edna Gundersen, 1989

Yokohama, Hiroshima, Nara. 1994. If you read no further in this essay you will have picked up the essential information contained herein, three city names that, used properly, can serve as a map to where the latest installment of the treasure is hidden. Dylan is a master. I weep with frustration at sitting down to write this column, because it seems so petty, almost demeaning, to follow behind a master artist as he works, rummaging in his shards, forever calling for attention to one more bold, unexpected, triumphant experiment, one more major statement tossed off in the course of a night's work, one more act of rediscovery, reinterpretation, musical spiritual emotional reawakening. Have I no life of my own? Haven't I said all this before? Yes, yes, but the other side of my dilemma is that the opportunity to speak about such marvelous new work is almost irresistible to me, I wanna put in my two cents' worth, wanna bask in the approval bestowed on those who lead their friends to Something Worthwhile. Wanna share my enthusiasm. And it's somehow both thrilling and exhausting—trying to keep up with this 53-year-old dynamo—that 1994 turns out to be yet another year for the Dylan connoisseur to be enthusiastic about. Not every show, of course, nor even every tour; but you almost can't go wrong grabbing a '94 tape if it says on the label—referring to the contents, not the object—"Made in Japan."

No two shows are the same. I wanted to write about Hiroshima here (2/16/94; a significant location, honored with an appropriate and splendid benchmark, the first acoustic "Masters of War" since 1963), a tape recommended to me by several friends, and then Yokohama (2/7/94, second show of the tour) started tugging at my sleeve, whispering, "yes, Hiroshima is a stunning performance, a perfect showpiece, but I'm so much more idiosyncratic, full of personality, unconscious emotional imagery, the kind you like, less impressive but more expressive . . ." I waffled. I'm fascinated by both. And these are long shows, close to two hours. Full of riches. I can't get to know their songs as well as I'd like to before I start critiquing. And good as they are, they make me curious about the other shows in the series, I want to check out variant "If You See Her, Say Hello"s, I want to hear a Japan '94 version of "Born in Time." And then there's this coda, return to Japan, May 20, 21, 22, "The Great Music Experience," that *must* be heard. Andy Muir called from England to say he thought the TV broadcast version (May 22) might be the best "Hard Rain" ever. At the very least, the Nara shows are one of Dylan's most unusual performances in a lifetime of musical innovation. The present-day artist refuses to roll over and play dead.

"The Great Music Experience" shows in Nara are unique because Dylan is performing with a symphony orchestra. What is significant about this is not simply the instrumentation or the sound—although I can't think of another occasion, except a couple of songs from *Self Portrait* that may well be overdubbed, when Dylan has performed with a string backing (a single violinist, i.e. Rivera or Mansfield, is something else). But what happened in Nara that is truly special is that Dylan, of his own free will (i.e. not some big benefit wingding group encore where he stands on stage looking trapped and pretending to sing, or a guest session where he politely mumbles a few words under someone else's instruction) and even with rehearsals aforehand, is singing (live) to arranged orchestration rather than with a band that is playing with him in the sense of following (or attempting to follow) his lead. The singer's relationship with the instrumentation is entirely different. Although he almost certainly arranged or helped arrange the

215

music as performed, what is unique, and very daring in terms of Dylan's artistic methodology, is that at the moment of performance he is singing to an arrangement that is essentially fixed rather than fluid, an instrumental performance that he cannot even pretend will be influenced (except disastrously) by what he as singer and guitarist does with the beat, the tempo, or any of the other structural elements that are the essence of the kind of music he makes when he performs with a band.

In theory, the outcome of this experiment should be awkward, stiff, and, to the true fan, weirdly fascinating, similar to Dylan's "acting" in *Hearts of Fire.* Dylan is trying to do something that is not in his nature, and as a singer he is nothing if not a natural. He has that natural, idiosyncratic swing, and when he connects with the ball it's partly because he can hear *it* singing to *him* from the moment it leaves the pitcher's hand. To such a talent, the freedom to be oneself is everything.

I do hear some of that expected stiffness and discomfort on "I Shall Be Released" (May 22; Dylan did the same three songs each night, but I haven't heard tapes of May 20 or 21 yet), but the problem if there is one lies in the peculiar inelasticity of this particular song, in my opinion. Dylan gives a fresher, more imaginative performance of "I Shall Be Released" at Nara than he did on almost any of the many Never Ending Tour and post-NET shows that this song showed up in . . . but it still defeats him. At the very least, the song needs a more original arrangement to give the singer something to work against; this version, like the NET ones, keeps drifting inexorably towards muzak. Maybe an impromptu TV performance with a neo-punk band like Green Day would work better (I can see him snarling "every man who put me *here!,*" looking directly at David Letterman).

But "Hard Rain" is an absolute triumph, and "Ring Them Bells" at least a worthy addition to the canon. Dylan the singer rises to the challenge gloriously. Rising to a challenge onstage as a singer, particularly of his own songs, particularly of his own familiar songs, is something that is very much in Dylan's nature, and so he aproaches this unusual situation not as someone else's idea that he's trying to come to terms with but as his own creative puzzle that he arrived at and accepted spontaneously and willingly. Not that playing with an orchestra was his idea, presumably, but neither are the various challenges that come up in the course of a lively band performance his idea or anyone's idea—they are simply circumstances that allow one to make new discoveries, depending on how brain and hand and mouth are hooked up this time.

I'm not sure I like the arrangement of "Ring Them Bells," but I love the way the musical circumstance seems to inspire Dylan to reinvent the song (which had fallen into a rather anthemic groove, albeit a lovely one, at the Supper Club shows) line by line and vocal phrase by vocal phrase. This version competes for vocal expressiveness with the original studio recording—with the result that simple phrases like "the world's on its side" suddenly burst into unexpected new realms of imagery and meaningfulness. This is yet another example of the huge gap between printed word and performed word in terms of communicative content. I've heard Dylan sing of "lost sheep" before in this song, but it never reached my heart, never began to mean as much to me, as it does now. "Bells." "Willows." "Mountains." "Sheep." Something is building from noun to noun, consonant to consonant, breath to breath—and when it climaxes, we feel, hear and see the breadth of the singer's great vision. Out on the intercontinental hookup, the song has started to become something closer to what it always wanted to be.

And "Hard Rain" is thrice as astonishing. I can see I'm not going to get to Hiroshima and Yokohama this month—I'm writing this by hand in a Montreal hotel room, the deadline is long past and this is the first hour I've had to call my own in two weeks (I'm road managing a low budget rock and roll tour)—but I urge you to check out those exceptional concerts anyway (with special attention to "If You See Her" and "It Ain't Me Babe" in Yokohama, and "Don't Think Twice" and "Masters of War" and "Under the Red Sky" in Hiroshima).

"Hard Rain." Watch the video a few times, maybe invite some friends over, and then stash that thing away. The audiotape is what matters, the proper and correct form (sez me) for appreciating this latest masterpiece. What a *musical* performance! It flows and flows, straight and steady up the ladder of attention and intensity from first questioning ("Where have you been?", gentle insistent hovering strings like they've never not been there) to final earnest apocalyptic response (". . . gonna fall!" Bam Crash Boom crescendo down all the funny stairs in creation all at once). And Dylan sings.

He has arguably sung better than this, but not a lot better, and he has certainly never sung in quite this fashion before. It's the national anthem at a baseball game. Absurd, bombastic, imposs-ible, and he pulls it off. With unspeakable dignity. And soul.

What matters is the way he as singer leans on and leans into the music. He is hearing something, and that's where all his great performances come from. Like Van Gogh, like Da Vinci, the man's a visionary. Goes into a trance. Makes a connection. I like to think the connection is with the individual (and collective) listener, but that's a leap of faith. What is more measurably true is that the connection is with the song and with the music being made in the present tense by his accompanists. He sings on, into, and with. He leans on something. That's when the magic happens.

Richard Meltzer once suggested that Jimi Hendrix reversed the polarity of our universe when he played the guitar with his teeth, because no one had ever played on stage from that side (audience side) of the guitar before. In my funny brain, Bob Dylan singing live to a fixed arrangement is a similar turnaround, like playing a guitar with fixed strings that cause your fingers to vibrate at various frequencies. Dylan has to turn his method precisely inside out here. He must lead this unresponsive band by making everything else in his perceived universe shape itself to the tempo and format the band (orchestra) is laying down.

Possibly the success of this particular performance stems from the fact that Dylan, in the course of these rehearsals and perform-ances, has found himself back in a space of total risk and total commitment that normally exists only when recording a magnum opus like "Hard Rain" for the first time. It is as though no one has ever heard the song before, and he cares mightily about getting it across, cares more than his conscious mind would ever want to admit to itself. Sings like there's no tomorrow, like he's recording "Mr. Tambourine Man" or "Like a Rolling Stone" or "Blind Willie McTell." Sings (as in those other instances) in a way he's never sung before, which is what makes it so risky, so exciting, so necess-ary. One does this for oneself, not for the fans or posterity. You do it because you find yourself in the middle of the work, and you can't rest until you finish and find out how close you could come to your felt vision.

Dylan (I've said before) is an artist. This is not a matter of my judgment, or posterity's judgment. It's a matter of why he does what he does, what really motivates him (regardless of what he may say in interviews). For the artist, the work itself is the leader—the unfinished work, not one's conscious ideas or intentions or pretensions but something inchoate, still seeking form, wanting to come into existence. Long after worldly ambition is dead and buried, the painter paints and the performer performs, driven by something inside (or wherever it is) that insists on taking form. Something new. Something (on a good day) unexpected. Something insistent. You ignore it and ignore it and it won't go away. You maybe run to the edge of civilization and beyond, like Jonah, and it pursues you. You try to die, and it won't let you. Might as well surrender. You could even learn to enjoy it. Again. And again. And again.

The price you have to pay to get out of going through all these things twice? Vulnerability. Willingness to risk. To surrender your crown. Listen. Listen to Bob Dylan in Nara, Japan, May 22, 1994, singing "I've stumbled on the side of twelve misty mountains." Like he means it. And he does. He has. And he's still stumbling. Like a beacon in the night. Or a thief.

You can hear it in his voice.

22. *Unplugged*

This is a review of the TV show (the album and videocassette would be released months later), written December 15th–16th 1994, not for a Dylan magazine this time, but for the general public, the readers of the San Diego Reader, *the weekly newspaper in my new hometown.*

Everything is a box within a box. Part of what I like about good music is that it cuts through the containers and makes them disappear, at least while it's playing (and I'm listening). Bob Dylan is one of a generation (or two) of modern artists who have found ways, at least temporarily, to present themselves within a box of their own invention, rather than one of the preexisting boxes that society eagerly provides for us to lay ourselves out in. Elvis was another. With the help of Sam Phillips and Tom Parker and happy accident, but mostly by the power and tenacity of his own inarticulate youthful vision (see Peter Guralnick's great new biography, *Last Train to Memphis*), Elvis opened a tear in the cultural fabric where none existed before and sat himself down in it. Dylan followed his example, and Woody Guthrie's, and James Dean's and Little Richard's and Billie Holiday's . . . And now at the end of 1994 I am watching Bob Dylan stick his head and his voice out of the box that is MTV (*MTV UNPLUGGED!*), watching the long string of quick slick ads for Calvin Klein, Kenwood, Chess King, Twix, Contour, Sprint, Levis, & MTV between each Dylan song, and wondering what I think about this.

I think, first of all, about the performance. Dylan is a musician, this is a musical performance whatever the context, and I want to hear it and watch it and feel it and receive it and like it or dislike it as the case may be. This is a little bit difficult, when it's two songs and a string of ads, two songs and a string of ads, one song and more ads, etc. How I am as a listener certainly depends partly on my ability to concentrate and pay attention, and I'm a little distracted here. And so is the performer. He doesn't have the ads to contend with, but he is confronted constantly with all the little aspects of Playing in a Box that Ads Built. How much thigh does he have to show (metaphorically of course) to be as worthy of attention as the Calvin Klein ad? Is he, like President Clinton, forced to find himself thinking about important issues like, if I keep my cool, will I be given credit for having kept my cool, or will I be vilified for not having been some other way that would have been more appropriate? How am I going to be spun?

Ahem. The performance. The performance. I'm amazed at what a good job Dylan does in an environment (standing before a TV camera) that he is usually extraordinarily uncomfortable in. Dylan fans are used to coworkers and others who don't share their fanaticism smirking and jeering after seeing "your hero" on Letterman or the Grammys or some such thing the night before. This MTV appearance was no embarrassment. It was probably a triumph. We shall see. (The official *Dylan Unplugged* album is apparently scheduled for release February 7th. Will it sell any better than the normal Dylan release, even a work of near-genius like 1993's *World Gone Wrong*? Up to #33 the second week, gone from the charts the fourth week after all the true fans have rushed to get their copies . . .)

It was not a great show. I read in the *San Diego Union-Tribune* that the November 18th soundstage performance that seven of these eight TV songs were taken from was "breathtaking in a way that no Dylan concert in recent memory has been." I believe that it was breathtaking. Bob Dylan is my favorite living performer. And I understand that by "recent memory" the writer (George Varga) means his own memory, the shows he's happened to see. But it sounds as though he's saying that it's the first outstanding concert Dylan has given in years, which is a very backhanded compliment and not true to boot.

Dylan has given a series of magnificent performances in 1994: at Hiroshima in February and those Japanese concerts in general; at Nara (Japan again) with a symphony orchestra in May, delivering one of the greatest "Hard Rain"s of his career; in Europe in July in fine voice (some say Prague was the high point, others Kiel, others Besançon in France); at the Woodstock Festival in August; at Roseland Ballroom in New York City in October (and other fall east coast shows). Quite a year. Collect the tapes. The Unplugged show provides some moments that give a very good indication of what all the fuss is about. A decent place to begin. But not to be confused with the kind of first rate, worthy-of-a-legend performance that you have a more than even chance of seeing if you go to any regularly scheduled (not made-for-TV) Bob Dylan concert.

Dylan's edited-for-TV (from two evenings of live performance in a New York City recording studio in front of an invited audience) MTV broadcast was an hour long (which means 48 minutes of music, eight songs). Surprisingly, this is the longest performance that Dylan has done specifically for television that has ever been aired in the U.S. (he recorded one other about as long for the BBC in London in 1965). He did have a truly great one-hour television concert (that baffled most viewers) in 1976, called "Hard Rain," but it was actually a well-shot film of a regularly scheduled concert, outdoors in the rain at Colorado State University, Fort Collins, the night before Dylan's 35th birthday.

On MTV, we see (amidst shots of airbrushed kids in and out of expensive clothing, and previews of upcoming Beavis & Butt-head episodes) (really) Dylan and his five-piece sort of acoustic band, performing "All Along the Watchtower," "Shooting Star" (from 1989's *Oh Mercy*), "Rainy Day Women" (not as appropriate as it was at Woodstock; at least, the cameras didn't show anybody lighting up), "With God on Our Side," "The Times They Are A-Changin'," "Dignity" (a sort of new song, first recorded in 1989 but unreleased until 1994, when it was redone to be the one unfamiliar track on a piece of record company "product" called *Bob Dylan's Greatest Hits Volume III*, just out for hit-filled Xmas shopping, to be followed by years as a loss-leader in record club ads), "Knockin' on Heaven's Door," and "Like a Rolling Stone." Of these, "All Along the Watchtower" is well played, maybe thrilling if you haven't already seen it even better in concert during the past few years or on the Woodstock broadcast. "With God on Our Side" is a striking song (though a little dreary musically, except in the lovely Wire Train version), seldom done by Dylan, and it starts with some fascinating uncharacteristic full-throated ballad-singer vocalizing. You can hear him thinking, "Ha, bet you didn't know I could do that!" Things taper off from there, a moody performance that highlights the words very well but doesn't seem to me to have the ring of conviction. Dylan delivers song as song here, not as statement, and he has a right to, but on this particular evening "God on Our Side" lacks the fire so evident, for example, on his 1994 performances of "Masters of War." "Shooting Star" also pulls its punches, mumbling instead of really asking the audience if he "ever became what you wanted me to be," but it does feature a charming little guitar solo from Dylan (the audience cheers). "Rainy Day Women" is its usual forgettable self except for some nice half-improvised lyrics (". . . stone you like being hit by a truck!").

Jann Wenner, in a special year-end editorial on the first inside page of *Rolling Stone*, usually reserved for high-rolling advertisers, calls the Dylan Unplugged performance "brilliant and passionate. I watched him sing 'The Times They Are A-Changin'' as if he had written it yesterday. The words 'He that gets hurt will be he who has stalled' sounded as true and urgent as they did 31 years ago." I love the kind words for my hero, and I appreciate and endorse Wenner's comments on the need for handgun control in the following paragraphs, but on the music critic level I have to disagree with my longtime colleague. Dylan's performance of "The Times" is tepid. And in this case, who could blame him? He was singing ten days after the November elections. If he really had written it yesterday, he would necessarily be singing it from a Newt Gingrich or Rush Limbaugh perspective, especially the quoted lines, which basically say, "get out of our way or you'll be flattened." If I were him, I'd have scrapped this number and done a cover of Jim Morrison's "Strange Days have found us," instead.

But everything comes together, and those "brilliant passionate breathtaking" adjectives become applicable (hey, if I'd been lucky enough to be at the taping, like Jann W. and George Varga, I'd have been over the top too—Dylan has that power, even when he's half faking it—and besides, they saw six more songs that weren't included in the broadcast), in the next two numbers, "Dignity" and "Knockin' on Heaven's Door."

"Dignity" is a very, very good Dylan song—until I heard this live version (second public performance; the first was the night before) I didn't realize how good. Like any proper Dylan fanatic I've had a tape of the song since it leaked out maybe three years ago, and I was charmed and impressed but I hadn't fallen head over heels the way I did for two other left-off-of-*Oh-Mercy* outtakes, "Series of Dreams" and "Born in Time" (oh what a fine songwriter he can still be when he gets in the mood!). But the new arrangement improves the song significantly, suddenly it's transformed from a clever bit of writing "in the style of Bob Dylan" to a playful profound witty rock-n-rollin' delight, words like tumbling tumbleweeds and almost all of them zingers, and the live MTV version is better than the album track. It cooks. Brendan O'Brien (sometime producer of Pearl Jam, the first keyboard player to accompany Dylan in concert in seven years) gets the organ pumps just right, the rest of the band hit that groove that is so fine whenever they find it, and Dylan is completely into the performance, putting his presence and per-sonality and energy and sly humor into every word he sings, all 16 verses of this somehow suddenly irresistible epic.

> "Got no place to stay, got no coat
> I'm on a rolling river, in a drunken boat
> Trying to read a letter to me somebody wrote
> About Dignity."

(The first of several tricks in the song is that dignity may be a character's name: "Someone got murdered on New Year's Eve/ Someone said Dignity was the first to leave." Narrator and everyone else in the song have been searching for it or him or her ever since. "Poor man looking through painted glass/for Dignity.")

I don't know if *Greatest Hits Vol III* is worth buying for this one song, but *Dylan Unplugged* will definitely be, and if we're lucky it will also include "Knockin' on Heaven's Door." This is the sort of Dylan performance I live for. The band finds a groove that makes the singer light up like a Roman candle, which just pushes them deeper into the groove, and the result is pure pleasure from start to finish. While Dylan on "With God on Our Side" seems to be "just trying to get the song right" (and doing a responsible job of it), here he is completely set free, his voice dancing between octaves till he sounds like he's duetting with himself, hamming it up but in that Hank Williams fashion that somehow opens a space for utter, hair-raising authenticity. Gooseflesh. We are feeling the singer's feelings, and they are huge and rich and visionary and complex. Suddenly the song becomes an open canvas, ready to take on whatever meaning may be hovering in the room and in the

224

collective attention of the vast satellite-and-cable audience. "Mama wipe the blood outta my face/I just can't see through it any more." Dylan's on top of the song and the moment, he has a tiger by the tail and he loves it, at one point he turns to the bass player and grins, and at the end of this second verse comes the predictable and necessary apotheosis, the first really heartfelt harmonica solo of the evening, beautiful mournful blast followed by some sweet rockabilly chugging, technically simple but there's such an enormous amount of feeling in it. The harmonica sounds like Neil Young as much as Dylan, and indeed they're doing the song with Neil chords (and, someone suggested, Eddie-Vedder-influenced vocals), it makes you think from the first notes, "helpless helpless helpless helpless" (as my girlfriend pointed out).

Speaking the language of rock and roll. And the language of pure feeling. And some kind of universal variation on the English language that is understood across a hundred cultures. "Mama wipe my guns into the ground," Dylan sings, it's a mistake (moving himself back to the correct verse after the first two words), but instead of faltering he leans into those "wrong" words so hard the audience cheers spontaneously (even MTV couldn't have set this up). Something opens in the listener, an emotional vulnerability and excitement, and the next words "I just can't fire them any more" seem to speak volumes. This includes but goes far beyond Jann Wenner's call for handgun control; it could speak for example of Dylan's guns of ego or intellect or fame or maleness or ambition or name-your-poison. It speaks to me of my guns, and to us of ours. It's full of energetic weariness, *fin de siècle* anomie while getting ready for the next millennium. A song also and always about personal death, how it hovers close, and as often as not I imagine Dylan sees that memorable scene he wrote the song for (from *Pat Garrett & Billy the Kid*), old sheriff dying dramatically (and with dignity), he and his wife saying goodbye. Dylan's voice soars. Everything has led up to this moment. The harmonica solo sounds partly as though he's just having such a pleasure of rediscovery, playing this song with an organ in the mix for the first time since Benmont Tench in 1987. Grooving. Just getting into it. And his voice wailing, opening those pipes like Sinatra on a good roll. Or Sam Cooke. Technical limitations seem to disappear as Dylan rests simply and magnificently on his genius.

One of the reasons there are fanatical Dylan fans is that this sort of performance is transcendent but not all that uncommon. The man lives to perform, does 80–100 shows a year every year for a decade without stopping, for relatively little money (often playing 3000-seaters). He's like an old Shakespearean actor. He lives (and finds God) on the boards. This ain't your Eagles or your Rolling Stones or your (sorry) Barbra Streisand. This is more like Jacques Brel or Edith Piaf. This is singing for the sake of music, for the sake of communion with an audience (yes, even though he never talks), for the sake of song.

One more thing that Dylan's amazing "knock knock knockin'" calls to mind is that the essence of Dylan's gift is idiosyncracy. He doesn't sing like other singers. The good things he does are not the good things you're "supposed to" do. They're weird and different and inventive and original and real. Even after 34 years on the road, and why not? His model is not the pop singers, who often lose their fire. His model is the old blues singers, who grew into their voices as the decades went by.

"Like a Rolling Stone," the final song of the TV hour, is anti-climactic. Dylan enunciates well and imaginatively, especially on the verses, but the song lacks feeling and even manages to be kind of shapeless. The band never finds the groove, not even close, and this one time the organ player doesn't seem to have a clue. (Are you sure we did this at rehearsal?) In general, the issue of Dylan's enunciation is an intriguing one. As I say, he has sung very well through most of 1994, as the pay-per-view world learned from his astonishing, riveting, truly masterful Woodstock performance. But on this Unplugged show he seems to be consciously working to project each syllable, as if this one time by God no one was going to accuse him of mumbling! Very good. I always like it when he finds new ways to experiment with his singing. It tends to awaken his creative juices. At the same time, however, I've seen and heard superb Dylan concerts that sounded like mumbling to the uninitiated (fans who haven't heard him in recent years). Good art is often a language, and when you come in in the middle of the conversation it may take a little while (unless you're very open and unjudgmental) to get into the flow of it. Dylan sounded strange the first time you heard him. He still does. I don't blame you for being disappointed if you paid all that money and you don't recognize any of the songs. But that doesn't mean he isn't doing something absolutely wonderful out there. Come back tomorrow night, it may start to make sense to you.

A Dylan-watcher will tell you that he sits down, or half sits down, during many of the Unplugged songs, which is very unusual. His odd posture of having maybe an eighth of his butt on the stool is perhaps his way of trying to cooperate with the show's request (we want you guys to sit here and strum your acoustic guitars) while continuing to do whatever it is he always does. What's also surprising is how relaxed he is, quite unlike his usual television demeanor. This may be a matter of having just the right amount of alcohol in his system (although that approach hasn't been too reliable for him in the past), and certainly it reflects a whole process of coming to terms with the idea of an audience of electronic strangers (his ability to do such a blistering performance at Woodstock knowing the cameras were on him, and broadcasting live, was the real shocker). But my opinion is that his secret weapon's the sunglasses.

Dylan wears sunglasses throughout the Unplugged performances, until a bit of pleasant semi-staged business shaking hands with audience members after the last song. This (the shades) is not normal for him. Certainly it's a way of dealing with the bright lights, but I think it's also a simple solution to the self-consciousness Dylan has always felt when showing his naked singing face to the camera. In this program we see his head but not his face. He's wearing a mask. And it works for him. It actually helps him to get into character. "Ya wanna see my soul, listen to the music. But you're welcome to stare as much as you want at my Bob Dylan mask."

I suppose you might envision a *Dylan Unplugged* program as a return of the pre-1965 folksinger, alone with his acoustic guitar and his harmonica rack. In fact, Dylan recently recorded two albums of completely solo performances—but he hasn't given a concert like that for 29 years, and every single song on this program is performed together with a five-piece band. (And the organ and pedal steel guitar aren't unplugged, but that's standard for this show. The word Unplugged is a brand name now, like Chevy Nova.) Apart from Brendan O'Brien on keyboards, the band is Dylan's road band. The newest member of the troupe, Winston Watson, an outstanding young drummer, has been playing with Dylan for more than two years (200+ shows). Bucky Baxter, who gives Dylan's sound a unique flavor with his gifted harmonics on pedal steel guitar, dobro, and mandolin, joined the band almost three years ago, March 1992. That leaves the veterans, John Jackson on guitar and Tony Garnier on bass (acoustic only on this show; but he plays both standup and electric in regular concerts), who have now been with Dylan longer than any other musicians he's ever worked with—four years for Jackson, an astonishing five and a half years for Garnier.

The band is only as good as Dylan allows them to be, which varies quite a bit. On a good night, they can be spectacular.

So the Unplugged show is only a half-good night, although any show that includes performances like Nov. 18th's "Knockin' " and "Dignity" gets a few stars beside it in my book. But to a certain extent the story of the Dylan fan is the fish story of the one that got away, that extraordinary track that was recorded at the sessions but didn't get put on the album, that amazing concert that was videotaped for TV but never released to the public because Dylan said no. And this Unplugged show, and its album (which could turn out very good or very uneven, depending on what's selected), will probably always live in the shadow (among the cognoscenti) of Dylan's first effort at providing a show for the Unplugged series (we think that's what he was doing, although it was also rumored that he might offer it to whichever cable channels, here or abroad, were most interested).

It was fall of 1993, same city, same band except for O'Brien, almost the same dates (Nov. 16 and 17). Dylan played four free shows in a 500-seat venue called the Supper Club (also midtown, also on the west side). The videos have not (yet) leaked out, but audiotapes made by audience members reveal a set of Dylan performances so rich and surprising and musically brilliant that they could make the case for Dylan as an important artist of our era all by themselves. With his own camera and audio crew under circumstances that he determined, Dylan sings and plays songs he's never played live before as well as reinventing seldom-heard classics like "Queen Jane Approximately" and "Ring Them Bells" and "Tight Connection to My Heart." The band is so tight and the singing so expressive and joyous and soulful I'd have to go totally over the top to begin to describe it (no, I wasn't there, alas). And then Dylan looked at the footage and decided he didn't like it, didn't like the way he looked or the way the audience looked or something. I mean I remember praying silently, if you don't like the video, why don't you please just release a double CD of selections from the shows?, but . . . And now with the *Unplugged* album coming out (allegedly—but with Dylan you never know till it's in the stores) the Supper Club shows are buried history. After 29 years it is rumored that the legendary "Royal Albert Hall" concert by Dylan and The Band will be officially released this year. Can Halloween 1964 and New Orleans 1981 and the Supper Club 1993 be far behind? Don't hold your breath . . .

I have my own ideas, not about why the 1993 acoustic show videotapes were rejected, but about why Dylan made the uncharacteristic effort to squeeze himself into the MTV box, your standard legendary performer in his casual (could I have a word with the assistant casting director in charge of the second two rows of the audience, please?) runthrough of semi-unplugged greatest hits and current misses. I don't think he's trying to sell records (though I trust he did get a fee or an advance or something, that's always nice). I think what really interests him is building up the audience for his live shows, which has been slowly but steadily shrinking so that it's harder and harder to find gigs that pay the bills and offer at least the hint of a profit to justify spending one's life at this crazy occupation. Woodstock was a gamble for Dylan, who doesn't like to play for audiences that may or may not be interested in hearing him (he was rattled when he shared the bill with the Grateful Dead, I heard him say to the audience at one of the shows, "I think I've got a line on you now"), and who has never been at his best when he's felt the hot breath of the camera on his eyebrows (not for nothing did he make a film called *Eat the Document*). The gamble paid off handsomely. He played extraordinarily well—you could see that he was really putting an effort into it, his intention was transparent and thrilling—and the kids loved it, and maybe Dylan began to dream again of shaking off the nostalgic boomers and the idly curious (wanna be able to say I saw Bob Dylan), and building a fresh/young audience of his very own. Maybe enough to make it back to the 5000-seaters. Whatever it takes.

Dylan and Calvin Klein and Beavis & Butt-head did not look particularly attractive together, but Dylan unlike Presley is in very little danger of living out his life a prisoner of popular culture. There was a lovely moment at the end of the vocal during Dylan's TV performance of his smash new single, the master singing "Sometimes I wonder what it's gonna take/To find dignity" and gesturing to his fellow musicians or himself or somebody, in acknowledgement of this MTV-rented, Sony-owned soundstage, and the camera pointed at him, and the unavoidable irony of the situation. He seemed to shrug. And then he sang and played a "Knockin' on Heaven's Door" to die for.

23. Prague and Glasgow, spring '95

This is another "You've Got to Hear this Tape!" column from On the Tracks; *this time I talked about a tape, and a show I saw, and some shows I didn't see. I'm not the only Dylan fan whose yearly travel plans are largely determined by where the concerts are. Thank you, Bob Dylan, for introducing me to Prague. I expect to go back many times, whether you're playing there or not.*

Hello out there. It's late July 1995, another busy, surprising, rewarding year on the Dylan trail. He's in Spain tonight, already performing his 70th show of the year, and if I were hooked to the Internet I could probably click a mouse and find last night's set list. What an amazing hobby we have! I do love being part of a community united by our common appreciation of and keen attention to the work and performances of a living artist.

"There's a certain part of you that becomes addicted to a live audience," Dylan told Edna Gundersen this spring. Well, Bob, it works the other way around, too. And those of us who've seen you in 1995 have reason to be more strung out than ever. "Well, it's all up from Florida at the start of the spring . . . we're following them dusty old fairgrounds a-calling."

1994 was another good year, but circumstances kept me from catching any shows, and I only saw two in '93. So I swore to myself that I would jump at the first opportunity, regardless of time/money considerations, to see a batch of Dylan concerts in '95.

Some of you know I cracked my head this spring in a bicycle accident, and by the time the Dylan roadshow returned to California at last (we do get impatient), I found myself in a hospital bed knowing I had a ticket waiting at the concert hall a mile away, but my doctors said no, I couldn't go. Gee whiz. My recovery has been quick and lucky and quite complete, and my thanks to those of you in our extended community who sent prayers and good wishes. Many more shows came and went without me (I'd already paid for my Las Vegas tickets), but finally I did get out of the hospital and my girlfriend was kind enough to drive me to Santa Barbara, where I saw lots of pals I'd met over the years following them dusty old fairgrounds, and a wonderfully friendly and inspired outdoor concert. What a remarkably good (and generous) mood Bob has been in so consistently this year!

Anyway, the really wonderful thing for me was that I didn't have to feel horrible about missing eleven shows within my driving range, because I did keep my promise to myself and flew to Europe (go on, use up those frequent flyer miles, what could possibly be a better excuse?) in March for a dozen Dylan concerts, the first shows of 1995, from Prague to Paris. The could-be dream vacation of a lifetime. And it was.

As I recovered from my head injury and from the drugs they tried to sedate me with, I was delighted to find a batch of tapes in my mail, some from concerts I attended, but I found it difficult to concentrate on tapes, or CDs or any recorded music, at first. Like learning to walk again. I was just hoping my love for music would return naturally, if I was patient. Patience has been a big word around here. A Dylan fan in Japan read of my accident on the Internet and sent me a CD of Beethoven string quartets, because it had helped him through a tough time. What a nice gift! Soothing. Oddly, the first Dylan music that really comforted me in my jagged state was a bootleg someone had given me of the Supper Club shows (I try not to buy bootlegs but you can't turn down gifts). They still sound so wonderful! (Forget the CD-ROM excerpts, a waste of time.) Probably the greatest and most universally accessible Dylan album of recent decades, but he decided not to release it. Oh well.

Anyway, the '95 tapes I've heard have been good, but most of the time I've just been wondering when I would have the time and energy and attention-span (still catching up on three months of unanswered mail) to really connect with them, if indeed those music-loving cells in my brain were going to totally click back on. Patience . . . And then a week or two ago I thought I'd try one of the April U.K. tapes I have, why not Glasgow, April 9? Cool place to have a concert. Dylan must have thought so too. What a thrill for me—lots of good shows this year, I'm not trying to say which was best, my favorite of the ones I saw was Brussels, and that tape sounds terrific too. But what an adrenaline surge to hear this Glasgow tape and suddenly find that old Paul I'd forgotten about returning to his body, consumed with that need to reach out and grab a fellow addict and shout joyfully, hey!, YOU'VE GOT TO HEAR THIS TAPE!!

Before I blather on about even a few of the wondrous performances on this Glasgow tape, let me first carry on briefly about what I can remember of that astonishing opening night show, Prague 1995. Hey, I sat (next to Allen Ginsberg) in a box in Carnegie Hall to see Dylan at the Woody Guthrie Memorial Concert, January 1968, and that was certainly an exciting and historic moment. But not the last. Imagine how we felt on March 11th '95, first worrying whether there would be a show or not, after the cancellation the night before due to illness, and then there he was, with his band—hey, he's singing "Down in the Flood"! First live performance ever—and without his guitar. And then another song with no guitar, and another, and Dylan stalking the stage with a hand-held mike, Elvis moves, crooner moves, and this fascinating look on his face like he doesn't know from one moment to the next whether to pick up the guitar or not or where he's going to stand, or sit, and whether to put the mike back on its stand. I noticed his antics with the microphone first, and only after a few minutes did the light bulb go off in my dim (not yet injured) brain, hey, he's not playing guitar! Clever guy, he's found a new way to reinvent himself, to reinvent his on-stage experience and restimulate his creativity, without anything as drastic as hiring and training a new band. It certainly seemed as though he'd done it that night to save energy because he was tired from the flu (he sat down a lot while he was on stage), we just sat there (and jabbered at each other in the bar later) trying to figure it out. And loving every moment. That incredible "Mr. Tambourine Man," a song he complained of being sick of back in 1986, but with this arrangement it's busy being born again every night on stage. And oh, that new-style "Shelter from the Storm," highest point of three extraordinary nights in the Czech Republic in spite of all the other high points. And then he came back the second night and left the guitar aside again (I suggested we call this the "unstrung" tour, and soon enough the phrase turned up on the Internet). A rumor from somebody who'd talked with someone in the band told us that he had rehearsed a few songs without guitar ahead of time, before the flu, so it did seem as though it was something he wanted to fool around with, and the flu, and his desire to save his energy to do a great show in this beautiful city (Dylan definitely had a warm feeling for Prague after his terrific reception there in summer '94), combined to make him try something a little more outrageous.

According to my sketchy notes, he only played guitar during pieces of three songs ("Watching the River Flow," "God Knows" and "It Ain't Me Babe") the first night. Even on those songs he tended to wait through half the song or more before picking up the guitar. My notes say that the second night he only picked up his guitar near the end of "Desolation Row" and near the end of "Maggie's Farm," and also on the second verse of "Don't Think Twice," and in the latter case picking up the guitar seemed to inspire him to do some especially great singing. A few shows later he began adding a little more guitar, but still, when the bandleader himself doesn't know what he's going to do from one song or one moment to the next, you have the potential for an extremely lively, inventive, inspired set of performances.

Bob Dylan invites you to buy a ticket and come and watch him invent his music, his art form, before your eyes and ears. Europe '94 was great, and Woodstock will stand forever as a terrific document of how powerful Dylan and his voice and band could be at that glorious moment. But '95, happily, has been totally different— new sound, new purpose—and just as great in its own way. On the continent in March, we went to the shows and critiqued them afterwards as fans will, some shows superb (Brussels) and others uneven, of course, and as the nights went on we heard more guitar from Dylan, but the magic of those first surprises was never completely lost.

And now let me say a few words about the 24th show of '95, Glasgow, Scotland, April 9th. I wasn't there (wish I had been), but oh this tape.

Tape recordings of live performances, circulating among avid music fans (and compulsive collectors), are an accidental art form. I feel certain the singer would tell us he's singing to the people standing and sitting in front of him, and no one else. The performance is a work of art conceived as existing only at its moment of creation. Performers sing and play and feel the presence of the audience. Audience sees, hears, and feels, as individuals and as a collective. For two hours only. After that there are memories, and anticipation of another show. And tapes. In an odd way the illegality of the tapes is important (as long as it's unpunished; in my view we are not thieves but true lovers, there's a difference) because it makes the artist's intention unambiguous. He is not recording some kind of live album (he has not yet released even one entire concert of his own as a consumable product, with the slender exception of *Unplugged* and the possible exception of the rumored future *Bootleg Series* featuring a May '66 concert).

So what we have here—Glasgow '95, 15 songs, including absolutely unforgettable performances of "Shelter from the Storm," "Tears of Rage," "Lenny Bruce," "Mr. Tambourine Man" and "Lay Lady Lay"—is a snapshot. But like the photo that accidentally reveals a murder in Antonioni's film *Blow-Up*, it is also a doorway to knowledge. Intended or not, this cassette tape is an extraordinary and durable, repeatable, work of art. Not just a document. An experience waiting to happen. If you hear it, if it catches you at the right moment, I suggest you may find it enormously expressive, affecting, moving, pleasing. Full of beauty and intelligence. Communicative in those very special ways reserved for great works of art to which we find ourselves responsive. John Coltrane's *Impressions.* Monet's *Waterlilies.* Dylan's *Glasgow '95.* Inside the museums, infinity goes up on trial. And is judged exceptional. Or inspires our sense of wonder. And our self-love and our joy at this privilege called being alive and aware. Vass you dere? No. But you can be. By listening to the tape.

Arguably, then, the tape is an anti-entropic device that puts extra seats in the hall. And lets us travel through time and space to be there. There, at a moment when Dylan is singing "Tears of Rage" from his heart, in an arrangement only shared with the public once before (London March 31) and with a freshness and presence that seem almost impossible.

The point is, to me a great performance is a miracle. I don't want to reduce it to something explainable or analyzable, which it is not.

But I do want to tell you about it. Because what I hear on this tape (most of the time, depending on my mood and the quality of my attention and whether I've dispelled my preconceptions) is a remarkable reaffirmation of my belief that Bob Dylan is one of the greatest living artists of our culture and time, and that the medium in which he works is performance, and that he is doing work now, in the 1990s and indeed in 1995, that is as good as and as powerful and distinctive as his best-known and most-praised work, from any era. And, perhaps more important, a reaffirmation that there's something here for me. Something so valuable it is a treasure beyond price. Something of outstanding aesthetic, spiritual (as opposed to material) value. Okay, enough wind-up. Let's focus in on the first two songs.

"Down in the Flood" is a new song. Of course it was written and first performed in 1967, but it went unperformed, as far as we know, from 1971 to 1995, when it was trotted out as a rockin' show-opener, new arrangement, new context (like "Hero Blues" in 1974), new purpose, new sound, and therefore new content. This is a conscious, intentional vehicle for the singer/artist/musician to express something that he wishes to share or launch or get across in 1995.

I mention "Hero Blues" because Dylan resurrected it and trotted it out at the beginning of his daunting '74 tour to make some kind of statement, maybe just to make himself feel better. I intuit that something similar is true of "Down in the Flood," which has so far opened every 1995 show I know of, always with that trademark rhythm-section riff that now electrifies me, every time I hear it, because I have been programmed to hear in it the message: "a Bob Dylan concert is starting, right now, Paul, in front of your eyes and ears."

Great sound. Reminds me I want to say something to John Bauldie and other doubters about the appropriateness and skillfulness of this band, these musicians, with this singer/bandleader, at this point in time. He's doing great work, '92, '93, '94, and '95. The proof of the pudding is in the eating. This team is doing great work together, year after year, not every night, but surely a great many nights. What more can we ask? I love the sound Dylan is creating with the help and cooperation of his band, for example on this track, and then on the different but equally remarkable "Lay Lady

Lay," and on most of the 13 songs that follow, including what may be the very best live performances ever of "Tombstone Blues" and "Everything Is Broken." What more can we ask? Well, for me, I'm thankful that my tape player has a rewind button.

The 1974 song this "Down in the Flood" most reminds me of, as a listening-to-a-recorded-track experience, is "Most Likely You Go Your Way," the *Before the Flood* version which I raved about in *Performing Artist*. I like the sinew of the song, the way it makes me feel, the way it keeps pleasing and exciting me when I play it over and over like a 45, and the way it somehow seems to speak mysteriously but relevantly (even wisely, like a Rolling Stones single in the good old days) to me about what's going on in my life now.

That part is all in the imagination, of course, but it's a measure of the artist's skill that he stimulates the listener's imagination.

The key words in the song are "crash" and "flood" and "best friend." Sometimes, standing out in the European audience, it's occurred to me that maybe he's speaking to me/us, the fans, who might have to find "another best friend now" if he quits or dies in the saddle or if we lose patience with following his eccentric, internal zigs and zags. Artist's privilege. And fan's privilege too. "Ain't you gonna miss your best friend now?" I hope not. But if you're asking if I love you, the answer is yes, I still do.

What does the narrative of this song mean? Well I rest on the notion I've had since I first heard it, at least 24 years ago, which is that it's sung by a guy who's crashed his car on a levee, maybe in Louisiana or east Texas, and is trapped in the wreckage with the water rising, soon to drown him since "no boat's gonna row" at this hour or in this obscure place or in this dangerous flood. So the man is thinking about the woman he'll leave behind, who perhaps has spurned him, maybe they even had a quarrel before he drove off, angry and maybe even somewhat tipsy. You'll be sorry when I'm gone, babe. "Ain't you gonna miss your best friend now?"

And a nice touch of Dylan apocalypsism: "Gonna be the meanest flood anybody's ever seen." So, that could be part of the song's relevance at this moment. The prophet is speaking. Ironically, *Before the Flood* would be the perfect title for an album featuring this great 1995 performance, rocking tougher than this song ever did before.

Now, my old interpretation of the song's somewhat mysterious narrative content still holds up for me—the words haven't changed, after all, although they've got more rhythmic punch now, and that could alter their meaning or implications somewhat. Perhaps because this is a Basement Tapes song (one of two in the concert— and there's a third song, "Watchtower," originally composed around the same time), I find myself thinking of the delightful liner notes to the *Basement Tapes* album, written by Greil Marcus who is now finishing up a book on the Basement Tapes which I very much look forward to reading. He quotes Dylan in those notes: "*Obviously death is not very universally accepted. I mean, you'd think that the traditional music people could gather from their songs that mystery is a fact, a traditional fact.*" Marcus, quite brilliantly and very accurately, goes on to say you can hear in Dylan's performances of the Basement Tapes songs the "plain-talk mystery and 'acceptance of death' Dylan found in traditional music . . . like Bascom Lamar Lansford's 'I wish I was a mole in the ground. Like a mole in the ground I would root that mountain down.' " Marcus goes on, "Now, what the singer wants is obvious, and almost impossible to really comprehend. He wants to be delivered from his life and changed into a creature insignificant and despised." Marcus is not speaking of "Down in the Flood," but he could be. "Well it's sugar for sugar, and salt for salt . . ."

Of course, especially while we're at the show, each individual may have particularly transitory and intense feelings of what a song means, to him or her, as she or he hears it. For a rather off-the-wall example, how about this? I was at the Santa Barbara County Bowl May 20th, fresh out of the hospital with a helmet protecting my head which was still recovering from my accident, and I heard Dylan sing (to me?) "Train on down to Williams point, you can bust your head . . ." Wow. I knew he'd been singing "bust your feet," like in the *Lyrics* book, when I heard him in Europe. Did I dream it? Close listening to the tape now suggests he was probably singing "bust your leg." But one could easily hear it either way. Hey, we always hear some mysterious combination of what we've been experiencing and feeling (flotsam, like in a dream, every concert a series of dreams actually) and what the singer is feeling and somehow getting across to us.

I remember being at a Grateful Dead show where the person

next to me decided, and I agreed, that this concert and the song we'd just heard were, this particular time, about Chernobyl and how we feel about the earth being wounded, since that disaster had recently happened.

We hear what we hear. Individually and collectively. At the show and on the tape. When Dylan gives a particularly strong performance, one where he seems very present, as though he's speaking directly to me (the listener) and to and from himself, in every song, I sometimes like to imagine that I hear in this concert or live album an unconscious or semi-conscious theme. I particularly feel this on *Hard Rain*, as Dylan and his wife moved towards divorce, spring 1976. How about that side two? ("Shelter from the Storm," "You're a Big Girl Now," "I Threw it All Away," "Idiot Wind.")

Two songs from the *Hard Rain* album appear, in new forms, on the Glasgow tape (was Sara at the show? I doubt it. Unless maybe in spirit). For me, this "Lay Lady Lay" could be considered the third major variant, number one being the gentle, seductive original on *Nashville Skyline*, and number two being the raunchy, cruder "let's take a chance!" version on *Hard Rain*. There have been many live performances since, but none sticks in my mind as having quite such a unique and memorable message or flavor of its own as those two, until now (though the assertive, "take me as I am" version on *Before the Flood* is a good one). What do I hear in this Glasgow arrangement and performance? Well, this may have more to do with me than with Dylan's private life, but suddenly I hear his "Stay!" in the context of a long-term relationship, whereas those other two variants usually struck me as one-night-stand situations, like "Tonight I'll Be Staying Here with You."

But my subjective interpretation is not the important thing. What's more important I think is the way the arrangement and performance directly seduce and exert a power over me, the listener. Faster than version one, slower than version two, somehow this new tempo makes it a new and very (newly) attractive song for me. There's a sincerity in Dylan's voice this time, and an unusual quality and beauty in the guitar sound, that make me newly receptive to the words I'm hearing, as though he never said them so directly to me before. I don't feel it as sexual;

instead, related to my "best friend" thoughts during the previous tune, it does strike me that "why wait any longer for the one you love when he's standing in front of you?" could be meant to call my attention to this singer who is in front of me, I/thou as singer/audience, as in any live version of "Seeing the Real You at Last." I don't mean that Dylan is boasting about being loved by us. Rather, I somehow imagine that as he gives himself the wonderful creative freedom to go his own way and continue to follow his muse, he may wonder whether we'll stay or not. After all, much of his audience must seem to have deserted him long ago, Tour '74 was a much bigger deal than Tour '95, remember . . . So I hear less cocky confidence than in versions one and two. Instead the song feels like a plea for acceptance.

But never mind my weird interpretations. Just listen to the sound of his voice. I don't think this could be called "ordinary" Dylan. Somehow it's special. At times this performance of "Lay Lady Lay" seems to me to have a fragile beauty like a landscape lit by the new light at dawn. A texture. And listen to that harmonica-playing at the end! Delicate and keen (penetrating), both at once.

A well-executed uptempo "Watchtower" follows—confident but not quite the overfamiliar version of last year, nor the different one of the years before. For some reason it reminds me a bit of the 1978 (David Mansfield) version, Dylan's own "Star-Spangled Banner." Anyway, I like the feel of it, a good night for this chestnut (good night for the singer and band, in any case), and it serves as a nice change-of-tempo bridge between "Lay" and "Shelter from the Storm." And somehow this particular arrangement does allow for moments of odd, moving, vocal tenderness in the midst of the frenzy—for example, "you and I we've been through that." So when that unearthly, delicate new-light beauty returns at the start of "Shelter," it doesn't seem too abrupt. Great transition, though. The sort of thing Richard Meltzer once called an "unknown tongue." The sort of thing that makes an album or a tape a favorite for repeated listenings. Mood shifts that pay off, that satisfy something very deep inside.

Much as I like these other performances, if I were trying to sell you this tape, I'd start by playing you "Shelter" and "Tears of Rage." If you're any kind of Dylan fan, you won't be able to resist the sound of his voice here. It's magical, that Dylan voice we all first fell in love with, not a precise sound but the way it's so full of intelligence and life, as though at these special moments he is able to offer himself as an immediate link to the oversoul, the huge lurking consciousness of our time, our place. Because the artist himself is plugged in at these moments, he is able to send the current through us as well. It's not a premeditated message. It's a direct connection with something large and vital and, as Greil reminded us, it draws on a deep intuitive awareness of and insistence on "mystery as inseparable from any honest understanding of what life is all about."   The artist is plugged in because he's faithfully doing his work, travelling the earth playing in front of live audiences, following his sense of his calling even as people complain to him that he should be writing songs, making more albums, getting a different kind of band or playing solo acoustic shows, etc. etc. Artists as committed as Van Morrison and Patti Smith have cited Bob Dylan, the present-day Bob Dylan, as a role model and inspiration to them because of his ability to stay true to himself in spite of all the pressures of the world.

He is also plugged in to something hot at moments like the night he sang these two songs because he has a band he feels able to lean on, not impeccable in their skills or their responsiveness but still very definitely worthy (based on results) of ranking among the very few groups of musicians who have been most able, during Dylan's long career, to respond to and give immediate form to his needs, his impulses, able to collaborate with him in the effective creation of whatever it is that he creates.

It's the victories that matter. Oh, I remember being furious at Winnie in Utrecht, when Bob had to interrupt a gorgeous gentle-voice interpretation of "You're a Big Girl Now" to turn and try to get Winnie not to play so damn loud, but the drummer didn't notice, Tony was equally oblivious, and J.J.'s gestures to Winnie also did no good. So they're not perfect. Oh well. But if you listen to the CD-ROM outtakes of "Like a Rolling Stone" you learn that the dream band that jelled into one of the most perfect realizations of "Dylan sound" ever was capable of botching the job totally on later takes as well as the earlier ones. But they did manage to come together and respond to spirit just once, and that one victory changed musical history as we know it, and still can be treasured today.

241

I point to the Glasgow performances of "Shelter" and "Tears" as more evidence that Watson Jackson Garnier Baxter and Dylan together have shown, over the course of time, an extraordinary ability to find "that thin, that wild mercury sound, it's metallic and bright gold, with whatever that conjures up; that's my particular sound." Yes it is. And when Dylan the bandleader finds that sound, Dylan the singer responds as though he's just been jacked directly into The Source of Mystery. Speaking for myself, I can't identify those moments by any particular element in Dylan's singing (and in my opinion Greil Marcus stands as an example of someone who criticized Dylan's art and missed out on his best performances for years because he kept thinking it wasn't the good stuff unless it had the recognizable vocal nuancing of *Blood on the Tracks* ; I've made the same kind of error—stubbornly looking for the treasure in the form where I last recognized it, and being rendered deaf and blind as a result). Instead, I identify them not with my ears but my skin. Gooseflesh. You know what I'm talking about. Try "Shelter" and "Tears" from Glasgow and see if you don't agree.

Please remember these concerts and performances are not in competition with each other. "Shelter" from Prague, March 11, is also wonderful on tape, and quite different. You'll want to listen to both takes. Dylan to me is unmistakably a conscious artist when he gets superior results, so I call your attention to one aspect of his craft, a deliberate process of editing. "Shelter from the Storm" in Prague features 5 of the 10 original verses, #s 1, 3, 4, 9, and 10. It starts off deliberately slow (like the summer '94 "Baby Blue"), moves into its own groove, and by the next to last verse has arrived at some unbelievably soulful singing. When he sings the words "In a little hilltop village" in both these versions, you will immediately see and hear and smell the sights and sounds and odors of that village. What a rush.

The Glasgow "Shelter" is 7 of the original 10 verses: #s 1, 3, 4, 5, 6, 9, and 10. "Little risk" has become "no risk." The rhythms and sounds of the band between verses, and the ways the singer responds to them, are miraculous. Despite the common notion that Dylan rehearses new songs on the road by opening his copy of *Lyrics,* he doesn't sing the book's "long-forgotten morn" but the original recording's "uneventful morn," now charmingly evolved into "non-eventful." Going back to that hilltop village, I was surprised to find that Dylan on *Blood on the Tracks* sang (unkindly, I think) "I bargained for salvation and she gave me a lethal dose." But in 1995 (and perhaps other live versions since; I haven't checked) he sings the more reasonable *Lyrics* version: "They gambled for my clothes/I bargained for salvation and they gave me a lethal dose."

What does the song mean now? I leave that for you to discover as it seeps into you. It still strikes me as being somehow delightfully autobiographical. I like that he does it at the same concert as "My Back Pages." "If I could only turn back the clock." In one song we are the history of our relationships, and in the other we're the history of our attitudes. And in both, whenever he sings them, anyway, we're still here.

"Tears of Rage" is extremely moving April 9th, wow, and this time I hear it as being more tangibly about a real daughter or child than it usually is for me. My habitual response to the song is to hear it as being about the republic, the U.S.A., and the way it turned its back on the good intentions of (us) founding fathers. This time, though, I'm hearing it fresh, and suddenly it strikes me how easily it could now be about the musical and cultural movement Bob and others long ago gave birth to. And the current state of the music business. "And now the heart is filled with gold, just like it was a purse. And oh what kind of love is this, that goes from bad to worse?" Indeed.

Lots of little edits on "Tears" that sound more like pencilled changes than words spontaneously substituted while singing. For example, "I want you to know just before you go discover that no one has been true, that I myself really did think . . ." And as for the false instruction, it used to be "which we never could believe," but now it's "that you never could believe." Significant shifts. Conscious author at work.

Preconceptions die hard. Somewhere back in '91 I guess I got the idea that "Everything Is Broken" is not an exciting song to hear in live performance. I haven't gone back to compare earlier versions with this Glasgow one (first in '95), but it does seem that when singer and band find their groove, anything in the songbook's ripe for transformation. I'll even cite this as an example of the pleasure these guys are starting to find (more and more, it seems) in playing together. Not a routine rocker. Yet another side

243

(quietly rediscovered) of Bob Dylan. Along the same lines, the '84 version of "Tombstone Blues" made me think it would always be just an easy-to-play oldie, stick it in when you need a rocker. But this Glasgow performance hits me differently. I find myself enjoying the words as if they were fresh. "God Knows," on the other hand, tends to make me look at my watch (actually I don't have one) in '95, though I remember it used to please me. Why? Maybe just my problem. But I do have this theory that certain songs, and their current arrangements and the way the singer thinks of them, tend to lull the singer/bandleader into unconsciousness, whereas others stimulate him, make him grin, remind him how much he enjoys this work. And when he's having fun I have fun. That's my theory. Hey, there were nights in Europe when I even enjoyed "Maggie's Farm" (Bielefeld was one, according to my notes).

It really seems as though the song's structure predetermines the singer's and the audience's emotional response. The new "Mr. Tambourine Man" is an outstanding example. One German friend talked about how it made him cry. It's almost set up to be a prayer, a hymn, a celebration of beauty. Lovely from start to finish in Glasgow, and then that extraordinary harmonica comes along and pulls together all those strong emotions you've been feeling, and releases them all at once. Pretty song. Made quite new. Pretty amazing.

Anyway, the point is it's there in the lineup just to get that particular emotional response. Call it an invocation. These song performances don't just exist on their own. They're intended to function as parts of a whole, movements in a new Dylan symphony. Notice also that while he stays within his particular spring '95 range, Dylan shows off a variety of different voices in the course of the evening. Song selection and arrangement is partly about arriving at the right combination and sequence of Dylan voices. So the parts will add up to the whole.

It's almost as if he's saying, well, even if everything is broken, and there are good reasons for rage and tears, there still is one source of comfort. A tambourine man who can be asked to play, not only him for us, but a higher tambourine man, for him. In Bob's little morality play, he is every character, even if he sometimes calls himself "you." So the next song is the startlingly pretty "Boots of Spanish Leather" (in Prague without a guitar he rocked back and forth while singing this song, using his body to beat the rhythm), a lovely, mysterious performance. The mystery is, what is this song about, after all these years? Still pining for or angry about that ancient girlfriend? Still waiting for those boots to come? I hear it/feel it as a sad sweet meditation on love, commitment, the problems we have communicating with each other, and the undying pain of separation. Well performed. Because he still knows where to find its truth. "Is there something I can send you?" Maybe he's not just playing her part. Maybe he's actually asking himself.

Still more beauty and sadness with "It's All Over Now, Baby Blue." To study Bob Dylan's new, surprisingly inspired technique, notice the ways this performance and arrangement breathes and dances. Not just a gloss on the 1965 version and all its meanings and memories. Delightfully (and profoundly), it's a gloss on the 1994 version (unforgettable at Woodstock) as well. And as such, the performance is also a continual exploration of and commentary upon itself. And the string band sounds great.

"Like a Rolling Stone" is another song that has rediscovered itself very successfully in '95. It's good at Glasgow, but methinks I remember nights in March when it was truly incredible, especially for the fierceness and intentness of the singing. As if the words meant something. Same thing with "Mr. Tambourine Man," even though a different mood; he sounds like he means every word he says, and every word feels like it means something. Good news for a performing poet.

"Like a Rolling Stone" is a good song for live performance. It fell on hard times during the G.E. Smith era, and was mostly a vehicle for silly endings on the '86 Petty tour. But this '95 version has more grit and integrity, and on the right nights has been a significant vehicle for the part of Dylan that still wants to be the Little Richard Hank Williams soul singer for the adolescent in us all. Glasgow's probably not the time capsule version. But the dignity and power of the band in this arrangement allow me to imagine a new version of that Nick Nolte movie (*New York Stories*) in which the painter is immersing himself and summoning his muse with a '95 "Like a Rolling Stone," instead of the (marvelous) one from *Before the Flood*.

So I have one more song to mention. A very interesting song,

"Lenny Bruce," and a devastatingly powerful performance. "What do you want written on your tombstone?" Allen Ginsberg asked Dylan in *Renaldo & Clara*. This performance of "Lenny Bruce" is Dylan's answer. It'll break your heart. And in the long run maybe increase your ability to have empathy, not just for Dylan or Bruce, but for your own self. The tenderness with which Dylan reveals his own inner dialogue, here, is indeed an empathy primer, very moving, once again just my (or your) ears and heart alone with his voice. And heart. (In a sense the other instruments speak for his heart, so that even after he's done singing, the words and spoken feelings keep sinking in.) You will want to listen to this one. I didn't think this was a great song when I heard it on *Shot of Love*. But over the years Dylan has taught me how wrong I was. He's found something in it equal to what he found in "Broke Down Engine" and "Delia." What a talent that performer has.

I forgot the encores. "Rainy Day Women" is another song I think I don't want to hear in concert, but I don't mind when it's reinvented as heartily and inventively as this. "My Back Pages" is in the group of ones I'm always excited to hear, and this is another very sweet reading of it. The string band, again (all those ringing guitars). This performance could also be considered something of a preview of the American shows, which I think were characterized by a great interest on Dylan's part in the sound of the guitars and the evocation of a certain crystalline sound and circular riff, for example "Simple Twist of Fate" in Santa Barbara. Like Greil, perhaps, I tend to think of "Twist" as a song about vocal nuance. But here Dylan shows us that that's only part of what it is for him. I got the feeling, sitting there in May, that he really does desire to share those sounds he hears inside his head. A passion that hasn't diminished in 30 years. Part of what makes a person a good—or great—performing artist. "Every thought that's strung a knot in my mind" is also a musical thought (head full of rhythms and melodies). And the news from Glasgow is that those stories are still being sung, for himself and his friends. Maybe he's addicted to live audiences because his farewells are still restless. Still got new thoughts to share. Even if he cleverly pours them from old bottles. But they sound new to us (as long as we acccept his minstrel's invitation to, figuratively, "lay across my big brass bed"). Just as our faces look new to him, somehow. And he goes on enjoying his ministry or minstrelsy. From what I hear, the one unmistakable truth about the American shows in spring '95 was that Dylan was happy and having a good time, and even very forthcoming in his little expressions of appreciation and affection for his audience. The fact that this burst of good-natured behavior coincides with a very creative and inventive stretch of performances is intriguing. Does he feel good because he's expressing himself, or vice versa?

I don't know. I just hope the work is as rewarding for him as it is for us.

24. The Paradise Lost Tour

*So the Bob Dylan travel agency brought me to the chilly northeast in December 1995,
and this time I got to see one of my other all-time-favorite live performers too, at the
same shows. Such a deal! This report was written for a high end audio magazine
called* Fi *which tries to include some articles about music amongst the articles about
hi-fi equipment. Gosh, imagine being a guy who gets paid to go to Bob Dylan
concerts! I can't help it if I'm lucky . . .*

"All you guys together is great too!" Thus spoke Patti Smith to
her audience in a college gym on December 7, 1995, in Danbury,
Connecticut. She was responding to an audience member who
shouted out how great it was to see her and Television founder
Tom Verlaine and Patti Smith Group veterans Lenny Kaye and Jay
Dee Daugherty on stage together. The shouter was presumably also
anticipating seeing Patti Smith and Bob Dylan together later on at
this, their first appearance on the same stage ever in the course of
their two legendary rock and roll biographies to date. "Mine have
been like Verlaine's and Rimbaud's," Dylan said of his relationships
in a 1974 song. It's not hard to imagine a 21st century minstrel
saying his or her relationships have been like Bob Dylan's and Patti
Smith's. Ah, history. Before our eyes and ears.

It was the Paradise Lost Tour, so described on a poster sold at the
T-shirt table at these ten Bob Dylan and Patti Smith shows in New
England, New York and Pennsylvania in mid-December. It was my
good fortune to be at the first five concerts. They were wonderful,
both sets, both artists and all their accompanists; and starting at the
fourth show, the second night in Boston, the two poets did appear
on stage together for one song, Dylan's haunting 1985 ballad "Dark
Eyes" (from the *Empire Burlesque* album), which he has never sung
before in concert except for a 20-second false start at one show in
early 1986. The name of the "Paradise Lost" tour is presumably a
humorous response (perhaps from someone in the Smith camp, or

could it have been Bob's prankish suggestion?) to Dylan's liner notes for his 1994 album *World Gone Wrong*, where he rejects the "Never Ending Tour" moniker and makes up funny names for many different (and arbitrary) six-month segments of his virtually nonstop itinerary over the last ten years. In any case, making up tour names is not entirely new to Bob; he named his fiendishly inventive fall tour of Europe with Tom Petty & band in 1987 "Temples in Flames." Don't you wish you had a poster from that tour to hang in your living room? Sure wish I had one. But anyway, I was there last month when the loss of paradise was celebrated as aptly as we're likely to experience in this wonderful corner of musical and pop cultural history.

Wow. Dylan, as he has so often been during these recent years of tireless touring, was inspired and full of surprises, full of inspiring musicopoetic performances, many breathtaking memorable high points during each of his sets, songs that even a very experienced fan could sometimes feel were the very best version of this particular song he (or she) had ever heard and seen Dylan deliver. (And the good news for centuries of audiophiles yet to come is that these shows, like every Bob Dylan and Grateful Dead performance since almost the start of time, were documented by fans in the crowd with illicit—and very good—tape recorders. Not obtainable at present unless you're in with the illicit crowd, but perhaps to be sold to happy music lovers someday by the artist himself or his heirs. Whatever. As long as that Danbury performance of "Never Gonna Be the Same Again" and the Boston performance of "Lenny Bruce" can be heard over and over again by gratified listeners imagining and indeed experiencing the soundstage.)   Dylan was superb, in great voice and full of keen desire to share life through music, through ensemble performance, and through this form of poetry called song. He also amazed even his most loyal fans by varying his offerings as energetically as the Grateful Dead in their best days: in the first four concerts, he sang 39 different songs.

Patti also was very good, at a moment that was important to her not only because she was finally co-billed with one of her true music heroes, but also because these were her first band shows (as opposed to solo, spoken-word-plus-song shows) after her astonishing fifteen-year absence as a live performer, a break even longer than and as momentous as Dylan's seven-year sabbatical '67–'73

249

(both poets were raising children during their breaks from tour-ing). She was nervous at first (as she acknowledged to the audience the second night), but also in terrific voice from the beginning and gloriously supported by a band more in the tradition of the early Stones than the later Stones themselves. New songs and old songs, and every one a delicious listening and watching experience. I'll tell you more. But first I want to note that in an evening (five evenings for me) of quite a few thrilling high points for Smith lovers and Dylan lovers, the single moment that most summarized the entire experience, and provided pleasure equal to the other highest points from both artists, was Patti Smith and band's per-formance of "The Wicked Messenger" ("with a mind that multi-plied the smallest MATTER!") from Dylan's 1967 album *John Wesley Harding*. What a great, unstoppable, irresistible arrangement. She reinvented the song as if she were the master himself, and in a way absolutely suited to her unique voice and temperament and packet of themes and messages. Oh my. You must hear this. And you will, because before the Paradise Lost Tour started, Patti and friends had already recorded this "version" for her new album that is expected sometime in spring 1996.

Before I discuss a few more specifics of the performances, I want to share with you a story I know I'll tell my grandchildren: hanging out backstage in Boston (my birthplace) way up the metal stairs with Patti Smith and Tom Verlaine and my old science fiction fan friend Lenny Kaye and other musicians from both bands, and other true fans, notable among them Michael Stipe of R.E.M. (I walked into Patti's band's dressing room and he asked if he could take my picture) (he traveled to the first five shows on Patti's tour bus, Resident Honored Fan) and ubiquitous poet Allen Ginsberg, who thanked me for reviewing his (very excellent) box set last year and told me about Paul McCartney volunteering to be his backup musician at a recent benefit ensemble poetry reading at the Royal Albert Hall in London. Allen won't exactly have grandchildren, but he is already telling them stories, because we are they, as we are also the respectful progeny of Patti and Bob. Such a night!

Patti's theme for the tour, don't ask me why, was feet. A high point of her set every night (and especially spectacular Thursday night, when it opened the tour) was her 1979 song "Dancing Barefoot," which she punctuated with the great stage stunt (and she made it feel like a ritual, invocation) of taking off her shoes. The Dylan song she chose to throw her very heart into, "Wicked Messenger," climaxes with the cry, "the soles of my feet I swear they're burning!" And the new songs she shared with us (and in five nights I came to know and love all the new ones, instant old friends) included "Walking Blind" and "Mortal Shoes." The theme seemed to extend even into the wonderful choice of 1978's "Ghost Dance" ("we shall live again . . .") and 1988's "The Jackson Song" (do yourself a big favor and find a copy of her 1988 album with her late husband Fred Smith, *Dream of Life*) for her first son: "Little blue wings as those feet fly." Great singing, never mind whatcha read in *Rolling Stone.* She has become one of our finest (most expressive) vocalists. And a nice choice to salute Jerry Garcia with a Buddy Holly song the Dead always did as a dance number, "Not Fade Away," concluding her theater piece each night by dancing fiercely to this and/or her own "Rock N Roll Nigger," and, on Saturday night particularly, rapping spontaneous poetry in the style of her masterpiece "Land" loudly over "Not Fade Away"s Bo Diddley beat. No, Jerry won't fade away. Not as long as we vote with our feet.

Walk up to the concert hall, and dance to the music. That's how the 20th Century cult called "Deadheads" practiced their arcane rituals. And the same is true for those who love and who have made time in their lives for any kind of jazz or rock or blues or R&B in clubs or theaters or arenas. Live music. Live performed art on stage in front of a live audience. I go on about this because, to me, the Paradise Lost Tour was an almost deliberate celebration of the art of performance. Smith recommitting herself after her long absence, in proximity to one of the primary role models who inspired her to pursue this calling. And Bob Dylan adding ten shows onto the end of what had already been a long year for a champion road warrior comparable (as Dylan himself has suggested) only to a B.B. King, or James Brown in better years, a performer committed to working as many nights as possible. In fact, these ten shows brought Dylan's 1995 total to 117 concerts, actually his biggest year ever (not bad at age 54), beating his previous best: 114 in 1978. Jerry Garcia was and is, I think, the patron saint of the dedicated live-rock performer, so it is appropriate that he was acknowledged not only by Patti but also by Bob, who sang a song by Garcia and Robert Hunter, "Alabama

Getaway," with tremendous gusto as his first encore every night. Not mentioning Jerry's name. Just throwing himself passionately into evoking his musical spirit, with every bit as much feeling as Garcia gave to the many Dylan songs he sang. There were moments, even, when you could see that Dylan feels he's now got a band like Jerry had. Soulful and tight and rockin'. I did appreciate Jim DeRogatis in *Rolling Stone*, even though he and I disagree on the overall quality of Patti's Monday performance, praising Dylan's band and noting that "it's possible that the artist who fills the cultural void left by the Dead's disbanding may well be the one who inspired them in the first place." Dylan celebrates the joy of performing most nights, but he played these shows as if playing on a bill with Patti Smith was as special for him as it was for her. Just what one might have prayed for: both artists speaking in tongues, like 1965, 1975. But in manners very much true to their experiences and artistic sensibilities in 1995.

"A lot of girls have come along since Patti started," Bob told the audience during their first moment onstage together, in Boston, "but Patti's still the best, you know." And he kissed her. And followed "Dark Eyes" with "Jokerman," one of his many theme songs. It was a playful, dramatic, deeply satisfying set of performances, each night different and each set at each show as high quality as the others (with the usual variables, such as where you happened to be sitting that night). I originally planned to go to four shows, and I emphasize that I didn't go primarily for the *event*, as exciting as the event of this co-bill was; I flew across the country to hear the *music*; both of these artists are among the very few that I will travel any feasible distance to see any time I have the opportunity to catch a promising series of shows. What a musical opportunity this was. Two for one. ... And then the fifth show was added when Michael Jackson collapsed at a rehearsal and had to cancel his HBO special and, secondarily, his nights at the Beacon Theater in New York. The Beacon asked Bob and Patti to add a date now that Monday had become available (and since their Thursday show had already sold out).

It seems strange to write about a live music experience in a magazine about the joys of listening to music recordings, although one of the things I most relate to in the audiophile community is the shared interest in preserving and re-creating the experience and artistry of live performances through good recording and good listening. Future generations will thank us for the preservation of vital art that we support and encourage now. So it would also seem strange not to acknowledge that while being at the five shows was the thrill of a lifetime, I am now having a different kind of thrill with the arrival (friends trading with friends, often with the help of Internet communication) of first-rate tapes of that fifth show, New York City, December 11. Future generations will write that much of the greatest surviving work of the 20th Century rock artists like Dylan and the Rolling Stones and Patti Smith, the Who, R.E.M., the Grateful Dead, is in the form of recordings (professional or other-wise) of their live concerts. A great legacy. So let me wrap up telling you about these shows I attended by sharing just a small piece of the ecstatic musical experience I'm still having listening to these first tapes. (More will likely come along, and if you're looking for a copy, don't write to me; post your needs to the appropriate Inter-net newsgroup.) And if you wanna know what tape to search for, you almost can't go wrong in my opinion, but the tenth show, Dec. 17 in Philadelphia, which I didn't see, is already a favorite of Dylan fans on the Internet. One woman on the Net describes talking to a member of Dylan's sound crew at the end of that concert, a guy who says he's been at every show since Dylan started touring with Tom Petty, which is ten years ago. "I told him it was the best show I've seen in six years. His response was, 'Best show *ever*. Even Watchtower was GREAT!'" (The fans and maybe the crew get a little weary of "All Along the Watchtower," a crowd-pleaser that Dylan and band have performed at virtually every show for years in a row. And it still does have nights when it transcends itself, even if you're not hearing it for the first time.)

So let's look at Dylan's Dec. 11 set, although Patti's is also worthy of repeated attention, starting (only this night) with a fiery unaccompanied reading of her own Corso/Ginsberg/Ferlinghetti extravaganza, "Piss Factory," a working girl teenage angst poem that was also her first single, on an indie label (quite rare). Dylan's first New York set—"I might seem a little sluggish tonight," he joked, "couldn't sleep last night, I was so excited about playing in New York"—showcased a very relaxed and confident (and not at all sluggish) singer and band. Working from an extraordinary songbook, which tonight yielded electric or acoustic string band

253

versions of "Mr. Tambourine Man" (gorgeous this night, as at most performances of this new 1995 arrangement), "Rainy Day Women," "Girl from the North Country" and "Watchtower" by way of greatest hits (he does want 'em to go away happy if possible), and a generous selection of less likely and highly desirable choices: "Tears of Rage," "Drifter's Escape," "Mama, You Been on My Mind," "Senor," "Most Likely You Go Your Way," "Silvio," "Masters of War," "Highway 61 Revisited," and the aforementioned "Jokerman," "Dark Eyes" and "Alabama Getaway." A splendid cross-section of an important artist's life work. But more than that, a very immediate cross-section of his mind and his feelings tonight, as though each song is coming into existence for the first and final time before your eyes and ears.

"Girl from the North Country," for example, as I rewind the tape and listen to it again and again with tears in my eyes, is an absolutely exquisite evocation of this 54-year-old man's intensely poignant feelings of loss and tenderness when he lets himself think about loves and scenes from his past. Particularly keen this night in New York. If you listen to all of the officially released live recordings of Bob Dylan, you'll have to go to the solo acoustic performances from 1966 on *Biograph* to find this particular degree of heartbreaking sweetness and vulnerability in the singer's voice . . . and you won't find the unique sound of his acoustic string band (guitars, string bass, mandolin) anywhere, because it hasn't been adequately documented on an official release. All Dylan has to do is hand this 12/11/95 tape to his record company and get it on the street to change forever the public and critical assessment of his ongoing revolutionary accomplishments as a singer and bandleader and working artist in the medium of live musical performance. The innovative, jazzy, small combo performance of this song is so richly textured and moving that the release of this show as an album, preferably alongside an album of the still-unreleased extraordinary Supper Club shows from New York City 1993, would I think serve to establish once and for all Dylan's preeminence among all American rock or folk performers of his era, not just back in the 60s but equally now in the 1990s.

I can barely begin to describe to you the treasures to be found on this Dylan tape. His self-confidence and expressiveness in front of his current band, and the results he and they achieve song after song after song, argue that this combo, John Jackson on guitar, Tony Garnier on bass, Winston Watson on drums, Bucky Baxter on mandolin and lap steel, and Dylan on voice, guitar and harmonica, is the equal of any band Dylan has ever worked with, even The Band itself. Listen for example to "Tears of Rage." This is a performance of almost unthinkable power and beauty, an epic re-creation (new words, new interpretation) that is every bit as timely and devastating as if he had written a brand new song in order to share with us his assessment of the state of the universe, end of 1995 and trembling on the edge of the next era. What artistry. The Paradise Lost Tour was more than a marvelous event. It was also the occasion of the recording, by amateurs if not professionals, of works by these great artists that will likely survive them and keep pleasing listeners for centuries to come.

What it takes to be present at a great moment is to have the impulse to go down to the show, and then to follow one's intuition. I can't help but remember a day at the end of June in 1975 when I had the impulse to finally go see this Patti Smith my friends had been telling me about. At the Other End on Bleecker Street, I found myself sitting in a booth next to Bob Dylan's, another music fan who apparently had had the same impulse. Patti and her group were great that night, and Bob went backstage to congratulate her. It was their first meeting. For some reason I found myself there. And twenty years later I found myself again a fly on the wall backstage, this time Patti had just come upstairs in Boston after her first conversation with Bob on the Paradise Lost Tour, and Michael Stipe was lovingly braiding her hair, helping her get ready for the show. Why was he there? Because Patti Smith, as he and other members of R.E.M., as well as their contemporaries Bono and The Edge of U2, have often said, was as important to his inspiration and career choice as Dylan was to Patti's. And so the wheel turns. And music lovers become music creators, and paradise is found again. I'm gonna tell my grandchildren. And better than that, I'll play 'em the tapes.